O Kukui,
Your branches turn and turn
      seeking the sun.
Your silver leaves gleam
      a bright beacon to the sea.
Your pyramids of white flowers
      are pointed tapers.
Your palm-strung nut-kernels
      are torches; their shells
Long-glowing coals in the fire.
      God is Light.

LOWELL AND ABIGAIL
WITH EMMA AND AUGUSTUS, ON THE
NEW ENGLAND FURLOUGH, 1865

LOWELL
AND
ABIGAIL

A REALISTIC IDYLL

BY

MARY DILLINGHAM FREAR

NEW HAVEN · PRIVATELY PRINTED
1934

Copyright, 1934, by
Mary Dillingham Frear

Printed in the United States of America

TO ALL SPIRITUAL DESCENDANTS

OF

LOWELL AND ABIGAIL

PREFACE

THIS *life story of the Reverend Lowell Smith and his wife Abigail Willis (Tenney) Smith (missionaries, under the American Board of Commissioners for Foreign Missions, to the Sandwich Islands), gathered from journals, letters, and a few written words of their daughter Emma, Mrs. B. F. Dillingham, is set forth by their eldest granddaughter as an offering to the gradually accumulating data concerning early settlers in Hawaii.*

The writer believes that inevitable repetition in these stories emphasizes the spirit of the day that gave them birth, and that inevitable variation springs from the different characteristics of the actors on the familiar scene and of their interpreters.

M. D. F.

PREFACE

This life story of the Reverend Lowell Smith and his wife, Abigail Willis (Tenney) Smith, missionaries, under the American Board of Commissioners for Foreign Missions, in the Sandwich Islands, gathered from journals, letters, and a few written words of their daughter, Emma, Mrs. H. P. Dillingham, is set forth by their eldest granddaughter as an offering, to the gradually accumulating data concerning early settlers in Hawaii. The writer believes that inevitable repetition in these stories emphasizes the spirit of the day that gave them birth, and that inevitable variation springs from the different characteristics of the actors on the familiar scene, and of their interpreters.

M. D. F.

APPRECIATION

My warm thanks are due Miss Ethel Damon, Miss Emily Warinner, and Miss Ethel Scott for comradely help in the making of this book.

CONTENTS

CONTENTS

ILLUSTRATIONS

*Appreciative acknowledgment is made to Jessie Shaw Fisher for
her drawings for the front cover, the end papers and the map of the
Hawaiian Islands.*

INVOCATION

ALL SAINTS' DAY

LOWELL and Abigail, I address you. Once you were my dear grandparents with whom I lived until my seventh year, that most impressionable time of life. Now you are disembodied spirits—whatever that may mean. If, as we hope, personality persists, you will not mind my talking to you. To be sure, along with your other concepts of Catholicism (Popery, as then called by Puritans), prayers to the saints were condemned—yet your letters, Abigail, confess talking to your absent mother and to your dying child. I have often talked to you since your departure, so why not write to you? If I do not consciously receive replies, perhaps the questions will answer themselves by their very expression.

The white-painted walls of your upper chamber in Nuuanu Cottage were bare save for the little mirror with the strange landscape in its top, and the flat portrait of Granduncle Lionel Tenney in throated-stock, long-tailed coat, and tall hat. But today they glow in the mind of a once little maid with tumbled curls who was twice moved up with her four-poster koa bed to your care while waiting for baby brothers to be born into the dainty crib downstairs. Do you remember the daily pilgrimages on tiptoe to that curtained shrine, and one morning the discovery in it of a gleaming egg brought by a hen through the low open window, and the next morning the pink baby in a blanket? All the grown-ups seemed so amused; the little girl wondered why. That upper chamber was so far away from Mama it was an adventure to cross the brick "lobby" between the two houses, climb the narrow, steep stairs, pass the dark storeroom smelling of heat from the unceiled roof, of camphor-wood trunks, of the cedar-shingled fleet of boats Uncle Gus had made in his childhood— one for every kind of craft that came to Honolulu—square-rigged, schooner-rigged, barks and barkentines, brigs and brigantines, etc. The chamber reached, one looked out of one window between the koa tree and the tamarind to sea, and to

the semaphore pole with its news of coming vessels. Out of
another, up the dusty-or-muddy lane bordered by Indian
shot and Chinese jasmine (how the scent comes back today)
toward an Hawaiian *kauhale* (cluster of houses). By day one
might wander barefoot up that lane and sit or lie on the
kuaunas (borders of taro patches) watching a man, with
only a loin cloth added to his suit of beautiful bronze skin,
leisurely wading in the brown mud to plant the *hulis* (taro
stalks), or, in a patch ready to harvest, a woman gathering
up her one garment of an unforgettable blue as she pulled
food for her family—green stalks with large, exquisitely
toned leaves from which water rolled in shining globes. How
serenely the huge white clouds sailed the sky! Like them had
sailed the white wings that brought the great English dis-
coverer, Captain Cook (undoubtedly a god, perhaps mighty
Lono returning). How quietly the taro grew! How sweet and
friendly the greetings of the Hawaiian neighbors! But by
night how the trade wind rattled Granduncle Lionel's picture
on the wall, or how the Kona wind moaned and drove the rain
up from the sea; and sometimes, oh, terrible memory! how a
hideous and indescribably mournful and frightening wail (*e
uwe kanikau*) poured from the neighboring *kauhale*, where
some one of the innumerable born or adopted relatives lay
sick or dead. After fifty years, the blood still curdles at recollection of the terror inspired. Then how soothing a grandmother's hand and understanding heart!

Can I forget repeating "Little Jack Horner" after the
sweet, sonorous barytone and ending it "What a good boy
was Grandpa"? or receiving a little purse with the injunction: "Now run away from Grandpa's study. Go visit the
folks and get some peaches." (But who were the folks?
And there weren't any peaches!) You did not dream, dear
Grandpa, of the vivid picture you made for child eyes as you
laid your spare figure, in the flowered dressing gown Mother
made new for you each birthday, on the haircloth parlor sofa,
your blue-gray curly head thrown back for a good ten-minute
snore between calls from the Hawaiians free to come at any
time. But, oh! can anything efface the sight in eyes too round
in amazement, but hidden in the shadow of the narrow

veranda, while you bled a patient's arm stretched out to hold the staff kept handily behind the study door for the common operation! Dear Grandpa, how could you of that day so freely give your blood when now we so cherish and build up ours? From the journal accounts of bleeding the passengers on the voyages to the islands one would think the missionaries would have been fairly anemic on arrival!

Do you recall, Grandpa, my scrambling up after you on the steep hip roof when you were reshingling your house, or my standing beside you learning to harness "Old White" for the carriage drive? How slowly he trotted, how often he walked—one of the "missionary horses," but how much one could see at such a pace!

After my father's mother came from Massachusetts and we went "to housekeeping by ourselves" how often was I your guest for overnight or a week at a time! Do you both remember my walking up the valley at sunset "come to stay all night, if you want me"? In daydreams I often return to the low-browed house in the tiny garden, bounded at the rear by a lichen-grown stone wall, but faced by a brightly white-washed picket fence and gate. There still purls the *auwai* (brook) where we sailed our "ducks" of wind-holding flowers; there is the pump on the covered well, the well you, Grandpa, dug, that called back to us when you let us shout down its wide throat; there, still, the "needle tree" from which we gathered needles and knotted thread to sew petal dresses for dolls made of lily leaves.

You haven't forgotten, Grandma, my complaint that my parents were so young—but I knew *you* could understand me?

Truly, to have no earliest memory in which your bright grandmotherly sympathy is not a part is to claim some knowledge of you, Abigail, as a woman. To have lain encircled by your arm, beside you on your necessary rest-couch, while you read from Shakespeare, your "favorite dramatist," or talked of your childhood where the air was scented with wild grape or the sumac caught your fancy in its autumn coloring, or when you clapped your face with mullein leaves to make rosy cheeks rosier as you neared the little red school-

house—that was to see New England years before it blessed
my outward eye.

Now, become myself a gray-locked grandmother, conning
pages written nearly a century ago in Massachusetts as you
peered awe-struck and breathless into a possible future far
away, or on that ship of your half-year voyage, or on Molokai, "the lonely isle," is a turning of the tables or a look
through the reverse of the telescope.

Your pages are precious to me. I want to make them
precious to other of your descendants. You won't object if I
lean on the shoulders of your pages and laugh a little with
you or nudge your minds with mine, or twinkle my eyes to
make yours twinkle back again? I who am now old know how
you both would laugh over some of the serious things of the
long ago.

Dear zealous Lowell, grown very tender in widowed grand-
fatherhood! Dear little girl grandmother, so wisely foolish,
so foolishly wise! Who would not be glad of your noble purpose, your utmost devotion? Who, not sorry for your lone-
someness, glad for your courage, sorry for your "dark-
hearted neighbors," glad for your unfailing light of faith?
Help me to understand you as you understood me! Help me
to picture you aright to those who cannot know you unless
I do! AMEN.

LOWELL AND ABIGAIL

I

"IN THE SPRING"

1. ABIGAIL

ABIGAIL, a graceful, harp-toned name! It seems rather
a pity that no one of her descendants to date bears
the name of which she was so proud. Although the
fourth daughter among the eleven children of Gideon Tenney, it was her portion to receive the full maiden name of her
mother's mother, Abigail Willis, "our revered grandmother,"
she would say, and "a cousin of Nathaniel Willis, the poet,"
she would add, as if a poet's blood were royal or might move
with latitude as well as with longitude. Some of her nieces were
chid by friends for their interest in this same poet who might
be "no better than Byron," but the "revered grandmother"
held place in her own right. A time-stained "Family Record"
in Gideon's own "precious handwriting," that ends impres-
sively "Remember Death," makes announcement of

Abigail Willis Tenney, born December 4, 1809, on Sunday.
Named in Remembrance & to bear the name of her Hon. Grandmother.

As her relatives stood about her wooden cradle did anyone
say

> *The child that is born on the Sabbath Day*
> *Is blithe and bonny and good and gay?*

It would have been as true had her motto been "Has far to
go," but, near or far, she was indeed Sunday's child or her
life would not have made the joyous triumph it did.

Of Abigail Willis and her husband Ebenezer Childs, one of
their sons wrote:

My father was a small farmer. By hard work he earned a
little property, and finally settled on a part of the farm of my
grandfather Willis, in Hardwick, Mass. This land he purchased
from Lemuel Willis, who had inherited the homestead. He was

*In the
Cradle*

*Abigail's
Grand-
mother
Abigail
Willis*

an honest man and held that truth and fair dealing were indispensable ingredients in a good character. My mother was a woman of energy, of an amiable disposition, and having a good constitution, took an active part in the labors of the farm. She could do any kind of work—to mow and pitch grass, and reap grain, no man could obtain higher wages. She felt the want of more learning, and labored hard to give her children a good common-school education.

Perhaps it was this same writer, if not a brother or cousin of his, who gives us the following rugged picture of one generation farther back, Hannah Spooner and her husband Benjamin Willis, the parents of Abigail Willis.

Abigail's Great- Grand- mother Hannah Spooner

They moved into the wilderness; no land was cleared. They had to cut poles and to make a yard before they could unyoke the oxen. [This was in 1749 when they moved from Dartmouth to Hardwick, Mass.] She, my grandmother, showed me the rock beside which she made a fire and baked a johnny-cake for supper. Grandfather got his farm under such cultivation as to keep a good stock of cattle before he died. Grandmother administered and settled the estate after great trouble, and carried on the farm. The latter part of one winter and in early spring, snow fell so deep that the fences were covered, and the crust was hard enough to bear both men and cattle. Men went to March and April town meetings in a direct line. Being short of wood, grandmother would yoke the oxen, uncle Lemuel drive them (he was then ten or twelve years old) to the edge of the woods on the crust of the snow; she cut down a tree, hooked the chain and he drove to the house while she cut another tree. I remember after grandmother was eighty years of age as she was singing one of her great-grand-children to sleep in her room a neighbor called. The door of her room being ajar, he inquired with some earnestness, "what young girl is in the other room singing?"

With such blood of determination in her veins no wonder our Abigail Tenney wrote her younger brother in happy pride, shortly before her death, of receiving from Thomas Spooner an autograph letter written one hundred and thirty five years ago by our great grandfather Willis to our great great grandparents Spooner . . . quite legible . . . a great treasure. . . .

I have often in dreams gone in search of the graves of our grandparents and our dear little brother Tyler, whom I never saw. And I found them too in my dreams. Our grandmother Willis must be buried in Barre, I think, as I was born there and she was living with our parents then and died when I was a year old. Her Husband I presume was buried in Hardwick, and Father's parents in Westboro I always supposed but do not know for certainty. . . . I have a copy of our "Family Record" in Father's handwriting and it is all I have of his writing. I had about a bushel of letters destroyed by a destructive insect a few years ago. All Father's and those of our dear sisters and many others had been securely packed away as I supposed and when I went about a year ago to overhaul them they were completely riddled. I feel the loss more and more.

Then her mind turns to things more colorful than gravestones. It must be remembered that in this day "parlors" were decorated with hair ornaments and even coffin plates. *Heraldry*

I am so glad you took copies of epitaphs and other things . . . the Childs Coat of Arms. . . . I could get it photographed here. . . . I used to think that the Tenney family had a coat of arms. When I was about thirteen years old sister Sarah told me there was a "title" in the family far back in England. Did you ever hear of it? Our parents never told us that I remember and of course it is of little consequence as it did not help us to an education when we were young!!

Those two exclamation points are significant. If there was one word engraved in capitals on the child mind of our grandmother and her brothers and sisters it was EDUCATION. Hannah Spooner yoking her oxen was clearing the way for Abigail Willis who felt the

want of more learning and labored hard (pitch fork and scythe) to give her children a good common school education.

Between this Abigail and our Abigail stood Betsey Childs
—only daughter of the first, beloved mother of the second—
Betsey, an older sister long revered and loved, as testified in
the minute and utterly tremulous handwriting of her youngest brother, Capt. Ebenezer Childs of Farmington, Maine.
Her face looks serenely from several daguerreotypes cherished by great- and great-great-granddaughters; and a
great-great-great-granddaughter, in the arms of an old
wooden rocker that once held Betsey's erect figure, listens to
the clock that ticked away Betsey's last minutes of earth and
in sweet tones struck the hour of her departure. To pass as
Betsey did at the age of ninety-eight, having just remarked
that she would take a piece of pie, argues a resistant constitution bidding for a boasted inheritance.

Vigor of mind as well as of a body that was to yield the
fruit of eleven children characterized this Betsey, who declared in her youth that if she did marry she intended to have
a husband who could talk "mor'n beans and molasses." As
was said of the little red hen in the primer, "She did," for her
husband knew a deal "mor'n beans and molasses."

Betsey! What wouldn't we give for one brief letter from
her. Her communications seem always sent in a joint letter
from herself and Gideon, in which he was phrase maker and
scribe, or as messages through her children. Moreover, her
children seem often to have written to each other about her
instead of writing to her, although we have a number written
her by Abigail. That she was quick of wit and swift of speech
several stories still extant give evidence. When she was over
ninety a grandson called her attention to some young
puppies, saying, "They haven't their eyes open yet!" and the
old dame retorted, "Humph! they're Democrats, a'nt they!"

Gideon Tenney was Betsey's choice, a young man thirteen
years the senior of her twenty-year-old self, son of Mary
(Tyler) and Stephen Tenney whose sheepskin Bible, "his
Book," was "Given him by his Honoured Father Daniel
Tenney by a Verbal Will and Delivered by his Brother Nathaniel Tenney June 6th 1770." How much of ceremony is
lost out of this generation when it is not customary to have
been "Born" or to have "Departed this Life" through the
engrossed extra pages of Holy Writ!

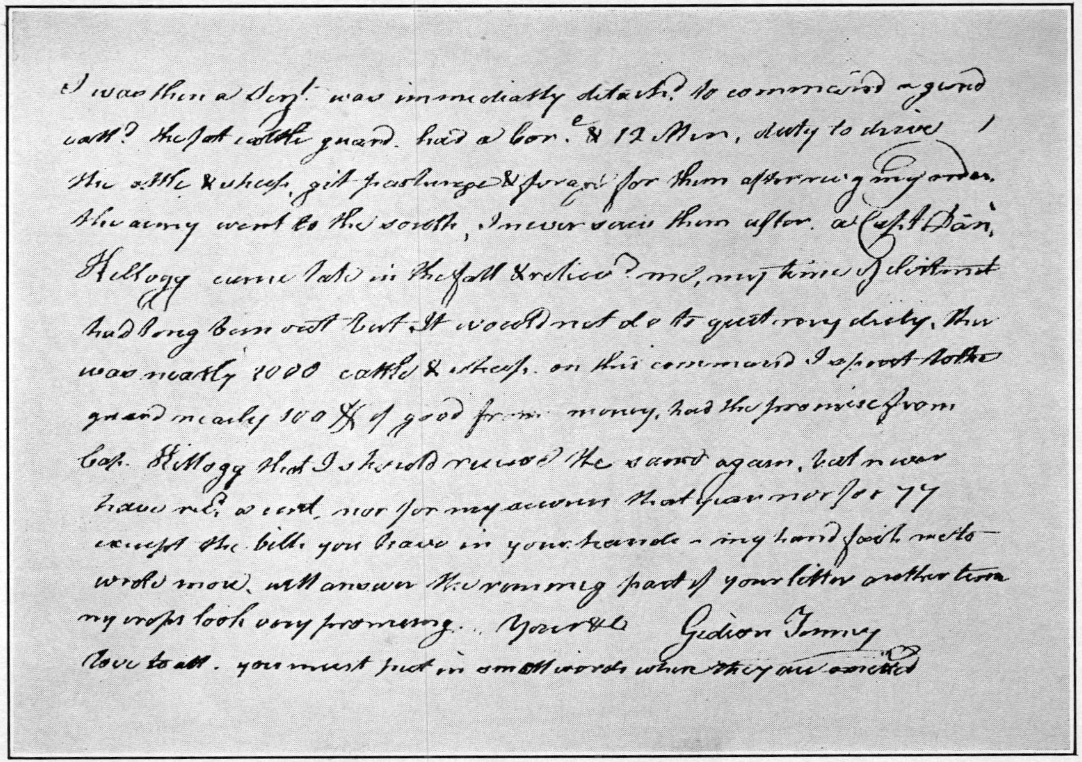
I was then a Sergt. was immediately detach'd to command a guard
call'd the 1st cattle guard. had a Corp.e & 12 Men, duty to drive
the cattle & sheep, git pasturage & forage for them after'rg my order.
the army went to the south, I never saw them after. a Capt. Dan.
Kellogg came late in the fall & relieved me, my time of enlistment
had long been out but it would not do to quit my duty. there
was nearly 1000 cattle & sheep. on this command I spent to the
guard nearly 100 $ of good hard money, had the promise from
Capt. Kellogg that I should receive the same again. but never
have re'd a cent, nor for my account that year nor for 77
except the bills you have in your hands - my hand foils me to
write more. will answer the remaining part of your letter another time
my crops look very promising.. Yours &c Gideon Tenney
love to all. you must put in small words when they are omitted

FACSIMILE OF GIDEON'S HAND

Gideon, who was to be a schoolmaster, began his career by helping to make lessons in American history. His daughter Abigail, the Abigail of this story, so long in beginning, invariably had the following dialogue in her successive generations of classes on the Revolutionary War:

"My father, because he was more than six feet tall, was allowed to enlist as a soldier although only fifteen years old."
"Oh, Mrs. Smith, was he killed?"

Would that this daughter who mourned

. . . the loss from Father's old desk of the Fourth of July orations and other writings of Father's of which there used to be such quantities, some of the old continental money . . . very old copies of the "Worcester Spy" . . . precious relics . . . Father cherished so, . . . those things that we used to look back upon with such awe in that old desk . . .

could have had the torn and time stained document that reads:

By His Honor
SAMUEL ADAMS, Esq.
Lieutenant-Governor and Commander in Chief
of the Commonwealth of Massachusetts.
To Gideon Tenney, Gentleman, Greeting
You being appointed Captain of a Company in the third Regiment of the Second Brigade, Seventh Division of the Militia of the Commonwealth, comprehending the County of Worcester.
By Virtue of the Power vested in me, I do by these Presents, (reposing special Trust and confidence in your Ability, Courage and good Conduct) commission you accordingly.—You are therefore carefully and diligently to discharge the Duty of a Captain in Leading, Ordering and Exercising said Company in Arms both inferior Officers and Soldiers; and to keep them in good Order and Discipline: And they are hereby commanded to obey you, as their Captain. And you are yourself to observe and follow such Order and Instructions, as you shall from Time to Time receive from me, or your Superior Officers.
Given under my Hand and the Seal of the said Commonwealth, the eleventh Day of November in the Year of our Lord,

1793 and in the eighteenth Year of the Independence of the United States of America.

By His Honor's Command, JOHN AVERY, . . . Secy.

Gideon or his father Stephen or his grandfather Daniel may have mislaid the Tenney coat of arms and, anywhere along the generations of disuse, the ancient family "title" may have vanished into a myth. Neither seems to have concerned the Captain, who took pride in matters far other. Abigail, his daughter, used to recount to her grandchildren how he would martial his flock of nine, stand them barefoot in close rank to give him the delight of stooping to look under the long arch made by their eighteen high insteps—to him a sign of noble birth. (Her grandchildren feared they could not measure up to such standards!) And as truly, if metaphorically, this same Captain made his little troopers stand face front to the enemy of sloth, take the aim of education, and believe in a fair goal beyond that aim.

For some reason, in spite of the impedimenta of so large a family, Gideon's residence has a nomadic appearance. Perhaps the Board of Education chose different pasturage and flocks for his shepherding. His children were born in Northboro, Gerry, Wendell, Barre, Massachusetts, and Ludlow, Vermont, and the family resided in Brandon, Vermont, when Abigail was married in 1832.

Of her father, Gideon, Abigail in old age wrote her younger brother Augustus:

Oh, how I have remembered his ambitions for us and all the helps he gave us. My reverence for him is very great indeed and our precious mother would "let everything go" that hindered the good we could get from our meagre opportunities. As I am following hard after them in years I love and honor our dear parents more and more continually. I long to sit at their feet and learn the ways of Heaven from their glorified lips.

I am keeping this day sacred to you and to the memories of our early life when father, mother, sisters and brothers, a numerous flock were about us and when I used to cry from loneliness if no more than two or three of us children were left at home at any one time. . . . My first recollection of you is you were standing in your "gocart" by the side of a chair on which you were playing. I rudely pushed away the chair, to see what you would do. You fell down and I hope I got a "spanking." I guess I did. I was then three years old and I remember a great deal of my own naughtiness—more than I remember anything else. I was dreadfully troubled with "worms" at that time in my life. I wonder if "worms" make children naughty? . . . I hope it *was* the "worms." The winter of my third or fourth birthday I went with Louisa to pay a visit and spend the day with some neighbor or friend a little way off. We wore our new red flannel dresses, bright scarlet I think they were. Observing a well-stocked poultry yard near the barn, I speedily paid it a private visit. But alas for me! An old turkey gobbler of immense size resented the intrusion of the scarlet lady. He flew at me with terrible force, seized me by the bridge of the nose, and laid me prostrate in an instant. I believe he would have killed me but for my cries which brought speedy assistance and rescue. I guess you remember the scar on my nose for it remained there for years.

Abigail's Childhood

Arethusa peeps out of a childhood picture as recorded in a letter to Augustus from Abigail just a year before her own death, when the sunset lights cast a pink glow on the opposite sky of her life.

Abigail's Sister Arethusa

Is it possible you remember our dear Brother Stillman? You were not yet six years old when he died. I was eight and I remember vividly just how our beautiful sister (Sarah) came in from Rutland village attended by Levi Long. She was all bathed in tears and our precious mother went to her and spoke cheerily and enquired the cause of her grief. "O, Mother, you would not smile so if you knew" was her sobbing reply, and then came the blow, and then the *agony!!* Tears fill my eyes now as I remember that dreadful sorrow that came to our dear mother while we awe struck little ones stood together in speechless grief— and then our poor surroundings. We were never so poor before or after as we were when that bitter sorrow came upon us. I know that God has long ago wiped away all tears from our dear mother's eyes, but mine still fall for her as I recall that time. Levi Long prayed with us and it was some time before our little sister (Arethusa) ceased to chide her kitten for its play-ful sallies, saying in her baby way, she was not four years old, "You don't consider, kitty, that Tippidee is dead." Do you remember that that was the name by which she called him? That dear good brother. He taught me to knit and he was most kind and tender to us little ones.

The name Arethusa recalls, like a nostalgic odor, an asso-ciation of those syllables with syllables equally exotic—trail-ing arbutus. It is like a sense of unrecognized rhyme, a matching of kindred ideas, the vague, girlish figure of one who left our planet so long, long ago reproduced in loving description and the stippled painting of that shy, brave flower of New England presented simultaneously to the con-sciousness of an island child fifty years back in the shadows. There was such a sense of mystery in the exquisite young woman who went into one of those obscure "declines." Later years brought the practical explanation that her descent to the grave was hastened, if not caused, by the fashion of the day that demanded the bodice be laced across a stomacher, i.e., a narrow board beneath the gown and over the vitals, the drawing of the cords to accomplish the desired slimness being accentuated by means of the bedpost as a stanchion. This evanescent one, her death following immediately that of her sister Louisa, called this cry from her sister Abigail across the world to her bereaved parents:

And she too is gone! That dearly loved one! The youngest lamb of our beloved flock, the child of your old age. She too has been cut off in the brightness of her youth and loveliness and when her life seemed so indispensable to her dear parents and friends.

Abigail's School Days

On receiving a letter from her brother Augustus in 1881, Abigail replied:

How many things you told me. . . . I am so glad you can keep the run of all these old neighbors. . . . What a far away memory came quickly back to me and they were all before my mind as of old. . . . Our old teachers . . . every one with his or her peculiarity rises before me. How did we ever get educated? Though Miss Severance was good. The best we ever had was Dr. Turnell and he was good every way. Then your old friend J. S. Green. Well he died a year or two ago at the age of eighty. . . . So we came up in spite of it all, owing so very much, almost everything, to the stimulus given us by our good father.

I have a whole chapter on our life at Sherbourne (which you cannot remember) to tell you, but not at this time. I am full of care now. . . . Lydia D. what a flood of recollections that name brings up. I do not remember ever crying in school but once and that was when she punished you one day, and her brother Dick was five years old and was not weaned!! . . . But you don't remember Mary Easterbrook who taught us in Sherbourne, for you were barely four years old, but I will tell you about it by letter another time. . . .

. . . I told my little grandson the other day how you at four years of age stood up stoutly and declared that you did not like school and did not wish to go to Miss Mary Easterbrook any more!! and how distressed I was and wondered what would become of you if you did not get an education! "And did he never learn to read, Grandma?" "O, yes, my darling, he did indeed, but not much under that school with its meagre equipment."

This school in Sherbourne was but one of the many dame schools that flourished over a hundred years ago throughout rural New England. It was a vague prophet of the nursery school, the kindergarten, and the primary of today, taking the children of the large families of a neighborhood, one after another, sometimes as early as the age of two and a half years, often as young as four, and, with all its faults, having the coveted feature of the best schools of today—individual instruction at the teacher's knee. Only, we hope, that the knees of today, if perhaps less often bent in prayer, serve as tables of better prepared and more suitable instruction. These schools were perhaps called into being by the crowding out of young children from the district schools because of the crowding in during the winter term of grown boys and even young men. The difficulties of the young men and the young women who taught these schools, with the hazard of discipline

Dame Schools

and the scanty pay and necessary boarding round, is a story by itself. A dame might charge

. . . for her services as caretaker and teacher nine pence a week for the older ones and eight pence for the babies.

Sometimes barter took the place of money. A married teacher accepted

. . . milk, butter and cheese, eggs, apples, cherries, tea and coffee, flour and sugar, candles, bay berry tallow, often in very small quantities. . . .*

as pay for her instruction. In some cases parents would offer service, like knitting socks or scouring a floor, killing a pig, or digging turf, in lieu of tuition. Moreover, sometimes school bills were long of settlement. As regards instruction, needle-work was added to the three hoary R's, and many a cherished sampler of today records long hours spent in the dame school. A picture of one such school sketches:

. . . Fifteen or twenty boys and girls attended, their hair short in the neck and a little braid each side of the forehead tied with ribbon. Their pantalettes reached nearly to their old shoes. The school began with a chapter from the Bible. When the teacher took it up she held a pin between her thumb and finger, saying "We must be so still as to hear this pin drop." She read some story of the Old Testament or a New Testament miracle, with such effect that the school sat entranced and one boy craved the privilege of taking the big Bible home. "Why you have a Bible!" "Yes, mam, but it isn't like yours, it hasn't any stories in it." When the school became restless she struck a little bell and the school broke into song,

> Haste thee Winter, haste away
> Far too long has been thy stay,

or they marched about the room singing,

> Children go, to and fro,
> In a merry, pretty row.†

* Thomas Franklin Waters, President of the Ipswich Historical Society, *Ipswich in the Massachusetts Bay Colony, 1700–1917.*
† *Ibid.*

The spelling match, patchwork for both boys and girls, the fool's cap or the stool in the corner for punishment, all had their place in the dame school. And such a school in various towns our Abigail was to teach between her periods of learning. Precious to the eyes of a granddaughter was the little gabled and clapboarded white schoolhouse in Gill, standing in the lush spring meadow grass, now refitted within to make of its small dimensions—twenty-two feet wide and thirty-two feet long, with nine-foot walls—the humblest of dwellings. In this very house Abigail in her teens was "School Ma'am" and experienced what more than fifty years later she confessed in words, that love of children was the strongest passion of her nature; and teaching, her normal condition. *Abigail's First Teaching*

Undoubtedly, before she was given her first school, she received a certificate similar to that of her younger sister Arethusa, a scrap of paper that, with its faded ink, has survived housecleaning adventures of more than ninety years:

GILL, May 6th, 1839

Miss Arethusa Tenney has been duly examined in the serious branches of Learning usually taught in our District Schools; & being found qualified, in the opinion of the undersigned Committee, is hereby recommended to instruct.

JOSIAH M. CANNING }
SAMUEL J. LYONS } *Committee*

Interspersed in Abigail's dame-school experience were radiant terms as student. No girl of today cherishes her college degree more than Abigail prized her privilege of instruction under Zilpah Grant and "That Mary Lyon who founded Mt. Holyoke Seminary." Ipswich Female Seminary, the forerunner of Mount Holyoke, was the high-water mark of Abigail's young womanhood, first as pupil and then as teacher.

This school, one of the first experiments in the higher education of women which have made New England famous for a century, was opened in April, 1828, under the principalship of Zilpah Grant, with Mary Lyon as assistant, during summer sessions until the spring of 1830 when, giving up her *Ipswich Seminary*

winter school at Buckland, she taught at Ipswich throughout
the year. Something of what this young principal of thirty-
three years was, may be gathered from a description of her at
the ripe age of twenty-five:

Zilpah
Grant

   . . . her brilliant mind, trained and developed by her long
and successful experience in teaching and her profound devotion to study, made her a conspicuous figure in the school.*

Mary
Lyon

Mary Lyon, two years Miss Grant's junior, also had been
a school teacher since she was fourteen or fifteen years old
and had performed Herculean tasks in learning, with some
air of nonchalance committing to memory the whole of a
Latin grammar over a week-end and, at the age of nineteen,
spinning, dyeing, and weaving two coverlets to meet the bill
of her first term at Ashfield Academy. No wonder that these
two young things were drawn to each other in mutual admiration for life. In 1824 Miss Lyon became assistant to Miss
Grant in the Adams Female Academy at Derry. Many
schools at that date had only one term, a summer or a winter
session. Miss Lyon, then spending her summers with Miss
Grant, conducted a school beginning with twenty-five young
ladies in Buckland.

Abigail
in Gill

It is evident that our Abigail spent at least the winter of
1828–29 under Miss Lyon's tutelage at Buckland. Alter-
nating study with teaching, the next winter she was teaching
in the tiny schoolhouse, already described, at Gill and boarding with a family of dear friends. In a letter to a niece in
Gill, Abigail writes in 1841:

   You all seem to my mind's eye little children just as I left
you and to think too that some of my little pupils have become
school teachers, and writers of poetry. That was a very pretty
piece written by U. Stoughton. She had a very fine mind and so
had A. Chenery. Give my love to them and to their parents. I
often think of them all. Sarah Ann and Elisabeth Chenery were
great favorites with me. I wonder if Elisabeth remembers how
she used to creep up stairs every morning when I boarded there
and call "Tenney-Tenney!"

  * Waters, *Ipswich in the Massachusetts Bay Colony, 1700–1917.*

That winter in Gill, Abigail received a long, ardent and introspective letter from Susan, a former schoolmate at Buckland. It makes rather painful reading, but reflects the strenuous occupation of soul-searching in vogue in the school that winter. On January 30, 1830, this Susan writes: *Schoolmate Susan*

Shall I not see you here this winter? You will realize something of my emotions when I tell you that I went into school last Friday confidently expecting to see Abigail. I had heard from one or two that you were at Major Griswold's. On going into school I cast my eye round upon between thirty and forty individuals who had taken their seats as spectators, to find the well-known face, but no Abigail could I see. I presume if anyone had observed me they would have discovered my disappointment in my countenance. I however soon recovered myself, not however without considerable effort and now and then an absent moment during the P.M. when thinking about it. Our school is so large that Miss L. has found it necessary to see company only Fridays. This will account for there being so many in.

. . . It is very different in many respects from what it was last winter. In reciting to monitors we occupy the hall and two chambers. There is necessarily more confusion than there was last winter. We have taken up the history of our country very extensively, have studied it in connection with Mr. Emerson's questions and explanations. It has been very profitable. Likewise Geometry, quite the first of the school. Part of the school are now attending to Upham's Intellectual Philosophy, the remainder to Natural Philosophy, Reading, Grammar, Definitions come in their order. Much pains is taken to have all the subjects profitable. . . . We have little societies now every Wed. P.M. to gain intelligence from newspapers. A President, Secretary and Assistant are chosen in due form. The selections are made previously—each to remember what they read and to repeat at the tea table. *Buckland*

In the same voluminous letter, its extremely minute chirography suggesting a tiny rill running between blades of grass, and flowing over every atom of the large sheet, Susan writes of

some very searching remarks made by Miss Lyon this morn

(and for several days past this subject has been under consideration) on the duty of telling faults to others. She ended by requesting those to rise who could recollect anything they ought to mention to any individual, or any confessions we ought to make. I rose with a fixed determination to go to my room and begin . . . with you, my dear. But you will enquire do you not feel that you ought to peform that part of your duty which would refer to telling faults. Abigail, I do not feel prepared to mention any now. Indeed I may say there are none that occur to me. Not that I suppose that dear A. has no faults for I believe there are none so perfect as to receive this character. I plead our short acquaintance as a reason, tho I think we were neither of us probably as faithful in this respect as we might have been.
. . . My dear Abigail, could you only hear Miss Lyon talk on "The Mississippi Valley!" "The American Indians!", "Our duty to each other," your heart would burn within you and you would feel that your life had been spent in vain.

After deploring the spiritual situation in the school, Susan suddenly comes upon this:

Abigail's Secret   The spirit which your letter breathed with regard to doing good, rejoiced my heart. I think I can praise God that he has inclined you to be willing to spend your days in labouring for the heathen and likewise that he is seeming to open a door of usefulness for you. O dear Abigail the subject upon which you have just hinted in your two last communications is one of deep interest, one which will involve your future happiness. I have no room, or time to enlarge upon it now. I hope and presume you will take it under serious consideration and make it a subject of earnest prayer. I do thank you for the information that you have given me with regard to it. I wait somewhat impatiently to hear further particulars. After you have told me more about it I will tell you my thoughts. I hope that you will be guided and directed in the right course and if it is the will of God that we be separated far and wide, let us say "thy will be done." It is of little consequence where our future lives are spent, if only they are spent in doing good.

If this thing which Abigail "just hinted" in her last writing to Susan was her engagement to Lowell, the discussion of the subject seems rather quaint for girls just turned twenty!

The twice emphasized idea of "doing good" and living a life of usefulness is a direct tribute to the very practical side of Miss Lyon's teaching. One who knew well the Ipswich Seminary of later years, Thomas F. Waters, has written:

The best features of the school in the days of Miss Grant and Miss Lyon were all preserved. In the early days it might appear that a morbid and self-centered type of religious life was fostered.

Even if that be true Miss Lyon showed a keenly developed sense for practical things which flowered later in her rules and regulations for Mount Holyoke, a school conducted on the

. . . principles of our missionary operations. . . . Style of living neat, but very plain and simple. . . . Domestic work of the family to be performed by the members of the school. . . . Board and tuition to be placed at cost, or as low as may be, and still cover the common expenses of the family, instruction, etc.*

Ipswich had been thus described to Miss Lyon by Miss Grant:

Ipswich Village

It is situated on Ipswich River twelve miles from Newburyport, twelve miles from Salem, and twenty-five from Boston. . . . The academy is a large, new building, and though it is not painted and has no blinds it is well finished inside and will be very commodious. Within a hundred rods of it twenty-five families would like to take boarders for the school and more than a hundred young ladies can be accommodated, no more than two occupying one room. Many of the houses there are handsome, and some are elegant, but there is a large proportion of old houses which have never been painted. It is said however that they appear better within than without. I understand that as a people, they are rather distinguished for their good morals and steady habits. The place is easy of access, from eight to twelve stages passing through the town every day. The leading

* Edward Hitchcock, *The Life and Labors of Mary Lyon.*

men of Ipswich wish to have a flourishing school here, partly
because they wish that their building (which has cost four thousand dollars) may not be lost, partly because they think it will
benefit the place to draw in strangers, especially to draw in
money and partly because they wish their daughters to have the
means of improvement. They think they shall supply thirty or
forty natives. . . . I believe . . . that by uniting our talents
and labors on the same school we may do more good than by
teaching separately.*

*Ipswich
Curriculum*

Miss Grant was followed by forty of her old pupils from
Derry, and by 1829 seventy-five girls answered the roll call,
of whom thirty-seven were "natives of Ipswich." The course
of study included the common English branches, botany,
chemistry, astronomy, ecclesiastical history, logic, Paley's
Natural Theology, Wayland's *Moral Philosophy*, Butler's
Analogy, and Alexander's *Evidences of Christianity*. Although no instruction was given in piano, French, or Latin,
vocal music was a subject of emphasis. Miss Grant lectured
on many practical and other valuable topics. Until another
building was acquired for the "boarders," girls were accommodated in the town for one dollar and seventy-five cents a
week "exclusive of fuel" (which, however, we trust was obtainable). The life was not lacking in discipline with the
rising hour "a quarter of five in summer, a quarter of six in
winter." Perhaps there was no objection then to extinguish-
ing lights at nine. But does youth ever appreciate a requirement of silence and solitude? Such a daily half hour would be
so welcomed by adults. What a pity that some things cannot
be shaken up and redivided! In three years Miss Grant had
her coveted paint and blinds, but never the endowed school of
which she had dreamed.

*Abigail's
Dreams*

Here in the fine old Colonial mansion—three stories high,
with dignified small-paned windows, three one way and five
the other wall of the house—for three divided but privileged
years Abigail passed in and out of the stately door, as eager
pupil and as devoted teacher. Her granddaughter has stood
under the graceful elms of Ipswich and looked from the old

* Waters, *Ipswich in the Massachusetts Bay Colony, 1700–1917.*

IPSWICH SEMINARY, IPSWICH, MASSACHUSETTS

stone bridge at the river, longing to see the dear ghost of the very tall girl with a waist only eighteen inches round pause to rest those high-arched feet, her father's pride, and to gaze downstream, letting her imagination flow with the river to the gray Atlantic and thence on ever adventurous waves far, far to the blue and balmy Pacific laving the shores of her long home-to-be. What of renunciation, what of adventure held the kind brown eyes that were to find those world-distant little dusky faces awaiting her as responsive to her teaching, as welcome to her love, as those of the old Bay State?

The matter "hinted" in letters to Susan had been ex-pressed at about the same date in a note to her friend Mrs. Urania Stoughton, mother of pupils in Gill. Although settled there for a winter of teaching, a deep-seated reserve made speech more difficult for Abigail than this guarded epistle. After a few introductory sentences the letter runs:

Abigail's Engage-ment

It is almost with fear and trembling I tell you, that since I left Gill a year since *Chance* or *Providence* has directed me to a place where I became acquainted with *one* devoted preparing for the holy ministry; and possessing so much love and zeal in his master's cause, that probably *heathen ground* will some day be trod by him. Can you think that such a one could even think of inviting such a one as I to accompany and assist him in his labors of love? Oh my friend my mind is distressed and I know not what to say. I so greatly fear deciding in some way injuri-ous to the cause and so bring horror and confusion on my own soul. I have for weeks been praying to God to direct me on the path of duty. As yet I am not convinced what is duty. I have not opened my mind to anyone in Gill on this subject. [Abigail's eldest brother and his family lived there.]

I feel my mind needs enlightening more on this subject. I long to converse with you familiarly. I have confidence in your judg-ment and I do long to go with you to a Throne of Grace and im-plore direction from that only true source. I know that the effectual fervent prayer of the righteous avails much, and I do ask that I may be remembered in your supplications at the mercy seat. I submit this to you in confidence that at present at least it will be kept a *secret*. Excuse this hasty scroll from your friend Abigail. I shall see you as soon as possible.

Abigail at Heath

The "place" to which "Providence" had directed Abigail was the village of Heath, Massachusetts, where in her course of "boarding round" as schoolmistress she was living under the roof of Lowell's farmer father. The meeting of Lowell and Abigail probably occurred when Lowell was graduated from Williams and about to enter Auburn Theological Seminary in his preparation for the ministry and in furtherance of his plan to be a foreign missionary. Abigail's daughter, Emma, visiting this old homestead in 1889,

. . . went upstairs into those beautiful chambers looking east and west. I suppose Mother slept in one of them when she "boarded round" and used to stay here. . . . I wish I knew which one. At any rate I looked out of *all* the windows.

Her loving imagination called the aged father to leave his desk in far Hawaii and the sainted mother to abandon her fields of asphodel to return to Heath and to their youth, that together they might look again

. . . on the same hills and valleys you used to see . . . and the beautiful meadows . . . often trod by your feet . . . I asked a dear old Lady, "Did you know my father when he was a young man?" "Yes, indeed, your mother, too. . . . She and I sat side by side on the bench when we were examined by the school committee for schools in Heath, your mother taught on the west side and I on the east."

Abigail, perhaps, long pondered Lowell's proposal of marriage and coincident departure, and as late as August, 1832, in Ipswich, wrote her brother and sister in Gill:

It is yet undecided where I spend my future days. Lowell completes his Theological course in about two weeks, he will come immediately to Mass. The Board have not decided where it is best for him to labor. His health has failed in some measure or at least it is not quite as good as formerly, & it is feared by the Board that he will not be able to endure a foreign climate, but all is as yet uncertain. I shall probably know soon.

However, the engagement was made by the summer of 1831, for on August 20 of that year, at Ipswich Female Academy, Abigail received as a gift from her pupils a little gold-tooled red-leather album in which within the following two or three days many of her associates inscribed their names and expressions of farewell. The book was thereafter a constant companion, gathering the sentiments of friends— even as her far descendants continue to do for themselves! But it was then the fashion to be sad. Even the book itself gives evidence of this, for the colored print on the title-page portrays three children standing beside a rose-decorated grave and beneath the picture, printed in delicate script, are the words

Autograph Album

> Here memory comes by true affection led,
> To commune with the distant and the dead.

Shakespeare may have declared that "Parting is such sweet sorrow," but to the girls of that day life seems to have been not only real and earnest but lugubrious to the earthly eye. For instance:

These are blissful moments snatched from the gulf of human destiny—moments whose bright gleams sometimes remain to enlighten the sad abyss, even after the orb of joy has disappeared from the horizon. . . .

> How oft the tenderest ties are broken
> How oft the parting tear must flow:
> The words of friendship scarce are spoken
> Ere those are gone we love below:
> Like suns they rose and all was bright;
> Like suns they set, and all is night.
> Remember me whene'er you sigh
> Be it at midnight's lonely hour,
> Remember me and think that I
> Return its sigh and feel its power.
> Whene'er you think of those away
> Or when you bend the pious knee
> Or when your thoughts to pleasure stray
> O! then, dear maid, remember me!

The last stanza is more than once inscribed by a friend, and was probably a favorite lugubriosity! One more selection penned in the delicate hand of Louisa Tenney, three years Abigail's senior and her favorite sister, was evidently written during a visit in Ipswich in August, 1832. Louisa was held up to Abigail's children and grandchildren as a model of feminine beauty and perfection, a model of propriety in her care for others and in her own decorum, who would even weep at her carelessness if in brushing her own long, luxuriant locks she should break a single hair. This beautiful and tender Louisa, whose quaint picture is treasured by a namesake of the third generation, copied upon two pages of the little red album, that was to go so far and survive the ravages of time, climate, and insect, an "Address to a Missionary," full of harrowing suggestions and closing thus:

Abigail's Sister Louisa

Hast thou considered well these sorrows? yea, more, a thousand more and greater? And dost thou bid them welcome all? Then go—go and thy God be with thee—go and thou shalt know far more of happiness than we who sit at home and bless ourselves that we have heard of God and idly wish that others might hear and love him too. Go to thy labors—to thy grave. Thy race it will be short but there is a prize to win—thy battles are soon over and a crown of glory waits for thee in Heaven.

Faded ink still prints a glowing picture in the inscriptions of August 26 and Sunday evening the twenty-seventh, when Abigail was spending a vacation with intimate friends in Andover. Over the signature of Daniel B. Woods is written:

Mills' Grove

We have this evening walked in Mills' Grove. We have threaded the paths which that sainted missionary trod. Here he prayed and wept—the ground is hallowed by his tears. Never will the recollection of the sacred hour be effaced. We stood beneath some branching cedars and listened to the soft tones of dying day. The wind seemed gently whispering back the sighs he breathed to their keeping years before. You asked, sister Abba, if Mills might not spiritually be near us at that very moment? There was a deep religious romance in the idea, to which we yielded ourselves. As the notes of the missionary hymn died away, you and sister were folded weeping in each other's arms. She said to you, "Abba, will you not think of this when far, far away among the poor heathens?" May we not think that this was a scene at which Mills was present? . . .

To the Missionary Mills

Thy soul is hovering o'er the scene
   Once hallowed by thy prayers;
Thy Spirit's near us, on the green
   Once watered by thy tears.

With hushèd voice and noiseless steps
   We tread the paths thou trod,
Thy name is whispered from our lips
   True servant of thy God.

     .   .   .   .

One of thy Spirit stands here now,
   Thy mantle falls on her
Lo! on the spot where Mills did bow,
   She weeps for nations sunk in woe,
     In Sin's dark sepulchre.

     .   .   .   .

Go, Sister, to the wretched go,
   God be thy guide and guard,
Our parting tears will—they must flow,
But God will grace and strength bestow,
   He will be thy *reward*.

The little red volume continued with Abigail as she journeyed with her husband immediately upon their marriage in Brandon, Vermont, October 2, 1832, to Lowell's old home in Heath, to Amherst, and on to New London, Connecticut. In that port their hosts, Esquire Learned and his wife, made their contribution of selected verse. The good Esquire copied a long poem by Miss C. E. Beecher, ending:

Farewell, blest New England, thy blue hills are flushing
In sunset's last rays as they fade from our view;
Land of our fathers! what fond tears are gushing
As we pour forth our blessings and heartfelt adieu!

The Esquire's lady, dear Betsey Learned, who was to prove a generous friend through many years lean in material comforts, lean also in messages of love from those who should not have been forgetful of their own, this new-found friend and hostess copied into the treasured volume the following sprightly and appreciated stanzas (with four others which we omit):

THE MISSIONARY'S BRIDE

Who'd be a missionary's Bride,
Who that is young and fair
Would leave the world and all beside,
Its pomp and vanity and pride,
Her Saviour's cross to bear?

None—save she whose heart is meek
Who feels another's pain
And loves to wipe from sorrow's cheek
The trickling tear—and accents speak
That soothe the soul again.

She who feels for them that need
The precious bread of life.
And longs the Saviour's lambs to feed
O, such an one would make indeed
A missionary's wife!

The Wedding   Sweet and plaintive as evening bells over the sea—all this —but oh, for a little earthliness mixed in for good digestion! Our times are overredolent with current "society news," but how much flavor an occasional note of a great-grandmother's trousseau, or a few comments on the wedding party, given by younger relatives, would have today! The wedding—what was it like? The departure—was it by farm wagon or by stagecoach? The event was surely an impressive one for the large village connections of this young pair. Babies yet to be born, children of cousins, were to be named for "That Lowell who went to the Sandwich Islands" and nieces-in-law were to bear the name of an Abigail they were not to see until women grown. How enjoyable would be a gentle dish of gossip about it all! A few young girls kept scraps of the bride's flower-sprigged house gowns as a bit of sentiment for a piece quilt. But the quilt must be gone with the hands that made it, leaving only the fact, a memory fragrant as lilac bloom. Evidently the wedding was without a ring, for the only ring Abigail ever wore was a tiny circle hardly more than a thread of gold that had been her mother's and was intended to hold an inset of hair, according to the fashion of the time.

Yet one memento of that wedding day remains—a frayed and cracked page of heavy paper browned by the passing of a century and bearing these words:

State of Vermont } Be it remembered, that at Brandon, in the County of Rutland ∫ County aforesaid, on this second day of October, in the year of our Lord 1832, Rev. Lowell Smith of the town of Heath and County of Franklin, in the State of Massachusetts, and Miss Abba W. Tenney, of the town of Brandon and County of Rutland, in the State of Vermont, were duly united in Marriage. By me. Charles Pomeroy. an Elder of the Methodist E. Church . . .

Let us return in thought from Brandon and the wedding to New London where Betsey Learned was writing in the album of her wayfarer guest. Of the sojourn in that hospitable city Lowell's journal records:

New London, Connecticut

Left our friends in Amherst, Mass. Monday, October 8, 1832 arrived at New London, Ct. the place of embarkation on the eve of the 9th, expecting to receive our instructions from the Board the 10th or 11th and sail the 15th. But on arriving we ascertained from the Captain that the "Mentor" would not sail for some weeks. Being one hundred, fifty miles from our friends, and having no desire to undergo the painful sensations of a parting scene the second time, we thought it not advisable to return.

Esq. Larned and his wife very politely invited us to take up our residence with them while detained in port. Accordingly we complied with their invitation and were treated by them with much kindness and christian hospitality.

The good people in New London conferred upon us many gifts and kindnesses which will long be remembered with gratitude.

During our delay in that city I preached nineteen or twenty sermons in the churches in the vicinity. The Lord raised us up many warm friends in Norwich and Stonington who did much towards our outfit.

With raised hands one is compelled to cry, "Why, why, had not the home villages of these young people, so long pledged to this foreign experience, made ample provision for every imagined need in years to come!" An exclamation from childhood days *"Kupanaha loa!"* (passing strange) is all that responds to the wondering question!

While Lowell is exercising his new art of preaching in a series of tryouts on New Englanders who have the church habit and is thus kept from being too restive to reap those whitening fields in mid-Pacific, let us peep behind the crimson pulpit curtain and view the background of this young man.

2. LOWELL

As the *koa* tree and the *palapalai* spring from the same soil, as the mystical and practical are both native to humanity, as prose and poetry are both expressions of the mind, so, with no inappropriateness, to William Langlande's "Vision of Piers Ploughman" in the Malvern Hills bordering the faery country of Wales, and to the faded memory of an engraving that depicted Burns the "Ayrshire Ploughman" visited by the Spirit of Poetry, we may bravely add a word picture of a college-bred New England farm lad inspired to leave his plow in its rocky soil and to furrow through unknown seas to a land awaiting gospel seed. This picture is found in the beginning of a sketch of Lowell by his daughter Emma.

At the Plow

In the year 1822 the Spirit of the Lord walked beside the plough of a young farmer lad at work among the Berkshire hills in Western Massachusetts and repeated the call given to Matthew the publican "Follow me." Like the Apostle of old, the young man was ready to "leave all" at once, but a year lacked to complete his majority, and his employer would not consent to shortening his term of service. The following twelve months, while filled with toil of every useful kind, were rich in lessons of patience and submission, and served to strengthen the determination of Lowell to become a preacher of the gospel. Clad in his "freedom suit" at twenty-one years of age he attended a preparatory school, which at the end of two years enabled him to enter Williams College. The influence of this institution, intensified by the spirit that brooded over the ground whereon had stood "the haystack" aroused in him the desire of self denial, and throughout his college course his purpose was to become a home missionary. The theological seminary in Auburn, New York, was his home for three years and here, in company with many others who were going to the uttermost ends of the earth, he received the touch of consecration which determined his heart upon Foreign Mission work.

New England! Sacred ground! The trail of the Redman is dear to the mind of the historian, but to the New England descendant the trail of his forebears is dearer. "Land where my fathers died" calls even to Pacific isles to come and trace precious footsteps in the dust of the past, to breathe with inherited love the lilac and clover that bloom in cherished tradition. Save for the painful destruction of elms in widening and straightening such highways as the one from Deerfield to Greenfield, more than a gesture of safety for the modern high-speed vehicle, the countryside is still blessed with glorious trees, beyond description for beauty, and fortunately preserved in a degree to posterity against the depredations of time, insect, or the ax of the woodman by a rare photographic lens with an artist's hand on the bulb. *New England*

Lowell's granddaughter, on a solitary pilgrimage in 1928, was suddenly of the elect, leaving trains and time-tables forgotten, and ensconced by tender hosts in one motor car after another. What peace of solitude, rest for tongue and ear in seclusion as perfect as that of the last glass car that lifts the body, but much more cheerful because eyes look out of the windows! A hearse driver is not conversational, but no more was the automobile driver who drove up hill and down, over bridges, beside singing river and mute lake, over the Mohawk

Trail, above the Hoosac Tunnel, through North Adams, still showing devastation of floods from Vermont just over the line, through Charlemont to Heath and back to Shelburne Falls, through Greenfield to Gill, to Deerfield, Northampton, Amherst, through Barre to the Brookfields, Wayland, Groton, Concord, Lexington, Weston, the Newtons, along the Newbury Turnpike to Andover and Ipswich.

Everybody everywhere complained of spring weather, "So wet!" "Still raining!" "Always overcast!" "No sunshine!" "More rain!" Had they no eyes for the half-tones, the twilight beauty of pale green grass starred with flowers, puddles offering broken bits of blue sky, white wreathing arms of streams, mirror ponds, and apple orchards filling the hollows with fragrance, climbing the hills over far-reaching meadows until their rose and white and evanescent hues between were merged in enveloping mist that knew no horizon?

Through all this region where had lived and died Tenneys, Childs', Willises, Spooners, Smiths, Browns, Prentices, farms have been restored, houses preserved, elms and lilacs cherished, barns expanded, wells kept. The white clapboarded buildings with their snow-shedding gables, green blinds, persisting ells, embrace the spirit of the old simplicity, frugality, dignity, with the warm appreciation of the new—a symbol of the faith in our fathers, if not always the faith of our fathers. Ever the spire of the church arose, a white dove hovering above the nest-holding elms from a building as uncompromising in structure as the granite hills, in pure shining color of full reflected light as lovely as the apple blossoms.

Heath   Heath was disappointing, raw and windswept, almost bereft of trees at the center with its post office where Lowell's daughter Emma lodged on her visit of forty-odd years ago.

The finest elm tree in the country, that is a landmark for miles around, standing beside the old cellar . . . of the place where your grandfather first lived when he came to Heath . . . on a hill commanding a wonderful view.

So Emma had described it in writing her father. It lay a prostrate wreck before the eyes of the granddaughter—but one must not expect everything of a tree that threw a mighty shade over one's great-great-grandfather! Although cremation was not in vogue in his day the names of Lowell's grandfather and grandmother, with their dates of departure, 1809 and 1817, are cut on gray stones adorned with urns and willow branches. How the fashions of men sweep in great recurring tides, even in our bodily attire, living or dead!

Emma, too, had felt the bleakness of the place for she wrote:

It is just the country to make men rugged in body and spirit and . . . in every direction the land looked like the billows of the sea. It seemed as if it beckoned one to sail them over and try the lands beyond. The severe wind was so chilling that it gave me a faint idea of what the winters here might be, and I could not help feeling thankful that your last days would be spent in a land of summer and sunshine. To breast this climate now would be a severe tax on one's vitality, I think. . . . Some one has said you went from Heath to the heathen, and I think in spiritual matters it would do the heathen in Heath good to have a missionary go among them and stay awhile. Everything spiritual as well as temporal is at low ebb here now.

One need not feel this to be repeating gossip, for in the last forty years Heath may have had such a revival as Lowell held responsible for the converting of himself and his parents in 1822. In replying to his daughter's "wonderful letter," Lowell writes:

Heath has been the birth place of many good men and women, whose blessed influence has been felt "*mai o-a-o*," East, West, North, and South, and is still rolling on like the waves of the sea. Glad you had a well informed pilot . . . of the second or third generation to pilot you all around town and off out West where my parents lived and brought up their family of children, but I dont take much stock in the genealogy of our ancestry of two or three centuries ago.

Accordingly, Lowell may not have known that his grandfather's grandfather Chileab was a great-grandfather of Mary Lyon. Undoubtedly numerous cousins in compact New

England many generations ago "knew not Joseph," nor many another of their brethren.

Not all of Emma's impressions of Heath was bleak. She wrote:

I can not possibly tell you all I experienced yesterday! I was living for you as well as for myself. I was going over the hills so well known to you, into the air that is so invigorating and life giving. We drove through East Charlemont and the way led us most of the way beside the Deerfield River. The opposite side of the river the railroad runs and we could see the trains flashing in and out among the beautiful trees. . . . After we passed the church we turned right up to the hills and then commenced the climb. But oh what a beautiful ride it was, almost every step of the way the trees met over the road and there was every possible variety of tree represented. Even the apple trees showered their red and yellow fruit into the road and we helped ourselves at one place to some Solomon Sweets. The autumn colors grew brighter the higher we climbed—the blaze of imprisoned sunshine shone upon us every step of the way. Brooks ran joyously by the roadside and tumbled into the ravines on either side. Down these we traced long rows of sugar maples and now and then the little cabins where the sugaring off is done. . . . In the afternoon . . . we started west. The view from the top of the hill was magnificent. The sun was flooding all those lovely hills and valleys—touching the woods that glowed in every direction with still more beautiful colors and illuminating all the farms with their sloping meadows and clusters of buildings. It was like looking into the "valley of blessing" or the "Promised land" or that place that "eye hath not yet seen." . . . We came to your old home. What a fine large house it was—how abundant the barns and what a beautiful situation! ! ! . . . The owner almost fell down at our feet in her pleasure at having . . . children of those . . . brought up in that house seventy-five years ago . . . come in. . . . Well . . . the ovation began! We went into the "east room" down stairs where your father and mother used to spend much of their time. The big fireplace with its crane, the convenient closets—all so handy—then into the sitting room west of the hall—the dining room back and the kitchen back of that . . . the pantries where nearly twenty pans of milk were set for cream—the back room, that was a sort of shop with the wood house still beyond. The back bedroom opening out of the kitchen—and then out of the kitchen door to the well, still able to furnish sweet water though not in constant use. The well sweep is gone but the curb and old oaken bucket looked . . . ancient enough to satisfy most everybody. . . . Upstairs . . . everything was as neat as wax but, I know, can not be nicer than when your mother reigned over them! . . . the garret over the kitchen—where herbs and dried fruit were hanging and old chests kept guard over treasured gatherings of a lifetime. . . . Another story higher . . . the floor was strewn with corn huskings to make beds of. They said no change had been made in the house since your day. . . . I tried to fancy your going in and out the side door that opened into the dining room and up and down the meadows bright in the setting sunshine. A home truly beautiful for situation. A short time ago an apple tree was cut down that was seventy-five years old. It probably bore in your day but had served its generation. Above the house was the row of sugar maples you helped plant when you were young, and the sugar house looked as if it might be a hundred years old! Near the road to Rowe we saw the spot where the old blacksmith shop stood that you worked in. . . . This is your wedding day—fifty-seven years ago and you and mother were married in Brandon and I suppose you came from there here. Well, I have thought many times in the last few hours that it was a beautiful place, uplifted by nature towards the heavens, from which to go forth on your life mission, to uplift others out of darkness into the light. How far you went . . . and how great is the fulness of your reward.

Here, then, on this Heath, uplifted from surrounding country, blown over by every wind of heaven, the powers of light and darkness stirred the cauldron of Lowell's soul, and from the stirring and scalding of such conviction of sin as this age little wots of, arose the submissive spirit that "thrice overturned" heard the still small voice commissioning him to seek those "uttermost parts" that were to be his long and congenial home.

Now the face turned for years to the blustering winds of outdoor toil, and hands that held the plow in spring, the scythe in summer, and worked at the anvil in winter were to be brought into the restricted space of a student's room with ill-smelling midnight oil and ancient text and cramping goose quill for company.

In a letter to his son Lowell Augustus, then working at Hilo, Lowell wrote in 1872:

. . . twenty years old today. That is just the age I was when my father allowed me to commence my studies, preparatory for college, Theological Seminary, the gospel ministry and a mission to the Sandwich Islands. Through my own efforts in keeping school with a little aid from the Education Society and the gift of my twenty-first year from my father, I prepared myself for the missionary work.

Williams College   Lowell does not name his preparatory school, but the chosen college was Williams, in lovely, sheltered Williamstown. What rewarding beauty greeted the eyes of Lowell's granddaughter after climbing the five flights of stairs in Memorial Tower! The white spire of the Congregational Church, the Library, East College and the growth of the modern town were not there when Lowell graduated just one hundred years before, but doubtless he had climbed to the highest window of West College, his recitation hall, or looked from his bedroom in the third floor of "Chapel," now Griffin Hall, on much the same picture. Although the village homes were not, alas, nestled under the arching elms, but were separated by straight-laced poplars, the stately mansion, now the residence of Williams' President, was a classic feature of the scene and the same fields smiled in the bowl made by the surrounding heights, Petersburg Mountain, the Taconic Range and Mt. Greylock seen through the famous "Hopper."

In the library Lowell is recorded as a "Senior Sophister of the class of 1828." Among his classmates was Samuel Irenaeus Prime, later the well-known and long-time editor of the New York *Observer*. The friendship between these two young men was lifelong and mutually stimulating. In the loneliness of his own widowed years Lowell wrote of the death of Dr. Prime:

Dear classmate, roommate, chum, correspondent, christian brother—gone—gone—Over the River—up to the New Jerusalem. Oh, what must it be to be there!

Williams College may have been chosen by Lowell for its propinquity to Heath, or from its interesting character. It is not unlikely, however, that its choice was made because of the religious redolence of the oft-quoted haystack under shelter of which during a sudden and violent thunderstorm a group of Williams College students had gathered for prayer.

Since even to the many visitors at Williams College who are shown the monument bearing a globe of the world the significance of its marking the spot of that "haystack" is obscure, it may be worth a pause to consider its meaning. It was on a summer afternoon of the year 1806 that Samuel Mills (the young man whose spirit our Abigail and her Andover friends so tenderly invoked that Sunday evening thirty-one years later as they walked in Mills Grove) and four other students were interrupted in a discussion of sending the gospel to Asia by the sudden clash of the elements. Mills said:

The Haystack

Let us make it a subject of prayer under the haystack, while the clouds are going and the clear sky is coming.*

Mills's was a spirit of great enthusiasm, yet it was so tempered by immediate calls of nearer duty and disciplined by true self-denial that he never saw Asia and made only one visit to "poor, degraded Africa"—a trip so exhausting as to cause his death on his way home. But his western tours in the home-missionary field were "remarkable achievements." Traveling over thousands of miles between the Gulf of Mexico and Lake Erie

he struggled with bridgeless creeks, dense cane-brakes, wretched fare, and the thousand hardships of pioneer life†

not to mention his encounters with practical and spiritual

* Leverett Wilson Spring, *A History of Williams College*.
† *Ibid.*

difficulties of creating interest in religion. Williams College today calls attention to the "One hundred, ninety thousand workers and the Fifty Million Dollars" that have sprung from the seed under the haystack and more than all cherishes the thought that even in its early life

the college encouraged men to think in terms of a world outlook.*

Williams College, as such, was born from the Free School (and the first of free schools) in West Township, established in 1755 by the will of one Ephraim Williams. In 1791 its

entire teaching staff and seven of the twelve trustees were graduates of Yale.†

A Lottery — Financial embarrassment seems to have been the portion of early colleges as well as early families in New England. It is an interesting circumstance that the first effort to increase the sum bequeathed by the founder, Ephraim Williams, which totaled only $11,277, eked out by a local subscription of $903.58, was made through legislative permission to establish a lottery "to raise a sum not exceeding twelve hundred pounds." Thus, this cradle of many a religious leader was, like Moses' basket of rushes, floated on a hazardous stream, the columns of the newspaper press announcing:

NOTHING VENTURE NOTHING HAVE
Not two blanks to a prize
Scheme of
Williamstown Free School
Lottery‡

Teacher — Early requirements in the qualifications of a teacher for Williams were

. . . good moral character of the Protestant type, all-round scholarship, skill in teaching and managing school boys, polished manners, and a mild disposition. . . . Good temper is a most essential requisite in a preceptor.§

* Spring, *A History of Williams College.*
† *Ibid.*
‡ *Ibid.*   § *Ibid.*

The curriculum in Lowell's day, blameless of any elec- *Curriculum* tives, was orthodoxically classic, giving large room to Latin, Greek, English, and mathematics through junior year, introducing Hebrew, natural philosophy, and chemistry in that year and anatomy, mental and moral philosophy, political economy, and theology in the senior year. Declamations in chapel were emphasized throughout the course, and also

. . . Punctual attendance is required at church and at morning and evening prayers, as well as on recitations and other collegiate exercises. An account is kept of all delinquencies in these duties, which is open to the inspection of parents and guardians and the corporation.*

The expense account of a student, including tuition, room *Fees* rent, library charges, ordinary repairs, board, washing, and food totaled from $77 to $102.25.

To young men designed for the ministry . . . assistance is given in board, money and clothing, by the aid of charitable societies in Williamstown and other places.†

A tremendous revival of religion "occurred in 1825." *Revival at* Years after, Dr. Irenaeus Prime referring to this revival *Williams* spoke of its "unexpected consequences." Referring to the period 1826–29 he said:

There were in the local classes of the college some of the wickedest youth I ever knew. . . . Parents who had profligate sons sent them here that they might come under the power of divine grace.‡

What would be the immediate effect of such a program as *Program* this?

From the opening of the college year until the first of May the day began with prayers in the chapel "at sunrise or a little before." Vespers . . . at sundown. On Sunday there were religious services morning, afternoon, and evening, with attendance required at the first two.§

* *Ibid.* † *Ibid.*
‡ *Ibid.* § *Ibid.*

Yet we are assured by those who seem to know that at that very time

the great majority were clean, earnest, studious fellows, who got their education at the cost of no little resolution and self-denial . . . and . . . in spite of . . . distractions . . . made a creditable intellectual record.*

Williams Commencement

One wrote of the commencement at which Lowell was a graduate:

Dr. Griffin presided . . . conferred the degrees, and figured as the master of the assembly with a grace and awe-inspiring presence, not only unsurpassed, but never equalled by any other personage, so far as I have had opportunity to observe. . . . For entire success and almost histrionic power of display and influence, I always recur to that scene at Williams, though all raining and storming without, in 1828 as . . . the climax of majesty, propriety, and excellence.†

President's Preaching

A History of Williams College, from which already quotations have been made, gives a portion of an undergraduate poem in blank verse descriptive of the preaching of Dr. Griffin. Passing over the dazzling picture of heaven, we read:

He spoke of Hell! and with instinctive dread
The affrighted heart recoiled, Despair's last
Agonizing shriek ascending pierced the
Soul and drunk its spirits up—the never
Dying worm with closer grasp embraced its
Victim and deeper thrust its deadly fangs—
The lurid fires that quenchless burn, arose
In forky flames, and threw their painful light
Upon the drear abode, where restless toss
On raging seas of flames the sinner lost,
While on their heads the wrath of God in one
Eternal storm descends.‡

Theology as thus described, plus the fervent intonations of passages from *Paradise Lost*, would surely make a lurid

* Spring, *A History of Williams College.*
† *Ibid.*   ‡ *Ibid.*

background in the expressions of faith in life, death, and
judgment of those young men who faced heathen ground as
their end and aim of endeavor. Doubtless such pictures inspired the cries of agony from the lips of Lowell when,
wearied with the heat and burden of the day in his far-away
mission field, he despaired of success in saving souls from
such a future.

Of Lowell's life and experiences at Auburn Seminary we   *Auburn*
know almost nothing save that it was very pleasant to him to *Seminary*
find as his first associate in the Islands "Brother Hitchcock,"
whom he had known at Auburn as well as at Williams. Some
years later he had a balancing unpleasant experience in
having for a time as house guest a chaplain from an American man-of-war, also an acquaintance at Auburn. The man,
to speak most charitably, must have been in the process of
becoming insane and was soon after removed from the navy.

Regarding the Seminary, this seems to be all obtainable
from Lowell's journal:

February 3rd, 1835;—As for metaphysical discussions on
the subject of religion, I think them unprofitable and worse
than vain. I was happy to get through that business when in the
Theo. Sem. I think I enjoy a meal of victuals when well served
up better than the dry speculation or discussion of the how and
why and wherefore the bones grew and the meat and skin, etc.
Sin I regard as an eternal enemy to God and holiness and
happiness. Repentance and faith in the Lord Jesus Christ is its
only remedy.

The rest of the short paragraph amplifying his freedom
from metaphysics, to his own satisfaction, is so dogmatic to
the eyes of his grandchildren as better to be left unquoted.
It is one more testimony to the infinite number of transla-
tions of our Pilgrim forebears' freedom to worship God.

While dogmatic assertions are sadly forbidding, Lowell's   *Lowell's*
descendants possess one document too sacred to profane by   *Covenant*
print—a sheet of mellowed paper on which is written his
"Secret Covenant with God." Adopted in 1823 and revised
in 1831, signed by himself, and laid away with his recorded
resolution "to read and renew . . . as often as every com-

munion day," its spirit, breathing humility, utter devotion, and submission, grips the imagination with its likeness in character to another covenant made thousands of years ago on the plains of Mamre, the heights of Hebron, when a man "believed in the Lord; and he counted it to him for righteousness," and received the word, "thy seed shall be a stranger in a land that is not theirs," also, "thou shalt go to thy fathers in peace; thou shalt be buried in a good old age."

Other documents extant record the examination and ordination of Lowell, who was already licensed to preach the gospel,

as an Evangelist with particular reference to his entering upon a Foreign Mission at the Sandwich Islands under the patronage of the American Board of Commissioners for Foreign Missions.

The ordination occurred at Heath, Massachusetts, September, 1832.

3. A LONG WEDDING JOURNEY

The Roster   While we have been reviewing the years of his young life Lowell has preached his last sermon, the *Mentor* is ready to sail from New London, Connecticut, the roll of passengers is called:

Mrs. Hannah B. Rice, Captain's wife
Rev. John Deill, Seaman's Chaplain for Sandwich Islands
Mrs. Caroline A. Deill
Rev. Benjamin W. Parker ⎫ Missionaries of the American
Mrs. Mary E. Parker   ⎪ Board of Commissioners for
Rev. Lowell Smith   ⎬ Foreign Missions to the Sand-
Mrs. Abba W. T. Smith   ⎭ wich Islands
Mr. Lemuel Fuller, Printer
Mr. Charles Burnham, Carpenter
Mr. Joseph A. Smith, Merchant to the Society Islands from
     England
Mr. John Toohane, Native of the Sandwich Islands

Are the real entities of our forbears shown to us much more than as silhouettes on the wall of our life? Familiar,

characteristic, sometimes, perhaps, a little grotesque, due to
necessary lack of perspective on their parts or ours; an influence, but full of unrevelation and mystery? What depths
lie behind the flat shadows? What inherited springs caused
the reactions of words, of motives? What changes in mental
and spiritual attitudes wrought by circumstances are visible
in the outlines sketched by a record of their years, told by
themselves or others?

Our years are like the shadows on sunny hills that lie . . .
a sleep, a dream, a story. . . .

Still, we love shadows of people as we do shadows on the
face of nature, tracery of trees upon the grass, the silhouette
of the austere mountain against the twilight sky, the shadow
of a great rock in a weary land. And in the shadows, the un-
discovered, the indescribable, we take refuge, we find comfort
from the burden and the heat of the day.

Lowell and Abigail with still-continued delays and false
departures now board the vessel at the call of the captain;
now, as a storm threatens, disembark with, one must think,
some embarrassing repetitions of farewell. At last on Friday,
November 23, 1832, accompanied for some ten or twelve
miles by a group of New London friends, who returned in a
sloop, Lowell writes:

We all took our final leave of America in good spirits and as
the city of N. L. and its neighboring hills was forever receding
from our view we sung the "Missionaries' Farewell," "Green-
land's Icy Mountains" and some other appropriate tunes.

Youth is youth, despite race or period. There must have *The Call*
been the thrill of adventure mingled with the call of conscience to go to the ends of the earth and preach the gospel
to every creature while crime flourished throughout the New
England villages they left behind them. There must have
been something alluring in the idea of the call. The shepherd
on a thousand hills halloes to his sheep and those that are his
come. Perhaps the young missionaries had no compunctions
for the drunkard in his gutter at home or the felon awaiting
the rope, since the gospel call had been sounded in their ears,

too—ears guilty of not heeding. Was not the burden that of *giving* the call and leaving the hearers to the mercies of the Lord, with possibly an unworded "the Devil take the hindermost?" The picture of the Hawaiian youth with his conch shell, in lieu of the bell of other civilizations, giving the call to prayer, as to this day the muezzin shouts from his watchtower, is an inspiring one. The ears that hear not are left to their doom.

Abigail, some years later, writing to a sister missionary obliged to return home from the mission, gave this comforting (?) philosophy.

The Sheep and the Goats

When you leave, I hope you will not allow yourself to be overcome by emotion. Your delicate health will not allow it. Try to feel as if you were only going to another Island. . . . Leave your flock in the hands of the great Sheperd—All that are his shall never be plucked from his faithful keeping. And the goats will go to their own place whether you go or stay.

There is no doubt that in these devoted lines conscience was as large as the heart. But, thanks be, they were possessed of a sanctified common sense—a saving grace. There must, too, have been a deal of curiosity and a great sense of adventure mingled with Christian devotion and missionary zeal and indeed the zeal of that day savored of an importance far greater and more romantic than that which attends the missionary of today. Was he not a chosen vessel set apart for a definite, clear-cut service? Experience was to test him on most prosaic scales and he was not to be found wanting; the banner of the Cross was not to go down in the mud and scum of things but was to represent idealism ever waving over the slough of despond.

The Open Sea

If only this, the first ocean voyage of Lowell and Abigail, could have savored more of adventure than it did! Probably it was Lowell's first sight of the ocean, as Long Island Sound opened its mouth to exclaim at the Atlantic! It is more likely that Abigail, also inland born, had enjoyed the ocean shore beyond the dunes of Ipswich during her days as pupil and teacher there. Perhaps she ran over the dunes, filling her shoes with sand—perhaps she flung her arms in the wind and

OLD CHOATE BRIDGE
THE OLDEST ARCH BRIDGE IN AMERICA, BUILT 1764
IPSWICH, MASSACHUSETTS

SAND DUNES, IPSWICH BEACH
IPSWICH, MASSACHUSETTS

chanted the lines of the young poet Byron, "Roll on, thou deep and dark blue ocean—roll!" Abigail may tell most of the story of the voyage, with Lowell looking over her shoulder, as it were, when she cons her journal, and interspersing his own versions now and then.

ABIGAIL: I shall not attempt to give you a particular description of the scene of our final separation from America. We stood for the last time on her shores, listened to the last prayers that commended us to the watchful care of our covenant God, exchanged the last tokens of affection with dear friends, dropped our last tears on the beach, and then said farewell to home and native land and friends until that day "when heavens shall be on fire and the elements shall melt with fervent heat and the dead from the four winds of heaven shall be assembled before the throne of Jehovah Jesus to receive a just reward for their deeds."

There is a gloom in this, recalling to me a scene of five and forty years ago—the prostration of a nun taking the black veil when a pall was lowered upon her motionless figure lying on the floor of the cathedral. Serious as this event was, perhaps Abigail would not so have recounted it had not Lowell shed this light upon her situation.

LOWELL: Abba had flattered herself that she should escape sea sickness and have the gratification of going from room to room as a public nurse tendering her services to each of the patients . . . but notwithstanding her plans . . . she was the first who came under the influence of the common foe. . . . I have had the gratification of waiting upon her. *Abigail's Ambition*

ABIGAIL: [on the first storm, thirty-six hours long, beginning December 1st, in Latitude thirty-four] We then witnessed what we had often heard from others, the violent contention of wind and wave which our little bark labored hard to buffet. At one moment she was riding high over some mountain wave—at another plunged between those that yawned as if to engulph her. Again rocking from side to side and receiving the waves that every few minutes broke over her deck and flowing down the companion way and steerage hatchway deposited themselves in *First Storm* the cabin and state rooms below. . . . We had often pictured such scenes as this to ourselves when contemplating our voyage, yet to a fresh sailor it could not fail of appearing terrific. At length He

> "Who rides upon the stormy sky
> And manages the seas"

spoke peace to the contending elements, and we were permitted to rejoice in his preserving mercy. There is something inexpressibly sublime in such a storm at sea if one can contemplate it without thinking of immediate danger but when the wind blows longer and harder and every successive billow threatens louder than the last to bury us in its embrace, we are more likely to yield to emotions of fear than sublimity.

LOWELL: [on the same storm] The "Mentor" groaned as if her task was intolerable. The Captain however cheered the crew and passengers. . . . "The ship" said he "is sound and strong, an excellent sea boat and she sails like a duck." A number of our little band spent a sleepless night fearful lest the next sea would close their probation. . . . But for some reason my mind was wonderfully composed. Some may call it "stoicism" others "fatalism" and others "unpardonable stupidity" but at present I shall call it *unshaken confidence in God*. I very deliberately reviewed the providences of God with me and the motives which induced me to enter upon this voyage and mission and I could not believe that I was a Jonah who must be cast overboard in order that the crew and other passengers might be saved. . . . Come life or death I have no wish to retrace my steps.

Jump Rope   ABIGAIL: [a fortnight later] My dear husband is suffering from dyspepsia owing to want of proper exercise. . . . I should rejoice if he could have an hour or two on land every day, he however does what he can by walking the deck, jumping the rope, climbing the rigging, etc. Today several fin-backed whales, a shoal of flying fish and the mast of a vessel were discovered.

Vault of   December 15th, latitude 25, 39, n. longitude 27, 50, w. Last
Heaven   evening at nine o'clock I went on deck with my husband and spent some time in contemplating the calm loveliness of an evening at sea. . . . There was scarcely the smallest cloud to obscure the brilliancy exhibited in the deep vault of heaven. I

never witnessed such a blaze of starry beauty. It seemed as if the broad canopy of the universe was desirous of displaying all her treasures and on the present occasion had decked herself in all her richest jewelry. We sat for some time gazing on the wonders of the vast creation presented to our view and our thoughts were led upward to admire the wisdom, power and goodness of the great Creator.

Moonlight and phosphorescence, the fireflies of America, are also her delight.

LOWELL: But what adds very much to the grandeur and sublimity of this planetary world is the "animal cula" of the sea. It is truly wonderful to behold the rolling sea all full of sparkling eyes . . . apparently striving to outnumber and out shine the stars of heaven.

ABIGAIL: December 18th. The sun begins to shed its tropical rays, but we have a fine breeze. . . . I rise early and sometimes walk half an hour before breakfast. . . . Have begun to study Latin, and hope to forward with it a course of reading to advantage. December 19th. [After describing a beautiful flying fish caught and examined] I could not but think they lead a sorry life. The dolphin is its deadly enemy. In escaping from the jaws of this foe by the use of their wings they often meet the fate they dread from aquatic birds in search of prey. December 22nd. We have been sailing for the last three days in sight of the Cape de Verds. . . . We approached so near Fuego that the smoke issuing from its volcanic top might be distinctly seen and also a little village of white houses on the beach. . . . My own feelings were little short of transport as we drew near enough to distinguish the green verdure that covered the valleys and . . . although . . . the Islands appeared little else than one irregular range of rocky mountains, my imagination was ready to convert it into a Paradise, so welcome was the sight of land. Upon a near approach however we could discover no trace of inhabitants along the shore . . . and the vessel put out to sea again. I was disappointed—for the Captain had intended sending on shore some provisions for the . . . inhabitants . . . suffering from severe famine.

LOWELL: December 24th. All on board, whether rational, or

Latin

*Flying
Fish*

Rain

irrational, men, beasts, or fowls, have been greatly refreshed today with a copious shower of rain. . . . As the clouds began to approach and give token of their particular errand, all hands were summoned on deck and preparations were made for catching water. Seven new whale boats were used for tubs . . . besides some eight or ten pails and buckets which were set under the rigging to catch the water as it came rushing down the sails and spars in torrents. . . . The crew appeared to enjoy it as much as the geese and swine which were then liberated from their unpleasant prisons.

Christmas Day

ABIGAIL: This day is observed by the sailers as a holly day. A sumptuous dinner was prepared for crew and passengers. Ours consisted of meats, chickens, baked geese, mince pie, etc., and the crew fared equally well. Captain Rice is as anxious to provide well for his crew as passengers. This circumstance gratifies me very much. . . . This is altogether the warmest Christmas I ever spent and forms a striking contrast with the one last passed in America. . . . We are now in Mr. Stewart's "swamp" rapidly approaching the line. We have frequent squalls of rain and wind. I think the name Mr. Stewart has given this part of the ocean very apropos.

December 28th. Last evening we were visited by a beautiful little bird which Captain Rice called a sea dove. It resembled in its whole appearance a land dove but was not quite as large. After examining it carefully we let the little creature fly, unwilling to circumscribe its range of happy freedom. It however expressed its disapprobation of our familiarity by pecking our fingers before it left us.

Fête Days

Both these young travelers failed not to mark the milestones of New Year's day and their birthdays, which came only a week apart, and to review the way they had come, asking divine blessing on their further path.

Before the day of typewriters or even the use of carbon sheets for hand-written letters, our young people faithfully copied their journals for their families and churches at home. Lowell's two volumes of diary record from time to time thus:

NOTICE ! ! My journal is transcribed and forwarded to Father up to this date.

Abigail sometimes varies a little her report sent home, leaving out little tendernesses of their private lives, for example:

January 1st, 1833, This morning I was awakened by some one whispering in my ear "I wish you a happy new year." I looked up and found it was my dear husband and I am sure that wish was heartily reciprocated by me. . . . Very ill all day yesterday. Kept my husband confined all day to our stateroom taking care of me. . . . My times are in the hands of a being who will do all things well, and leaning on his kind arms I will go cheerfully forward. . . . Before this year is over may I and my beloved companion be permitted to rejoice over sinners converted to God through our instrumentality. What a privilege this! Who could desire a greater?

With the active interest in youth already noted, Abigail writes of John Toohane the native Islander now returning to his country: *Toohane*

He gives good evidence of genuine piety. Could we indulge the pleasing thought that he is a fair representative of his countrymen we should not feel that we were going to a heathen land. But he is, I believe, a fair specimen of what they will be when the gospel with its mild rays and attendant blessings has had its due influence upon them. In alluding to the darkness in which his countrymen were involved . . . he was affected to tears. He takes lively interest in missionary operations and appears delighted that a new reinforcement of missionaries are now on their way to his native land. He is in judgement and information on many subjects altogether a man. He bears two marks of former heathenism about him which cannot be effaced. One, the tattooing of his arms and the other the loss of the upper and lower front teeth, which were extracted when the queen died.

LOWELL: January 9th. . . . an event . . . which caused some anxiety not only among the passengers but even the Captain was alarmed. In the afternoon a sail was descried about two points off the windward bow, sailing across our track, apparently bound to Rio Janeiro. It having been some time since we had forwarded letters to America, the captain was anxious to *Mysterious Boat* speak her. At ten in the eve he despaired of falling in with her by plain sailing, being almost becalmed and she was like to pass our bow. She was then about two miles distant, but it was thought best to send a boat and board her if practicable, notwithstanding it was night and the distance so great. At eleven o'clock two of the mates and four or five of the crew set off, the moon shone bright but soon the boat was not to be seen. The captain had given them orders that if he should raise two lights to return to the ship without delay. Soon after they left the ship, the breeze of wind stiffened and we sailed nearly as fast as they could row. Indeed one of the men felt sure that they had fallen in the rear. Two lights were immediately set—after a suitable length of time for them to return, but nothing was seen of them, the ship was hauled to and two more lights were raised, one on mast head. Soon two lights were discovered on the neighboring sail. This gave a momentary relief, still the Captain was in suspense. In a few moments the boat returned safe and sound. They had spoken and boarded the vessel. . . . The return of the boat cheered us all especially those who convert every other innocent vessel into a habitation of pirates.

Sharks, with attendant pilot fish "guarding their sovereign's life," and whales as neighbors are reported. Any pupil of Abigail will remember *The Child's Book of Nature* as a favorite textbook and so will not be surprised that Abigail must describe the albatross, although we wonder she did not quote Coleridge's *Ancient Mariner*.

Albatross

ABIGAIL: January 25th. The sea around our vessel is thronged with a large sea bird called Albatross. Three have been caught today. This is a very large bird about three times the size of a goose and is the largest of marine kinds. The color is grayish brown or whitish color with lines of black upon the back and wings. The hinder part of its body is white. The end of the tail and a great part of the wings are black. The bill is very long, thick and straight, terminating in a hook. The toes are long and are webbed and membrane. There is no hind toe or nail. The nails are short and blunt. The tail is rounded and composed of fourteen feathers. Its wings when extended measured from ten to twelve feet from tip to tip. These have three joints and are very narrow, but the albatross being very strong flies to a great distance. At night it sleeps upon the waves. It is very voracious and is said to be a perfect emblem of gluttony. When it finds abundance of food it eats to such excess that it can neither fly nor swim. It is often seen in this state with a fish partly swallowed and partly hanging out of its mouth. It builds its nest on land. It is said that neither the flesh or feathers of this bird are good for use. . . . Captain Rice says that the seabirds have no gizzards—a fact hitherto unknown to us.

ABIGAIL: February 5th. We lie almost becalmed near Cape Horn. A shoal [of whales] was discovered so near the ship that we had a distinct view of them when they rose to the surface of the water and the noise of their blowing was distinctly heard. Some of them were probably seventy feet long. I am astonished at the wonders of the deep with which we are from day to day made acquainted. . . . Dew that wets my bonnet makes me think of evenings at home. *Whales*

LOWELL: [also astonished] When I was a lad and went to a common school, memorizing the geographical description of Tierra del Fuego as the most southerly land of South America, the southern extremity of which is Cape Horn, I little thought then that I should ever make this land from these wide waters. But so it is. I am a wonder to myself . . . verily a sojourner and a pilgrim—may I improve by . . . every distinguishing providence. A number of porpoises were seen playing around the stern of the ship this morning and this afternoon a large fin-backed whale came right along side and blowed a number of times. *Porpoise*

February 11th. Captain Brayton of Nantucket returning from a whaling expedition on the coast of Japan, came on board our vessel and breakfasted with us. . . . He brought us intelligence direct from the Islands whither we are bound. Said the mission was in a prosperous state. . . . This news to us is like cold water to a thirsty soul. We can hardly wait to reach the islands so anxious are we to engage with our brethren in their delightful labors. . . . While Captain Brayton was on board, another ship hove in sight. . . . While these three ships were all lying within speaking distance a fourth came along side *Island News*

and proved to be going in the same direction with ourselves
. . . a most cheering sight to us in this distant latitude.

Courtesies   On February thirteenth Captain Brayton won the hearts
of our voyagers and Lowell describes an exchange of courtesies between the two captains of oranges, lemons, and yams
(which excited Abigail's curiosity as probably a part of her
Island diet but which disappointed her as well), on the one
hand, for bread, onions, and dried apples, on the other. But
in the aftermath of the visit the host called his departed
guest "liar, impolite, barbarian, hog." Lowell tried to solve
the "mystery of iniquity" in the man who had seemed to him
"like a father and brother" and lined the two seamen up thus
on combative points:

1.	Jacksonian	Anti-Jacksonian
2.	Mason	Anti-Mason
3.	Tobacco	Anti-Tobacconist
4.	No Christian	Zealous Christian

Iceberg   ABIGAIL: February 18th. Early on the morning of the six-
teenth an iceberg was discovered several miles to the windward
of us and we were all to see the wonderful and to us new spec-
tacle. Its form when first discovered was like three large conical
pillars, but it changed its appearance frequently as it moved
with the current. We were becalmed most of the day and it
gradually approached us. Its appearance when the sun shone
upon it was truly splendid, being of the purest, brilliant white.
But I regarded it as such an enemy that I could not think much
at the time of the beauty of its appearance. Captain Rice said
a vessel and an iceberg would mutually attract each other in a
calm though ten miles apart. We did not however approach
nearer than two or three miles before a breeze sprang up that
bore us beyond its reach. About sundown a multitude of these
floating islands were discovered to the leeward of us. Captain
Rice judged there might be a hundred of them. They were most
unwelcome visitors. . . . I felt more agitated than I ever have
since we sailed. But our Heavenly Father was better to us than
our fears.

Doubling   February 20th. Captain Rice cheered us all this morning by
Cape Horn   announcing the joyful intelligence that we *have doubled Cape*

Horn. . . . We have accomplished the most difficult and dangerous part of our voyage. Indeed we have experienced nothing frightful except the icebergs. . . . Captain Rice says we might make the voyage a thousand times and not find the like success. We had all made such calculations for a tremendous time that it had proved quite a disappointment, although a happy one.

Lowell takes the same occasion to philosophize. Since he is so young we will indulge him. He writes:

Lowell Philoso- phizes

Various circumstances contribute to render the minutes about to be recorded in my journal for this day worthy of considerable attention. In every person's history there are certain eventful periods which seem to be very prominent in his history to be summed up. The child looks forward to the day when he shall become of age as of great moment to him. The student anticipates with great interest the day when he shall receive academic honours as a reward for his anxiety, studiousness and good behavior during the four years course of mental discipline, acquisitions etc. The Traveller often anticipates various hardships in his journey, certain dangerous bridges that must be crossed, steep and difficult mountains to be traversed, etc., and when these have been safely passed his heart leaps for joy and he proceeds onward with new zeal. So the skilful and experienced mariner about to sail for some port across wide waters, looks forward to certain latitudes and longitudes through which he must pass, as the most dangerous, as places where many a ship has been cast upon her beam's end, foundered and lost, and having made these islands, passed these rocks, and quicksands, and doubled such and such capes, he feels that he has encountered the most difficult and dangerous part of his voyage. . . . Our passage has been unusually short and pleasant, about thirteen days, and I presume one third part of this time we lay becalmed, drifting with the current, which by the way was against us.

But doubling Cape Horn was not all the excitement of that day. Abigail resumes her story:

This afternoon we were all exceedingly alarmed by the cry "John Jepson is overboard." A scene of great excitement en-

Man Overboard

sued and the orders "down with the helm—bring the ship about
—throw over the tubs—throw over the sky light—cut away the
lashing of the boat—dont stop to untie it—dont let him drown
—save him—save him—" followed each other in quick succession from the presiding officer. He caught by one of the tubs
until he saw the boat when he was taken up by the second mate
and soon brought on board. The lad is about fourteen years old
and was thus mercifully rescued from an early and watery
grave.

Lowell's comments on this incident are:

It is thought that he (John) was extremely careless in falling
into the water. It is hoped that this event will constrain him to
remember his Creator in the days of his youth and seek first the
kingdom of God. . . . This event led the brothers and sisters to
relate a great number of anecdotes of a similar kind, and mention some of the hairbreadth escapes through which we had
personally passed, etc. . . . It is presumed as many accidents
happen on land as on the water.

On the twenty-second, Lowell is again inclined to be medi-
tative, writing:

Medita-
tions

To a person of considerable imagination and who possesses
strong nerves to bear the sight, the rolling of the sea, the
ascending and descending of the vessel upon the mighty billows
is among the most grand and sublime objects in the world. A
ship supplied with provisions, manned with officers and a crew,
in other words with rulers and ruled . . . having travellers or
passengers on board, all floating on the wide waters may be considered as a world in miniature, or as one of Earth's satellites.
Here nearly all the mechanic arts are in operation—here are
almost every description of character from the parent to the
child, from the serious devoted chaplain to the profane and
heaven provoking blasphemer—temperate and intemperate—
learned and ignorant—the sick—the lame, sane and insane;
some who are laying up their treasures on earth, others in heaven
—some seeking the praise of men, others the praise of God;
some who make the chart, binnacle and compass their constant
resort and guide to their desired port, others who go to the

sanctuary and the word of God as their pole star and guide through time to the haven of eternal rest and peace.

The suggestion of insanity on board was only too real a horror and disturbed the peace of the whole voyage. For despite enough "blisters" and "bleedings" administered according to the custom of the day one of the passengers had had repeated attacks of the sort thus described:

LOWELL: Brother F. had today another turn of insanity and madness. . . . Pondered awhile upon committing suicide and then threatened the lives of others with his jack knife in his hand. No one dared approach him except with a long weapon of defence. He came to about eleven o'clock, delivered up his knife and wept like a child.

ABIGAIL: February 28th. It has pleased our Heavenly Father *Hurricane* to shake us over a watery grave and then snatch us from its embrace. Yesterday morning about seven o'clock another gale of wind commenced which so rapidly increased that before eleven o'clock it blew a hurricane. Captain Rice and the third mate ascended the rigging and took down the gallant yards from the mainmast. . . . Captain Rice had not performed such a duty for many years but there was not a sailor that dared to undertake it. Everything was secured in the best manner possible. About noon while our little bark was laboring hard to keep herself above water a dreadful sea broke over her weather bow and dashed with overwhelming force the quantity of one hundred tons, as it was judged, upon it. The shock was dreadful and the damage done, much. The bulwarks and davits were under the water which stood above a man's head upon the deck. The forecastle was open and two men coming out of it, the water rushed with fury down the hatchway knocking them down, filled some of the berths with water and one sick man was nearly covered in his berth. Two whale boats on deck were instantly stove to pieces, one lashed to the side of the ship was instantly carried away, the stern boat was so injured that it was cut away and lost. Two gallant yards fastened under the boats were broken in several places and a grindstone weighing one hundred sixty pounds was swept overboard. The head of the ship and parts of the bulwark were broken. After one or two rolls the ship cleared

herself so as to rise above the water. Fears were entertained
that some of the men were lost but on examination none were
found missing although one of them was swept over board but
he caught by the rigging and saved himself and another was
carried by the water on deck against the side of the ship, when
had he not caught by the rigging he might have found a watery
grave. Some of the officers and most experienced seamen have
since told us they supposed our case hopeless, that we should
never rise more. Captain Rice says had ours been an old vessel
she would probably never have survived such a scene. He says
he never knew so heavy a sea break upon a ship before, although
he has been a sailor more than twenty years and that he might
make a hundred voyages and never experience the like again.
. . . Captain Rice has been unable to get a lunar observation
for some days, which causes considerable anxiety as we may be
too near land. . . . Our confidence in our Almighty protector
is strengthened and we trust we shall be preserved from harm.

This experience drives Lowell again to philosophizing:

Cause of
Storm?

The wind blew a hurricane. Indeed I do not know but it was
equal to Paul's Euroclydon Acts 27, chapter five. . . . The
reason of our being thus driven about is unknown to us. It may
be that there is some Jonah on board, fleeing from the path of
duty. It may be owing to the awful profanity among the crew,
or God may be answering a very unwise and inconsistent wish
of "an officer" "I hope we shall have a head wind for six months
so as to be obliged to sail with doubled reefed top sails"!! God
sometimes takes such men at their word. Again, it may be because the missionaries on board have put too much confidence
in a firm, well built ship and in experienced, skilful officers,
rather than in the arm of Almighty strength. . . . Or it may
be because we have been unfaithful as christians, both towards
God and man. It certainly becomes us all to inquire honestly
and immediately and individually "Lord, is it I? Lord is it I?"

ABIGAIL: March 4th. We shall be unable to say we doubled
Cape Horn in thirteen days for thirteen more elapsed before we
were beyond the reach of its dangers and the owners of the
"Mentor" will have six and seven hundred dollars done to their

ship to repair in consequence of our trespassing on its briny
territories.

March unexpectedly brought calms and the exasperated
captain declared he would "never ship any more females from
America," as the voyage had been "nothing but gales and
calms." Indeed, the rolling of the ship in the calms is so disagreeable that Abigail is

constrained to say,

> "Far more the treacherous calm I dread
> Than tempest bursting on my head."

Abigail viewed the calm morning of March 19 thus:

When I awoke this morning the golden rays of a bright sun
were reflected through our little skylight into our state room.
The cocks were crowing, the hens were joining their notes with
these and I almost expected to hear the sweet well-known notes
of the robin awaking man from his slumbers and calling him
forth at early day to enjoy the beauties of a May morning. I
arose and went early on deck, when instead of the fresh green
grass and early flowers glittering in fresh dewdrops—nature's
jewelry, a boundless ocean met my farthrest gaze. But the
morning scene at sea was far from being without its attractions.
The light clouds scattered here and there over the blue heavens,
the reflections of the sun's rays upon the deep colored waves as
they rose and fell in regular undulations, our noble ship loaded
with canvas, its tall mast towering to the heavens as it glided
calmly through the deep waters of the Pacific, together with the
many animated countenances that met my eye, all presented a
scenery worthy of admiration, so that I was far from being
discontented with my situation.

*Morning
at Sea*

When the wind is fair Abigail cons her Virgil and says her
tutor commends her proficiency. Crossing the Equator brings
extreme heat and debility.

Abigail: There has scarcely been a well person from fore to
aft in the ship . . . oppressive it is to lie perfectly still day
after day and constantly exposed to the searching rays of a
vertical sun.

At last the trades, and the log tells of two hundred, and, as the end of the voyage is reached, two hundred fifty miles in a day.

April fifth brings the death of a seaman and burial at sea. Lowell is deeply impressed by the circumstances and writes:

Burial at Sea

The body was properly wrapped in a winding sheet and then a large piece of canvas wound tight about the body. About eighty pounds of iron, sewed in a bag, was attached to the feet which caused the body to sink. . . . The crew and . . . passengers . . . assembled. . . . Dr. Deill read a few verses of scripture and then a hymn "Hark from the tombs" etc. He then offered a short prayer and made a few remarks on the resurrection of the body. The body was then carried to the starboard side of the ship and . . . the Chaplain read a few more verses in the latter part of the Seaman's hymn book. The captain then with uplifted hand exclaimed "dust thou art and to dust thou must return." These words being uttered, the body was instantly plunged into the deep and sunk among the pearls of ocean no more to rise till the resurrection morning. The scene was novel and to me in some respects more affecting than a funeral ceremony on land.

April also has fateful calms depressing bodies, exciting minds. Lowell's spirit cries out from a harassed body:

Becalmed . . . becalmed . . . becalmed. . . . Crew sickening. . . . Captain has bleeding enough to do. . . . Air seems to be completely burned. . . . "Guarantee" fails—reason absent —passions rage. Jesus wilt thou come and dethrone thy rival Satan and reign in the hearts of all on board.

Booby

April 16th, a Booby lit upon the stern . . . and was caught. . . . It appeared to sicken and immediately vomited up four flying fish two of which appeared as fresh as if just taken from the sea. It . . . much resembled a pigeon hawk—his wings from each extremity measuring about a yard and a half.

Maui Sighted

The trade winds now bring swift and prosperous voyaging and in the evening of April twenty-ninth both Abigail and Lowell record the sight of Maui. Says Abigail:

As it is deemed unsafe sailing in this region during the night the ship will lay to until daylight. I imagine there will be little rest among us however. The sailors are so overjoyed that they can do nothing but sing as loud as they can all the time.

But the young lady thinks no apology is necessary for a little joyful excitement on such an occasion as the present. Next day Lowell adds:

Land ho at day break. . . . We are about twenty miles North of "Mowe." All the canvas is spread to the wind, every person on board seems to be inspired with enthusiasm. . . . Hoped to make Oahu before dark. But hark! what is that crash. Ah! by a too great pressure of sail, the mizzen top mast has given way and but for the rigging, the mast, gallant yards, etc., would all have unceremoniously landed on deck.

ABIGAIL: May 1st, A bright morning and fair strong wind finds us twenty miles from Oahu, steering direct for the harbor of Honolulu. . . . We have just doubled Diamond Hill and begin to distinguish considerable diversity of appearance in the face of the country. Mountains and vallies alternately meet our view—very few trees near the shore—only here and there a row of cocoanuts, answering exactly in their appearance to the idea I had formed of them. The grass does not look fresh and green, but exhibits more of the appearance of our fields in autumn than the ever verdant spring. *Oahu Sighted*

An idol temple, or more properly the ruins of one, has just been pointed out to me. Thanks be to God that precious prophecy predicting the utter abolition of Idolatry and the universal reign and worship of King Emanuel is already beginning to be fulfilled. May all who nominally acknowledge him worship him in spirit and in truth, and those who yet cleave to gods their own hands have formed speedily hear, believe and receive the only Savior as offered in the glorious gospel. Several large ships are already seen in the harbor. We are borne on with great rapidity. Our national banner waves proudly over our stern and the Bethel Flag raised top mast high—exhibiting the dove bearing the olive branch—gives token of the embassage we bring. *Idol Temple*

Nine o'clock A.M. Our anchor is just dropped among several other ships in a safe harbour about two miles from land. One or *Anchor Dropped*

two boats from the other ships are already alongside us. It is
cheering to see some of our countrymen here. But what do I see
on board that ship near our stern? For what purpose are so
many females seen among the crew? Ah me! Their bold and in-
delicate figures indicate their characters. But can this be a ship
from a christian land? Let me look again. Ah yes, I read the
well known name of the port from which she sailed. But is this
the character in which I must first see these poor heathen for
whose salvation I have come to the ends of the earth? And are
my endeavors to do them good to be thus counteracted by men
who bear the name of Christian? My faith almost fails me. I
have come to tell them of the dreadful consequences of their
vicious courses and to point out a better and happier way, but
one directly contrary to their sinful propensities. These men,
who have like myself come from a christian land, by their conduct say we are false. And will not these poor deluded heathen
be most likely to pursue the course they best love? And scorn
our message, although brought in love to their souls? But hush
my desponding heart!

Darling young Abigail, we weep for you with the burden
of this naughty world on your heart! But you are bravely
continuing:

Let me remember in whose name I have come here. . . . It
stands written "He shall give him the heathen for his inheritance and the uttermost parts of the earth for his possession"
Then we will not be discouraged but will endeavor to rely im-
plicitly on the sure promise of God. *It will not fail us.* . . .
Animated with hope we will enter upon our labors.

A boat full of half clad females just came along side our ship
with the intention of coming on board, but were driven away by
one of the boys. I shall never cease to remember with gratitude
the commendable stand our Captain and his officers take in
regard to such things. Although there are several ships in port,
I have seen females on board but one. No doubt there are many
who visit these distant shores who abhor such vile practices and
I ardently desire that the age may come when there shall be none
among sailors so lost to every sense of principle and shame as
some now appear to be.

Probably our precious young grandmother would have been surprised at the quotation familiar to our generation "Human nature is so prevalent"! All morning while the captain went ashore with the welcoming missionaries who had boarded the *Mentor* to make what seems a strangely lengthy preparation for landing a few people so long expected, Abigail confessed to her journal a burden that seems appalling for so young a woman to bear.

How awfully responsible is our situation! In what a peculiar manner will all our future conduct have an important bearing on the destiny of souls. O that we might have the spirit and character of primitive christians.

Her courage rises as the first natives come on board.

Their countenances are bright and they appear active. But we can not talk to them. Our tongues are as it were tied. Well we must make haste and acquire their language. Their word for salutation is "Aloha."

Methinks, Abigail dear, the time spent on your Virgil *Where* might better have been employed with a Hawaiian primer *Was the* and John Toohane as teacher. Could he have been coaxed to *Home of* tell you some of the Hawaiian nature legends would you not *Interpre-* have felt a charm in this childlike people that would have *ter?* associated them in your mind with your delight in the poetry and mythology of Greece and Rome? For you as for so many of us we could wish a different introduction to favor a truer translation of the life about us. Even John Bunyan created for his need "Interpreter." We sigh with relief that in the afternoon you had

some fine fresh watermelons from land . . . far more delicious than any . . . ever tasted in America. Much larger.

What thrills, Abigail, next morning to have the Queen *A Queen's* Regent, Kinau, send her blue handcart, the royal equipage, *Carriage* to conduct you, your slender feet dangling at the rear, to the mission station. But, poor dear, you saw such sights on the way as to bring the blush to your New England cheek and make you long for a shop where you could purchase a veil for protection of your sense of modesty. Lowell was as shocked as you, confessing his thought as he viewed the kindly throng with their welcoming "Aroha oe," thus:

O the first thing I teach you will be to cover your naked bodies.

With what swaddling clothes the people of civilization in that generation covered the facts of life and also ignored their own scriptures that the beginning and ending of our mortal life is made in nakedness. The sons of a brother missionary were to tour among primitive peoples a generation later and to report that the most chaste tribes were those utterly destitute of attire, which is now conceded to have been used in all ages for allurement rather than any form of protection.

4. KINGS' PALACES

From the beginning the American attitude toward the tiny kingdom in the heart of the sea was one of respect. All deference was shown to the rulers. No landing, no building, was made without invitation. Not only the gospel which its author declared He brought first to the poor but also the civilization calling itself Christian, was in the case of Hawaii brought first to the chiefs and through them to the people. The evening of May 2, the day of landing, Abigail wrote:

House of Kinau

We were informed that the King had made an appointment for our introduction to his majesty at two o'clock P.M. We accordingly repaired to the house of Kinau, Queen Regent, at the hour specified. We were accompanied by some of the missionaries. On our arrival there we were informed that the royal youth was otherwise engaged and would see us the next day. We were ushered into a large and handsomely finished grass house and upon our introduction met with gracious acceptance from the rulers of the nation. They were all richly dressed in European style and were very dignified in their manners. Much reserve was manifest on all sides for considerable time. . . . We were told that we were at liberty to converse with them if we liked. After a time I took my seat by the side of the Ex-Queen of Kauai and held one of the most interesting conversations with her I ever did with any christian. Dr. Judd was my interpreter. She exhibited a meek and christian like spirit. Indeed hers was a missionary spirit. Our conversation turned on the inhabitants of the Marquesas Islands where the missionaries at these Islands contemplate sending a mission. She said with tears that she was in pain for the salvation of the poor Marquesans. She said her desire was very great to go with the missionaries if any were sent there. (At the time the Catholics were sent away from these Islands this woman salted the pork with her own hands for the vessel's supply). On the whole our visit with the chiefs was very interesting. Most of them are professedly pious. . . . [History tells us that rather than be conquered in battle the King of Kauai capitulated to the great Kamehameha.] *Ex-Queen of Kauai*

May 3rd. We went . . . agreeable to appointment to the house of the Queen Regent (the King's house was under a state of repair) and were presented to his Majesty, Kaukeouli, King of the Sandwich Islands. This monarch exhibited much ease and urbanity of manner, unaccompanied by haughtiness. I was exceedingly interested in his appearance. He is, I believe about nineteen years old, has an open, frank and generous countenance. He was richly attired. . . . There was more formality observed than during our visit yesterday. . . . The King is not pious. He rules a people sunk in vice and superstition. His youth requires good and experienced counsellers. We have some fears that he will not follow in the steps of the excellent Kaahumanu, who died a year ago. The spiritual interests of this people may be materially affected by the course he pursues. His heart is in the hands of the Lord, and we earnestly hope he will turn it to himself. *Kamehameha III*

Lowell adds to the description of the royal visit:

Presented our letters of introduction from the Board . . . our certificates as licensed missionaries of the American Board, etc., to all of which he expressed his approbation and promised us protection, etc. To crown all, I presented the letter forwarded by those one hundred young men convened at my ordi- *Reception by King* nation. This almost raised him from his chair. High emotions were visible all round the room. The King requested Mr. Bingham to take it home and translate it for him, etc.

A Page
Turned
Back

In the civic center of Honolulu stands the statue of Kamehameha the First, or Kamehameha the Great as he is well called. To have any conception of his people, the people to whom these devoted missionaries, their predecessors of thirteen years and their successors for many another long day, came in love and with the gifts of healing, learning, and truth-as-they-saw-it, we must unroll the scroll of history a little farther and try to read it with as little prejudice as the scientist brings to his findings, or the artist to unfamiliar designs in carving or the tattooing, or the marking of *tapa* (bark cloth).

Simultaneously with the first slight contacts with men of other races, some fifty years preceding the advent of Christian teachers, began the breaking down of native religious ideas and expressions. The pomp and circumstance that had surrounded the hierarchy of gods expressed in idols, the *heiau* (temple) ceremonials, and, in scarcely less degree, the sacred persons of the chiefs (who, like the kings of many another race, received at least a semi-deification) were losing power. The *tabu* system built up from the first recognized ancestor in the mists of antiquity, Wakea, was weakening before the brave Kaahumanu dared to defy punishment, ate with the young king whose regent she was, and declared the *tabu pau* (restriction removed). Once emerging from the shadows and mystery of an old and elaborate system, things that glittered in the light brought by the stranger, metals, silks, firearms that gladdened or startled eye, hand, and ear, fruits for the palate, or customs—all were given the aloha of a childlike people. Together with the wreckage of the *heiau* would naturally come the gradual abandonment of the ceremonial dwellings. Always there had existed a wide gulf between the chief and his vassals and later pages of this book will show a sad remaining fear on the part of the commoner of being despoiled of his own by his superior.

It is not only not strange but quite to be expected that, as their frail domestic structures were replaced, a people freeing itself from *tabu* would build more in accordance with new ideas. Had the missionaries come earlier they would have seen not only the rude, congested huts of the poor which they decried with such distress, but would have found among the chiefs and the well-to-do a plan of life claiming great interest and respect. For Hawaiian civilization at its best, untrammeled by crowded conditions of a seaport town, and untouched by the life of the beachcomber (an unfortunate acquaintance of more than a generation), would have revealed a ceremonial of house building, arrangement, use, and beauty, possessing a dignity undreamed of by the farming folk of the Atlantic coast who came as missionaries.

Doubtless to eyes used to the hayfields of England, whether Old or New, the Hawaiian *kauhale* as Abigail described it would have seemed a cluster of haystacks. But examination would have proved a scheme of living and a quality of handiwork far from mean. A chief's house might be forty by seventy feet long, built of timbers carefully selected and hewn in the mountains and carried on men's shoulders to some waterway or to the shore. It would stand upon a platform of stones carefully laid and projecting beyond the roof. The poor might thatch their homes with leaves of *ti* or fern or any convenient grass but a house for a chief must be of fine *pili* grass deftly tied in bundles with cord made by hand from *olona*. Due ceremonial must be observed throughout the building of the structure, for even as the Hebrew poet said, "Except the Lord build the house, they labor in vain that build it." In one of the modern hulas, a poem in motion, is a suggestion of the cutting of the thatch over the door of the house, the last ceremonial of the builder. A complete establishment would consist of at least six buildings. The idols, or rather let us say the household gods, *aumakua*, must first have their house. Because of certain *tabus* the women must have beside their house for beating tapa, a separate eating house (as they also had their separate *imu* [oven]) and an infirmary for *tabu* periods. Their common sleeping house would be the largest and provided (somewhat in the fashion of Japanese houses) with raised portions for the spreading of the mat

Hawaiian Homes

beds, soft and fine, as still to be seen in the Bishop Museum, and offering as bedding five thicknesses of tapa (bark cloth), white and foamy, with coverlet of heavier quality decorated in vegetable dyes with unique designs. Less inviting to the European or American was the Hawaiian pillow, a short bar of wood covered with matting finely braided from the *hala* leaves. This also suggests the oriental idea of comfort as the matted floors and scarcity of furnishing reminds us of Japanese custom. With little clothing or bedding to store, a few large calabashes carved by patient industry and skill from the boles of trees and painstakingly polished by coral, pumice, rough leaves, and, finally, with the "palm oil" of the hand were sufficient containers for treasures as well as for the frequently renewed food supply. The *lanai*, literally a roof, was a valuable adjunct to the establishment, offering shelter for the canoes, a cool and pleasant place for the pounding of the *poi* or doing other work. It was often erected especially for some feast in celebration of an event, even as today. Light timbers covered quickly with coconut or other leaves are all that is necessary, a gala day calling for bunches of *ti* or *ie ie* branches, and *lei* (wreath) of *maile* and fern for garnishment. Undoubtedly, life in the open, at work or play on the beaches, on and in the water, made possible (though one cannot understand how it could be enjoyable) the large lack of windows and doors in their abodes. Considering their ideas of dress one can hardly think it a need of privacy. Probably it was felt to be needed protection from the cold of the night air and from rain, also from intruders, human or otherwise. Few examples are extant, but these show the steep sloping roofs protected by the covering of a large fish net against the wear and tear of the weather.

But no such establishments do we find in descriptions by the missionaries. The glory had departed before they came and the study of primitive arts was not yet. Hawaiians of rank or financial ability were aping foreign ways. Bales of damask from China in exchange for sandalwood were brought by the early queens to the lady missionaries, with requests for garments to be made them immediately, the king being not less demanding in his desire for "hand-made ruffled shirts."

Mahogany tables were possessed by that queen, who, returning from a swim in the sea, dressed in her altogether and
unabashed at her nakedness, paid a call upon a lady from
New England. It would of course be the majority and not
the exception in building that would give general character,
and we have no reason to think Abigail's eyes played her
false in the following account of impressions written home.

5. THE VILLAGE HONOLULU

It is worthy of note that even to the eyes of a New Englander as brisk and occupied as Abigail was from her childhood in a large family through her days of earnest study and
teaching, Honolulu is at once recorded by her as "a busy
place." Within her first three weeks ashore she writes:

Honolulu . . . occupies a barren sandy tract of land. Very   *Old*
little vegetation. No rain for months together. All the water for   *Honolulu*
drink is brought from the mountains. All the washing of the
missionaries is done upon the mountains [rather in the valleys
between] by natives. They wash in the brook and generally
pound the clothes between two stones to make them clean. Of
course they wear out fast. The roads here are broad and very
sandy. Not a spire of grass grows by the wayside. When the
wind blows a cloud of dust arises which is enough to put one's
eyes out, besides putting a dirty coat upon his back. A little
back from the mountains the soil is very fertile, and productions
abundant so that there is no lack of provisions on the Islands.
The population of Honolulu is between eight and nine thousand,
including nearly two hundred foreign residents. The houses are
generally of native construction. Those resemble as much as
anything an oblong haystack. They are built by fastening poles
into the ground some five, six or seven feet high. Small rafters
are fastened on to these and meet at the ridge pole and the
house is covered with grass. They use no nails in building.
Everything is fastened with strings twisted from the fibres of
the cocoanut, and sometimes grass. They frequently have but
one door and one room in the house. No glass windows. The
whole family not infrequently includes besides men, women and

children, dogs, hogs, and goats with which the Islands abound. These animals, especially the two former, are exceedingly doted upon and oftentimes receive more attention than children. Many of the natives who have become more civilized build large native houses and have separate apartments.

Here Abigail meant a number of rooms in one house, foreign fashion, rather than the ancient separate houses in a single establishment, for she adds:

The partitions are made of mats or tapa. The houses are so closely huddled together in this village that if one should take fire, a hundred might be destroyed at once, and owing to the very combustible materials of which they are composed, burn with great rapidity. The Meeting House is of native construction.

Kawaiahao Church

This was the predecessor of the Kawaiahao Church, the restored coral structure, sometimes called the Westminster Abbey of Hawaii, because of its memorial tablets within and gravestones without, naming chiefs and teachers of the early days of the mission.

It is one hundred ninety-six feet long and sixty-eight feet broad and will admit four thousand five hundred persons. There are no galleries. The pulpit is built like those in America. The bell is hung in a small building erected for the purpose several yards from the front side of the church.

School-house

There are quite a number of large stone buildings of English construction here. Among them the mission buildings. There has recently been a convenient school house erected where a school is in operation for the benefit of foreigners who have native mothers. This school is at present under the care of Mr. and Mrs. Johnson, missionaries of the Board. There is English preaching in this house twice on the Sabbath.

This may have been the quaint building near the rear of Kawaiahao Church later used by Lowell for his girls' school. Sacred to the memory of many of the conferences of the annual General Meeting of the missionaries gathered from different parts of the group and also hallowed by the prayers and tears of the missionary mothers wont to gather there to make intercession for the conversion of their own lively offspring it is now the property of the Hawaiian Mission Children's Society, the descendants of those same offspring. It is used as a training school for kindergartners, whose present methods of teaching little ones would have delighted Abigail, a woman in many ways more than a generation ahead of her time in ideas of education. But let Abigail continue:

There are several American and English merchants residing here. Not only whale ships but merchant ships visit these Islands. This is one of the principal ports. I believe there are but a few foreigners residing at the other Islands. We have of course learnt but little of this people. We can give you more information as we become acquainted with them. *Ships*

These missionary journals served a double purpose of diary and letters to families and churches at home.

As to their dress I can hardly know what to say. One thing is pretty certain, there is no prevailing fashion, either as it respects the *make, quality* or *quantity* of their clothing. The chiefs dress like civilized beings. There have been hundreds of natives to see us since our arrival and we have observed a great variety of dress and a great deal of undress. Those who are under the influence of missionaries dress better and with more propriety than others. Many others wear nothing but a narrow strip of tapa about their loins, called a *maro*. Others wear besides this, just what they can obtain. A piece of tapa perhaps two or three yards square is thrown over their shoulders and tied in a knot under one arm. There is evidently a great desire for dress and not understanding what is most proper they often expend as much for one rich garment as would purchase a suit of plain clothing. A few days since I met a woman dressed in *white crape*, perhaps the only garment she wore. I recently saw a woman dressed in *rich satin*, she was barefoot and had not another article that could correspond with it. Sometimes I have seen them with scarcely a garment to cover their nakedness who would nevertheless have a rich India silk pocket handkerchief or shawl, and the other day saw a woman with an expensive white merino shawl wrapped closely around her otherwise indiffer- *Dress*

ently clad body. Still I do not know that they are particularly
attached to rich clothing. We have seen men who wore nothing
but their *maro* and *one old shoe* they had found, apparently
feeling that it was one badge of civilization. Others we have met
who wore a vest buttoned closely around their naked bodies and
sometimes a thick sailor's jacket.

How sincerely I hope, Abigail, that the stains on this page
of your delicate script are from tears of excessive laughter
as you sent your people at home these word snapshots of
Nature's children wreathing themselves in anybody's grotesque cast-offs, or some sailor's gift of India's shawls or
China's silks, with not a thought of conforming to any much
boasted civilization, but with the delight of masquerading!
The plumage of birds, the gay colors of the flowers, the veils
and earrings of Isaiah's day, the wimples and crisping pins
of Chaucer, the haori coats on or off at the displays on the
beach at Waikiki today—do they speak civilization or something far more integral in the pursuit of life itself? But do
go on, dear!

As I before remarked, many of this Island appear in decent
clothing. I recently attended with Mrs. Bingham a meeting of
the female members of the church where I saw forty or fifty
women respectably clad, with the exception of their feet, which
I believe are generally bare.

Native   As to labor, I am informed that idleness is a distinguishing
Character trait of native character. The productions of the earth necessary for their subsistence require little effort for cultivation,
and they never think of the future. There is no winter here,
consequently they are not obliged to provide against cold.

But I must drop this subject for the present. I have written
from my own observation and the information I have received
from others. Sometime I may tell you more particulars.

We must bear in mind that Lowell is writing thirteen years
after the pioneers came when he states that:

Mission   . . . The mission families here have very comfortable houses.
Homes   Their dooryards, gardens, trees, vines and fences very forcibly
remind me of the many blessings I have left in America. The

FIRST MISSION HOUSE SENT AROUND THE
HORN AND ERECTED IN 1821

REAR OF THE FIRST MISSION HOUSE SHOWING
THE CORAL STONE COOK HOUSE

missionaries have many things to render them comfortable . . . enough that is good and wholesome to eat and drink and clothes enough when they can get them. Those families which depend entirely upon the Board for clothing are often most straightened. Most of the families receive boxes yearly from some of their friends, which are very acceptable. Their flour is all brought from America. About one and a half barrels a year to each family. Vegetables are very rich and delicious. The tarro is a good substitute for bread and sweet potatoes are excellent. Some milk and butter, watermelons, muskmelons, cucumbers, grapes, bananas, etc., in abundance the year round.

Insects

Not many melodious birds. The most troublesome insect is the cockroach which is almost as numerous and quite as impudent as the frogs of Egypt. They are about the size of those large bugs which fly about in your yards at milking time in the summer. They show mercy to no one. They enter every trunk, chest, bureau, bookcase, cupboard, pantry, etc., when it is practicable. Hence obliged to keep everything locked up tight. The climate is very mild and agreeable—May and June weather in New England.

Ride to Nuuanu Pali

May 29th: A circumstance of note and even of lasting remembrance occurred yesterday, Mr. Smith and wife, residents of this village, had the politeness some few days ago to invite the mission families to ride up the valley of Nuuanu to see the parry [*pali* (precipice)] which is seven miles distant. They proposed to go up the evening before and make preparations and the company to start at an early hour in the morning and breakfast with them about five miles from here; then proceed to the parry—return and dine with them before we came to the village again. The opportunity of visiting the parry seemed favorable and the last reinforcement were advised to go, whether others did or not. Arrangements were made. . . . Arrived . . . at the breakfasting place. Abba . . . after breakfast . . . concluded that she would go no farther. . . . The verdure, mountain air and delightful scenery were all calculated to revive and invigorate. A ridge of mountains on our right and left at a short distance, on the tops of which rested the clouds. The path for our horses was quite rough in many places, but having been trained to such business they carried us very safely. Having arrived at our journey's end, the prospect was truly grand, sublime and overwhelming. I shall not attempt to describe my emotions. Suffice it to say my expectations were more than realized. One of our company purchased a muskmelon which served as a good treat. On returning to our dining place, found

Illness   Abba quite ill. Stopped two or three hours to refresh our horses and ourselves and after expressing our gratitude to our kind and hospitable friends we all set out for Honolulu. But as every cup of earthly felicity has in it more or less that is bitter, so in this Abba had not rode more than one half mile before she said she must either get off or fall off her horse, for she had not strength to sit on. . . . She could neither ride nor walk. The natives assembled around her and expressed their sympathies. I requested them to make a bier and carry her upon their shoulders. The thing was no less novel than interesting. They immediately obtained some poles, sticks, cords, and mats and a pillow and four of them conducted her at least three miles to our lodgings; another led her horse, for which they charged me fifty cents apiece. She had a very sick, restless night . . . today she is a very sick woman.

Dear Lowell, you did not dream how many years that bitter drop in your cup would last. Thirty years of more or less invalidism lay in wait to try the faith and patience of the sufferer and you, her caretaker.

II
SUMMER SUNS
1. TO WINDWARD

WITHIN a week of this excursion Lowell and Abigail embarked on a modest craft for the General
Meeting at Lahaina. It was their first taste of a
common and necessary experience to folk whose abiding place
is a group of islands—inter-island voyaging. Their fore-
runners, the Hawaiians, conquered the channels in their
great outrigger canoes. Of late years the Japanese have
built refrigerated sampans and developed an industry of
deep-sea fishing. Moreover, American men and women, descendants of early settlers, dare the mountainous waves on
their own fishing sampans as a rare sport. Others bent on
swift business or pleasure trips cross to Lahaina by comfortable steamer in six hours, or, mounting the Sikorsky, fly
in one hour. In pioneer days a schooner, paralyzed by calms,
might spend six days on a crossing and on one delayed and
rough passage a missionary mother triumphed over the
hazards of childbirth.

Lahaina once reached, is now, as it was then, nestled under
old groves of coconut and other trees on a narrow margin
between the sea and lofty, eroded cliffs, the mountains of
West Maui. Its quiet waters provide a haven for our American fleet in times of maneuvers. Lahaina makes little boast as
a town, but cherishes her history of being one time capital of
the group. On the heights back of the village an industrial
school for boys was established by the missionaries and
proved its worth when recognized, together with a like school
at Hilo, Hawaii, by Gen. S. C. Armstrong as the inspiration
for Hampton Institute in Virginia.

Let Abigail tell of her first inter-island experience:

June 27th, Lahaina. Agreeable to previous arrangements the
missionaries from the several stations assembled at this place on
the first of the month for the purpose of concerting on the measures best calculated for the promotion of the Redeemer's King-

dom the ensuing year. We embarked with several of the brethren
from Honolulu in a native schooner of thirty tons burden . . .
pretty well crowded with natives. Our accomodations of course
formed quite a contrast with those of the good "Mentor." The
cabin was too confined to allow of our remaining in it. We accordingly remained on deck most of the time. At night we lay
down among the natives, thus making ourselves all things to all
men rather from *necessity* than a better motive.

On the morning of the third day we drew near Lahaina. I wish
I could give you an accurate description of the scenery the
village presented at the entrance of the bay. A rising sun was
shedding its mellow rays upon a landscape of the richest green.
Vegetation appeared in all its glory. Numerous trees with their
thick foliage grow along the shore for several miles, the banana
with its broad leaves, and the taro seemed so completely to cover
the earth that I could discover nothing of that barren nakedness
of land that struck me so unpleasantly when we entered the
harbor of Honolulu. Native houses in abundance were scattered
along the beach. Here and there a good stone building met the
eye, and soon the large white church with its cupola rose among
the trees, thus indicating that a dwelling place had been prepared for the most High on this Island also.

Two or three miles back of the village the high school buildings—groups of native houses surrounded by cultivated patches
of ground, increased the pleasantness of the prospect. The
mountains and hills that rose beyond exhibited the same autumn-
like appearance with those of Honolulu.

We landed about noon and met many brethren and sisters of
the mission not before seen. Perhaps you will find it difficult to
imagine what were my feelings when, in this far distant land—a
land of darkness and heathenism, I pressed the hand of Mr.
Green, my former teacher, and also my beloved school companion, Mrs. Spaulding. I believe mine was a privilege with
which few missionaries are favored. We took up our residence
with Mr. and Mrs. Green during the first two or three weeks and
have now been a few days with Mr. and Mrs. Spaulding. Mr.
Green is stationed on the same Island about twenty miles from
Lahaina.

*General
Meeting*

At this, Lowell's and Abigail's first General Meeting, the
first topic for discussion and decision nearly swept them far
across the ocean to another field. One of the greatest evidences that the charge of Jesus to go into all the world was
cherished by this little group of disciples is that only thirteen
years after the arrival of the pioneers on these shores they
were burdened with the need of sending the gospel to the
Marquesas Islands, miles away, and for this purpose were to
take leaders from their own number of missionaries and send
them with converts among the Hawaiians. Although consent-
ing to be "held up as candidates" Lowell and Abigail were
greatly relieved not to be chosen and Abigail's lack of health
was probably the deciding weight added to "debilitating climate, lack of expertness in languages and no prospect of a
physician going at present," Lowell's objections. He adds
regarding the second topic, the location of the missionaries:

. . . After much deliberation and discussion and many
powerful and urgent pleas by brethren located alone for an
associate, the committee reported that Mr. Tinker be located
at Wairuku [*sic*], Myself at Morokai [*sic*], and Dr. Chapin at
Lahaina for the present. . . . Abba and myself joined the Hawaiian Church. We are located with Mr. and Mrs. Hitchcock.

Leaving Abigail in Lahaina and returning to Honolulu
for his goods, Lowell found a complication unexpected in
missionary plans. He tells it thus:

*Kinau's
Hand*

June 24th, 1833. . . . This morning waited upon the chiefs
accompanied by Mr. Bingham and Mr. Emerson. Kinau and
husband expressed an utter unwillingness that Abba and myself
should go to Morokai; said they would not carry my things to
Morokai but would carry them to Ewa about fourteen miles
from Honolulu on Oahu. Kinau wishes us to settle upon her
land, will build us a house and do anything to promote our
happiness. They will send to Lahaina for my *wahine* (wife), etc.
Though the missionaries had unanimously decided that we shall
go to Morokai, yet they, the chiefs, can alter the decision and
send me where they please (as they say). But after mentioning
Mr. Hitchcock's illness etc. Kinau consented to let me go to
Morokai for one year. The chiefs are all assembled at this place

to transact political affairs. The King carries on at a desperate rate, tramples upon the Sabbath, drinks and carouses most shockingly!! . . . About four P. M. . . . an attempt was made on the part of the chiefs to remove the king from this island to Maui. Proceeded as far as Frenches' and by the combined effort of the foreigners he was induced to refuse to go and the project was given up. Three vessels stood ready to embark the moment his Majesty could be induced to go on board, but all to no purpose.

Molokai   June 29th. . . . Arrived at Lahaina yesterday. . . . At half past two A. M. this morning A. and myself, Mr. and Mrs. Hitchcock, accompanied by Mr. Gulick and Miss Ogden embarked from Lahaina for Morokai; dropped our anchor in this port about half past five A. M. Our goods were all landed before twelve o'clock (half barrel beef went to the bottom of the sea but was obtained again). I was not filled with very high enthusiastic emotions at my first introduction to this place. But from the memorable hour of my landing on Morokai my expectations have been more and more realized. I find the climate to be very salubrious and congenial to my health. The natives appear kind and friendly. A new house and a garden spot have been presented to us by the chief. A meeting house spacious enough to contain some hundred persons is nearly completed and has been already occupied.

2. FOUR STATIONS OF THE CROSS

a. KALUAAHA

Kaluaaha   Ten days after arriving, Abigail writes thus of Kaluaaha:

. . . Owned by one of the best and most pious chiefs on the Islands, the place we are to call home for the present, . . . we found ourselves in a region quite different from those we have seen before. This mission station was established about six months ago. There had been none before on the Island. Every thing is purely native. No great improvement as far as outward things are concerned. I mean in relation to their land, etc. All native houses. We occupy a house 12 by 15 feet. No glass windows, no door and no timber to make one. Mr. Smith has accordingly constructed one of mats. Moreover, according to the native pattern the house is almost all roof coming down to walls but three feet high. The climate is cooler than at Lahaina. Fresh trade winds blow constantly. Rains frequent. Our house does not defend us very well, as it pours in a stream over the door, and several places in the roof afford it an easy entrance—also our open windows. But we are in good health and manage to defend ourselves from the rain although the dampness is considerable.

Lowell more bluntly called the roof a sieve and said their clothes and bed were damp, but neither he nor his cheerful wife apprehended the prostrating illness but a week ahead of her. Abigail continues:

We feel perfectly contented and happy. We have set down to the native language with all our might, have also commenced assisting our associates in the schools. We cannot do much yet owing to our ignorance of the language. We are improving a little from day to day. It is much easier to acquire a language where we are situated among the people and obliged to talk with them. . . . The people here dress much less than at Lahaina or Honolulu. Their clothing is mostly native tapa. They are very ignorant and very many on the Island do not desire instruction. Many who live around us are glad to improve and I hope we shall be able to do them good. We have plenty of native neighbors living about us, who favor us with as many daily visits as we know how to attend to.

Before long Abigail was to be driven almost to distraction by her neighbors who wished to learn the arts of foreign life by observation, and, when she begged that they terminate their calls and go home to their household duties and the care of their children, leaving her free for her own tasks, they cheerfully assured her that they had no duties and continued to occupy her dooryard despite her discomfiture.

Here is an inside view of social-settlement work as carried on by the mission families. It was surely practical and sometimes, if not always, rewarding.

We have taken three natives to live with us, to whom we are

Neighbors endeavoring to teach the arts of domestic comfort. . . . Let me tell you a little of the manner in which the common people live. Their habitations are small, never contain more than two rooms and generally but one. Their beds are mats spread on the ground. Besides these, their furniture consists of a few calabashes for their food and water, instruments for making their tapa, a stick of wood or a stone for their pillow, a few books, slate or a little paper, and among the more wealthy we find a few extra mats, or tapa, twine of their own manufacture, and perhaps a fish net. Their clothing is tapa—which is worn loose and requires neither needle, thread or washing to keep in repair. Their "staff of life" is poi, which is made by baking taro in the ground and pounding to the consistency of thin flour paste. After it has fermented, they eat it with their fingers out of a calabash. A whole family gather around one common dish which is placed on the ground, and themselves seated in the same posture, enjoy their social repast. Fish is a favorite article of food which they eat raw, not even allowing the entrails to the numerous vermin that infest their habitations. The same may be said of hogs, dogs, etc. which are very delicious food. The sweet potato is much used for food so also is sugar cane. . . . They have naturally no care but to eat drink and sleep. . . .

Station Letter   The Station Letter to the Home Board sent about this time by Lowell and his associate uses stronger language than would become the bride of New England. With Abigail they point out the extreme poverty of the people and dwell on the heavy taxes imposed upon them although no High Chief is resident on their island. Many of the houses, they say, are not more than five or six feet long by a width of four to five feet, the height from the ground to the ridgepole being not more than five feet. In such huts dwell two, three, or sometimes more individuals of both sexes. Even if the huts are larger the state of things is no less distressing, there being no window, no chimney but the one humble door. In this one-room apartment are men unclothed save for the "wretched *malo*," women perfectly naked above the loins, children naked, cats, dogs, swine, and goats, plus lice and fleas without number.

No word or phrase in their language is proscribed and their *Credulity* bodily functions are performed as openly as by the brute creation. Moral principle is rarely to be found. There is indulgence in all those sins which fall not immediately under the cognizance of the laws of the land. The people are credulous to the last degree without why or wherefore. That this credulity is a result of mental indolence is by no means a benefit to the cause. They are of a pacific disposition, but this being from fear rather than principle adds little interest to their character. They have learned that the Christian religion, unlike the old pagan, inflicts not immediate death. Fear therefore has ceased. Sermons which would cause a congregation in New England to quake with forebodings of eternal death would produce no consternation in the hearts of this people.

We rejoice to say there are many precious exceptions. . . . *Church* The church already built, 120 by 30 feet, accommodates one *and School* thousand persons. A spacious school house is almost completed so that the station already begins to assume the appearance of a small village.

Abigail thus describes Molokai:

This Island is forty miles long and seven broad, seems to be formed of a chain of volcanic mountains. Inhabitants not far *Descrip-* from 6000. It is impossible to traverse all parts of the Island *tion of* by land owing to impossible parries [*palis*]. There are no roads, *Island* only foot paths. The mission is situated on the south side of the Island, about 25 rods from the sea and that is about the whole width of the plain here. Mountains then begin to rise; their ascent is at first gradual, then more abrupt. The height of the highest from the level of the sea is perhaps 8 or 9000 feet. We are not troubled with so much sandy ground as at the stations I have visited.

The mountains and vallies alike are covered with grass, and, owing to the more frequent rains, exhibit a verdant appearance compared with some other parts. The native population is like that of Lahaina. No foreign fruits. Few trees on the beach; these are lauhala. They afford a pleasant shade, but the roots rise above ground and form a bulk as large as a hogshead. This circumstance renders the tree less desirable for our door yards.

They produce a yellow, oblong fruit an inch or two inches long; these are highly prized by the natives for beads. They wither in a few days. There are forests of trees upon the mountains. The "Ohia" or native apple tree yields a fruit resembling in form and color our American apple, although inferior in taste. It contains a stone like the peach instead of seeds like our apple.

Ignorant of its forbears, dear Abigail, you seem to consider it an American apple gone native!

The animals are goats, hogs, turkies and hens.

Native Teachers   There are schools on various parts of the Island taught by native teachers, but the teachers are ignorant and unfaithful and their schools of little use. I hope we shall some time have better teachers. The novelty of instruction has subsided and the people seem to care much less about it than they did years ago. They are contented with a very little knowledge. The schools at our station are under the direct instruction of the missionaries with native assistants. And even here the scholars are very unsteady.

A Normal School   The Station Letter of the fall of 1833 describes the organization of a training school for teachers

with *60* to *70* pupils including *20* females. . . .

Value of Example   July 2nd. . . . Nearly a thousand attended worship last Sabbath. Have been busily employed two days in making an outside door to the house which is to be our residence for a time and also in arranging our furniture etc. May I now be enabled to enter upon the acquisition of the language with success and delight. The heathen are indeed heathen and in order to benefit them I must acquire their language. I may mourn over their degradation in secret, but tears and grief will never civilize and christianize them. A godly example and a decided, persevering [*sic*], untiring effort to bring the holy principles of the gospel to bear upon their lives and conversation is my duty. . . .

Visit of Chiefesses   July 17th. The princesses Harieta and Auhea have been here about a week with their attendants. Have embarked this morning for Lahaina. They called the people together on Monday and addressed them in reference to the "pono" (good), reading their books, attending to the instruction of the missionaries, etc.

Auhea talks of coming to Kaluaaha to live and she prefers the house and lot that have been formally give to A. and myself. Hence she has given orders to have another house built for us.

No comment follows this statement. Evidently it was a fact to be accepted if not expected.

Lowell thus describes a burial scene:

One of the Chiefs recently departed this life. The kanakas assembled about 9 A. M. and commenced digging a vault, bringing stones, gravel, grass etc. . . . It was really a novel scene to me to behold some 40 or 50 men, women and children in single file marching to the burying ground, each with a stone on his or her back. The tomb was completed about half past 2 P. M. Religious services were then held, Brother H. officiating. The audience was attentive and solemn though there was no wailing. *A Burial Scene*

Another episode a few days after that interested Lowell was this:

Today have been about six miles with Br. H. in a canoe to see Auhea who on her way to Oahu had stopped on this island. Had a very pleasant ride in a single canoe. On arriving at the landing place we were carried some rods on the backs of natives to the shore, a scene which would be very novel to our friends in America. But we find it necessary to become all things to all men. . . . Attended conference meeting about a mile from this; took a seat on the mats with the natives; hope we shall be the means of saving some.

Abigail writes with a lively interest, July 1:

I have today for the first time attended a native wedding. Marriage ceremonies are performed in the meeting house at the Wednesday lecture. You know it is but a few years since christian marriage was instituted at these Islands and as far as the ceremony is concerned it claims the attention of the natives. Two couples were married today. They made their appearance attended by some of their friends and were seated in front of the desk. They were probably dressed as nearly like civilized people as they could be. The two brides wore loose calico dresses, unpinned, one had her dishevelled hair partially con- *A Native Wedding*

cealed by a native straw bonnet, the other wore a turban made
of a cotton flag handkerchief. She wore about her neck a small
India silk shawl; both were barefoot. One of the bridegrooms
had on a ruffled white shirt washed quite clean, but wanting
starching and ironing; his other clothes were decent. The other
wore over his other clothes a large great-coat made of scarlet
broadcloth of ancient fashion. This was buttoned closely around
his tall body, giving him a truly primitive appearance. I
thought he felt his consequence and superiority for he deigned
not to look to the right hand or the left. He appeared to be
about 22 years old, as also did his bride. The other pair were
younger, the bride not more than 13 or 14. When they arose to
take upon themselves the marriage covenant, the little bride
appeared extremely bashful. She held down her head and continued to bite the top of her dress until the minister pronounced
them "no more twain but one flesh" when she raised her head,
smiled, and appeared as much pleased as any other child would
be who had borne a conspicuous part in a ceremony that excited
so much attention. When we left the church at the close of
service, the man in scarlet walked forth in the pride of con-
scious superiority towards his home. His wife followed after,
although she did not keep up with him. He showed her not the
slightest attention. I soon lost sight of them, and returned to
my own happy home sighing to think that although they were
tied together for life how little they would probably know of
true conjugal felicity. I have been told that love is not the great
motive in forming the marriage connection, that although they
marry, they are oftentimes quite indifferent towards each other,
or rather that the parties do not seem to realize their particular obligations. Still, I understand they do not often leave each
other. There are undoubtedly some who know something of
domestic love, but the cases are few compared with the people.

A few weeks later another double wedding was arranged.
Lowell describes it as follows:

*Another
Wedding*

A singular circumstance occurred today. At the afternoon
lecture two couples presented themselves to be married. Brother
H. called upon them to rise and take each other by the right
hand. He proceeded as usual to marry them, completed half the

ceremony and called upon the gentlemen to assent to what he had said. One answered in the affirmative and the other in the negative. The question was repeated but he positively refused to be married on those terms. They were then commanded to separate their hands and sit down. The other couple were made fast. What could have been the object of the fellow to come to the sanctuary to abandon his intended I know not. He had not many to comfort him after meeting. He probably will have his affections placed upon some one person before he attempts to be married again.

Fortunately, Lowell had a sense of humor which one can only wish had been always as ready as it sometimes was to spring to his relief in many exigencies. The following gives us a pleasant slant upon his situation:

This day has been sanctified by the advent of a young Paul, who drew his first breath upon Molokai. One of our church members who has assumed the name of Hezekiah, has had so much of an apostolic spirit on this day of a man child being born into the world that he has named him "Paul." By listening to the names of many of the people on this Island a stranger would be induced to think that either the old prophets have risen again or that the days of the apostles have returned. For among our neighbors are Abraham, Isaac, Jacob, Joseph, Benjamin, Moses, Hezikiah, Zachariach, Naomi, Martha, Mary, Elizabeth, Lydia, etc. etc. It has long been predicted by some that the millenium is to commence on the Sandwich Islands and is not here incontrovertible evidence of the fact? Truly this must be a favored place—an enviable station. Who would not be a missionary on these Islands in 1834!

Names of Parishioners

This "favored place" was not, however, without the ordinary trials, among them the servant problem. Replacing Oihu and Kane, natives who did "not agree" with Br. H's. natives and were "too dirty to have about" was a lad "twelve or fourteen years old, bright, active, promising to do well." Departing from the scriptural choices of his flock, Lowell renamed this Kanelaauili after Leavitt Hooker. Within a fortnight the lad was baptized. In five months we learn of a circumstance . . . worthy of note. For some two weeks or more Hooker has been very unfaithful in the duties assigned him, especially in washing and ironing clothes. Many of the articles we have made him wash the second time. He has also been quite impudent and saucy to Abba and myself. In addition to these things he has been at war with Kenai; has also been ugly in school. Moreover this P. M. when catching the goats to milk them he abused one of them unmercifully, for which conduct I rebuked him sharply. I also reminded him of his other misconduct of late and told him that he must either do better in future or he must leave us. He immediately replied that he wished to leave. Went and got all his books, tapa and clothes that we had given him and threw them down apparently in anger and retired. . . . We regret that he has so soon concluded that it is easier and better for him to throw off the restraints and duties of civilization and turn again to folly. May the Lord interpose, arrest, convict, and save him from shame here and ruin hereafter.

The Servant Problem

Abigail in a letter to her sisters in New England writes:

When our natives, (three) came to live with us I questioned them concerning their knowledge of domestic affairs. I said to the woman "do you know how to make a bed?" "Aole—(no)." "Did you ever sweep a house?" "Aole." "Can you sew?" "Aole." "Can you wash or iron?" "Aole." "Do you know how to cook after our manner?" "Aole loa" (No indeed). "Do you think you can learn?" "Ae, paha" (Yes, perhaps). You will not be surprised that with such a want of qualifications and also considering their former indolent habits, they are unable to perform that amount of labor which three individuals in America could do. They do best to have a certain portion of labor allotted to them and let that be of one sort if possible. . . . They require superintendence.

House Building

Continuing in a domestic strain, both Lowell and Abigail write of the new home built by the arrangement of the Chiefess Auhea, already mentioned. The most of the building occurred during Abigail's absence of five weeks in Lahaina. Although Abigail struggled to be cheerful and appreciative of everything good in her lot, the Molokai climate with its dampness and cold penetrating her little grass house was hard to bear and moreover a serious illness of two weeks in July had left her weakened. So October first Lowell writes:

Brother Richards came over from Lahaina . . . in the Pupuka to carry Abigail to Lahaina. . . . I staid there until I had an opportunity to return in a canoe with our chief Lazarus. . . . Mr. Laurence has come over with me to plaster our house.

November 7, 1833. I crossed the channel this a.m. from Molokai to Lahaina on a canoe. Had a very pleasant time. Neptune spit at me a number of times but it did not at all frighten me. Have been labouring for some weeks in preparing a comfortable habitation. Have come to L. today to accompany Abba to Molokai. Find her health much improved. Shall return in a few days.

Years later Lowell wrote reminiscently:

Not being satisfied with our grass house and there being an old *heiau* or pile of good stones near by, I resolved to build a stone house, using common mud for mortar. Having been brought up on a farm I felt assured I could make a door and window better suited to keep out rogues, dogs and pigs than a lauhala mat. So I employed natives to go out into the mountains for plates, beams, and rafters; and others to bring stones and help lay up the walls of the house; and while the work was going on I learned to say, "hele mai," "hele aku," "lawe mai," "lawe aku," "hapai," "hana pono," "hana paa," etc. . . . In due time my stone house was finished, with a good thatched roof, a batten door hung on hinges, and a glass window for light and ventilation. This at the time was considered quite a step forward in civilization.

Such work with its inspiration had been stimulating to the young man, but he was not without his troubles. Loneliness of itself may be a burden, but when it could induce such thoughts as the following the cheerful song of hammer and saw were insufficient to ease his spirit. The climate of Molokai, salubrious and bracing to him, had proved disastrous to his wife, and, at Lahaina, said he:

Depression

I left her to enjoy the influence of a climate which saps the very foundation of my constitution. Can it be, that one half of a person needs such different treatment from the other!

Poor Lowell! Being of one flesh with an invalid demanded strenuous mental adjustment. In September he had written:

My dear Abba has been quite ill for the last ten weeks. Although I am unable to determine for what particular sin or sins this affliction is sent upon us, yet I am fully satisfied that God has a good reason for rebuking us in this way. It will be plain another day, although obscure at present. May we feel to kiss the rod and him who hath appointed it.

A Doctor's Fee The beginning of Abigail's illness in July had occasioned the immediate summoning of a doctor from Lahaina by double canoe manned by five men. On his return from his two days' visit, with a twenty-mile channel twice crossed, the good man was given as fee a barrel of potatoes, seven fowls, some taro, three or four bunches of ohias, one and a half dozen eggs, etc.

Kindness The kindness of the native people in making provision for the wants of their missionaries is often referred to by both Lowell and Abigail. Kindness on the part of the parishioners was duplicated sometimes by captains of visiting sailing vessels, who often seemed to show interest in these lone countrymen of theirs. For instance, Lowell writes of them:

One presented Abba with a pair of shoes, another with four yards of cloth, another with a wash tub, another with a bucket, and one of them presented me with two good water pails, and two others with thirty bricks each, and one with a rope three fathoms long, and another with a bottle of lemon syrup.

Sailors It was a life of give and take. Lowell who, when in Lahaina, often preached to large congregations of seamen felt his

compassion for the weather beaten sailors . . . much excited. It is seldom that they enjoy any means of grace. Said one sailor to me "We have no Sabbath at sea." They will most assuredly testify against their employers who "cared not for their souls."

Guests The "packet" which brought Lowell and Abigail home

from Lahaina brought with them Miss Ogden and three of
the Richards children who were to be the first guests in the
new house, sharing it a week after their hosts had entered it.
That happy day was November twentieth, when housekeeping was begun with the statement

One room is now completed, the rest is *kokoke* (soon).

As if to celebrate the joyful event, on the following day
Lowell

commenced a singing school . . . under quite favorable auspices—seventy scholars. The voices generally are quite rude and   *Singing*
uncultivated, though there are evidently some natural singers   *School*
among them. By patience and perseverance I hope to improve
their voices and taste for music and thus do something towards
preparing them for serving God in his lower temple.

Years after, his daughter wrote of him:

Having a good knowledge of music and a sweet voice, he had
regular singing school sessions himself and introduced the reading of music by note into these schools. The returns from this
branch of study were ever most satisfactory.

Abigail, making as light as possible of her burden of frequent debility and, at best, frail health, writes her sisters:

We have been busy today in moving into our new house. Have
not arranged our things in much order yet. We think it will be   *The New*
very comfortable. It is quite a wonder to the natives who never   *House*
saw so fine a house on their Island before, although the missionaries at the older stations occupy good American houses. The
walls, windows and outside doors exhibit all of American archi-
tecture about our house. The walls are of stone which we
gathered from the ruins of an idol temple. The idol had long
ago been cast out and we thought it would be no sacrilege to
appropriate to our own use what was once impiously devoted to
one of those abominable things which God hates. We have endeavored to consecrate it to the true God and if anything can
be calculated upon beneath the sun, we think we shall be happy
and useful in it. The roof is covered with grass which is tied on
to the rafters and lined with sugar cane leaves. The partitions,

inner doors and floors are of mats of native manufacture. It fronts the sea and is about 25 rods from it. About five or six rods back of the house is the little eminence from which we gathered our stones and on whose summit once stood the idol temple. Beyond this "hills peep on hills" and mountains rise several thousand feet above the sea. Directly in front of us, across a channel 10 miles wide, lies Lanai, and a little to our left lies Maui, some fifteen or twenty miles distant. Our nearest white neighbors dwell on that island. We are levelling a yard in front of our house where we intend to rear some shade trees.

Poverty of the People

One prominent feature in the condition of this people is *extreme poverty*. And what renders this circumstance more trying is the fact that it is likely to continue so long as the present system of government exists. An absolute monarchy exercised by those who were so recently actually savages, is not a very enviable form of government. To republicans it seems intolerable. This people possess nothing that cannot be taken away at the will of the chiefs. The king and chiefs are at liberty to levy taxes as often and to as great an amount as they please. Besides the public taxes if an individual obtains by his private industry a little property, the chief can take such a portion of that as he deems fit. The people have a very great respect and fear for their rulers and never withold anything they ask for.

Here it seems to the point to insert extracts from an "Unpublished answer to a criticism of the Missionaries" written by Abigail a good many years later:

Chiefish Rule

. . . Establish a "savings bank" here! Why, man alive, there was nothing that could be saved from the rapacity of the chiefs! Everything belonged to the chiefs. That was a fundamental principle throughout in the whole system of Hawaiian Government from time immemorial. If a man a little more thrifty than his neighbor managed to get a little ahead in anything, such as a better cultivated taro patch, fowls, tapa, etc., his great care was to conceal the fact lest a Chief or a petty underling should take it from him. If a man sold any article for money—even a chicken or turkey—the half always went to the Chief.

During the year 1833 our home was on the Island of Molokai which was then thickly populated. The Island was said to be-

THE HIGH CHIEFESS, KEKAULUOHI

*From "The Hawaiian Islands" by Rufus
Anderson, D.D., published by
Gould & Lincoln, Boston,
1864*

long to Kekauluohi (Auhea), a sister of Kinau who was Regent at that time. Our Chiefess did not reside on her property but placed over the Island one of her servants and his wife, who assumed in a good degree the manners and state of their superior. These two persons had embraced christianity and were diligent in learning from the missionaries the arts of civilized life, especially in the matters of dress and household appointments. They did this sometimes to an absurd degree noting carefully any changes even in our attire and copying the same, whatever it was. One time my associate had an attack of "salt rheum" in her hands. She dressed her fingers in cabbage leaves as a remedy and in this guise went to church. Our "Head Woman" noticed it and supposed it to be some new style of glove and the next Sabbath, sailed into church with each separate finger enveloped in a cabbage leaf! Well, during the year Her Royal Highness Kekauluohi came with her train of attendants to visit her possessions and receive the tribute from the people. Then it was "as good as a play" to watch the change in our Head Man and his wife. Every evidence of thrift was removed from sight. Their good clothes disappeared and to our surprise and disgust the man went about dressed in a shirt only and his wife in the *holoku* worn by the common native women. Their lofty bearing was laid aside with their good clothes and they were as abject as the rest of the people. This continued during the stay of the High Chief's lady. On her retirement our Head Family resumed their former state.

Why did we not teach the chiefs better? We did. Long before the good Kamehameha III gave to his people a "constitution" which guaranteed to them certain rights of property and other privileges the missionaries had taught the chiefs the higher law —the christian law—of honest dealing, sometimes with and sometimes without success, but this I affirm, that they were never allowed the indulgence of oppressive acts after they professed christianity. I will illustrate one case only. More than forty years ago a petty chief of some consequence united himself with Kaumakapili Church. He had received a good deal of instruction and certainly knew right from wrong. He was of course a land owner to a considerable extent. In looking over his territory one day he lighted upon a nice piece of land and

coveted it. This was held by a native woman who refused to give
it up. With scant ceremony the chief took the land to himself in
accordance with the old customs. The woman came to her teachers in great distress and made her complaint. The chief was sent
for and remonstrated with. The right and the wrong ways were
set before him, until he confessed that he had done wrong, and
promised never to repeat the act, but though he was instructed
and labored with patiently for six months he would not restore
the land. He was accordingly cut off from the church. Numerous instances might be cited to show how light gradually
dawned upon the chiefs and people in all matters connected with
right living even before a Constitution was adopted.

I will relate one more incident of those old times which had a
more encouraging ending. A chief of much influence and importance on account of his connection with the royal household,
saw and appropriated a large pile of wood which one of his
people had collected, intending to sell it on his own account to
some shipmaster. The man thus wronged complained to the
pastor of the church of which the chief was a member. He was
remonstrated with and patiently instructed, when he returned
the wood to its rightful owner, remarking meanwhile to his
pastor that he didn't know that christianity had to do with *such
things*. This chief lived to become an intelligent christian, a
"civilized" man and a cultivated gentleman.

Turning back to Abigail's journal we read:

When in the presence of the chiefs, the people often dress in
their meanest apparel lest that which is more decent be taken
from them. 'Tis true there has been a great change for the
better since the tabu was removed, for then it was death to a
common native to come within the shadow of a chief and they
were slaves to them as well as to sin, but still there must be a
great change before this people will rise to a level with civilized
society in their habits of life. The consequence of such a government, as you would suppose, is an insuperable obstacle in the
way of external improvement to a great degree. The people have
no motive to exertion, except to pay their taxes and provide
what they consider the *bare necessaries of life*. There is no public spirit for general improvement among them. As a general

thing they are content to live and die like their fathers. You will ask whether christianity does not influence them in this respect? It certainly does in a degree. Those who live around the missionaries and are most attentive to their instructions, are much influenced by their examples of order, comfort and propriety. But those are not the great mass of the people. When we find our way to habitations but seldom visited we find poverty, filth and idleness reigning with supreme power over the inhabitants. They mingle promiscuously with the goats, hogs, dogs and vermin, all having an equal right to the habitation. And then notwithstanding all that has been done for their souls, the great mass are very darkhearted. You can not think how dark is the mind of a heathen. It seems almost impossible to make them comprehend the simple doctrines of the cross. Although they no longer worship gods their own hands have formed, I sometimes think they are like the Athenians who worshiped the "unknown God." . . . They have little idea their hearts are evil.

Dark Hearted- ness

Sweet girl-grandmother, the doctrines of the Cross, simple? What children we all are, ancients and moderns, of whatever color, under whatever skies! Reaching with ever so little a reach of intellect or heart, how quickly we make and unmake gods of our own. How even the church of Christ has followed one will-of-the-wisp of doctrine after another over the swamps and quicksands—sometimes to disaster and death! And of this "dark-hearted" people? How little the first foreigners knew of the great legends mixed with a faith in great invisible gods, a hierarchy far above the petty penates of their own hearths. In my youth I was deeply impressed by a tale of a missionary son, long grown to manhood, who was known as "the *kamaaina*" (child of the land) in many a hamlet, on many an isle. On a visit to one family he had not seen in months he found trouble in the sickness of a child:

Faith

"And did you pray to Jehovah?"
"No. For Jehovah is the great god among gods and he might be busy or gone on a journey so we called on our own *Akua Aumakua* [household god] for he is near and understands."

Faith of our fathers! Here was something that persisted,

something real. Under this guise (and what is in a name?) God is a spirit. "Closer is he than breathing, nearer than hands and feet." Paltry as are our superstitions, yes, ours of the present day and those of dusky minds in the dawn of what we call civilization, even these superstitions prove to us a life beyond the ordering of the body, beyond the dictates of any social code, a mysticism, a spirit-life. One wishes it had been possible and feasible to the missionaries to draw from this affectionate and childlike people what in their former religion had been of love and gentleness. We seem to know little of what they observed or learned except that of pro- hibitions or *tabu*.

Having told us of the painful depression of the people by the chiefs, Abigail shows another picture of the relationship in results:

"A Provi- dence"

But I ought by this time to say something on the other side, which may be more cheering. . . . There are apologies to be made for them (the chiefs). They have never seen a better form of government than their own. It is very merciful in many re- spects compared with what it formerly was. . . . As they be- come more enlightened and more anxious to do their duty we believe . . . they will give to the people those rights which the God of nations designed all his creatures to possess. . . . It was a most wonderful providence that caused the authorities of this nation to abandon their idols even before any missionaries had arrived on their shores, or they had been convinced by the truths of the gospel of the inability of their gods to save them, and it was an unheard of thing for almost all the chiefs of the nation so soon to adopt the laws of the Bible for the foundation of their national code. When the commands of the chiefs went forth for men to abandon their gods, attend upon the preaching of the gospel, collect in schools, etc., they were obeyed by the people just as they were in everything else. Some turned with their hearts unto the Lord, but the great mass, time has shown, only obeyed their rulers. They turned because the chiefs did. Yet even these are full of self righteousness and think they are good because they no longer worship idols and destroy their own offspring, not realizing how desperately wicked are their

"As if His Whole Vocation Were Endless Imitation"

hearts. . . . Christians in America have great cause to continue their prayers and their charities *for all these Islands will yet be converted to God.*

The first of the year 1834 Abigail was strong enough to resume her school of thirty native children, and, added to her period of religious instruction of the neighboring women, comes an interesting Pauline touch!

We have also commenced a school for the purpose of teaching as many females as we can collect to sew themselves bonnets. The braid is made of a part of the stalk of sugar cane and sewed makes very decent bonnets. We have no means of whitening or pressing them. Neither Mrs. H. nor myself are very skilful at the business but we are able to give them considerable aid. Necessity you know is the mother of invention. I feel deeply interested in my work and cannot but hope I shall be the means of benefitting this dying people.   *Bonnets*

Few pages remain of Abigail's journal, for her frail health so recently regained was soon to be overtaxed and after going to Oahu she seems not to have kept a diary. Letters sent back from America after their recipients died have been a boon to Abigail's family in giving many disconnected pictures of her life on to the time of her death in 1885. The thanks of the present are due to the past for the habit of preserving such things as now perish for lack of time and space. On the evening of January 4, 1834, she writes:

We often say to each other how happy we should be could some of our dear friends step into our cottage and make us a visit. But I feel this evening in a particular manner that such a visit would be agreeable for I am all alone. This morning Husband left me to go twenty miles to the leeward part of the Island to pass the Sabbath. I have mentioned before that we have an outpost there. He will return on Monday. We have no society but that of each other and our associates who live near us (Brother and Sister Hitchcock) so that when one is absent the other naturally feels rather solitary, but I felt when I was fitting him away that he was going where the people were more dark-hearted than those directly about us, and I was glad to   *"Two Is Company"*

see him step into the canoe that was to take him to the field of
his labors. I have been busy during the day in baking and making necessary preparations for the Sabbath. This evening I
have been reading with our native domesticks and a few others,
the third chapter of Matthew and explaining it as well as my
knowledge of the language will allow. I have commenced reading
the New Testament with them in this way, one chapter with explanations every Sunday evening if my health will allow. I find
by my labors that it is not yet confirmed. Still I hope it will
improve. Monday Eve. Husband returned today and gave me a
full account of his voyage and labors.

Such an account was newspaper and magazine in the life
of an island bride. As such we may as well give that account
as recorded by Lowell in his journal.

January 2nd. Have this day completed my tenth sermon in
the native language. Light just begins to dawn, though it is
with difficulty that I can distinguish the rays of heathen science.
. . . Expect to spend next Sabbath twenty miles below here.
May the God of missions go with me—protect me from all harm
—render me an instrument of good to his creatures and in due
time return me again to the embrace of my dearest earthly
companion.

*Two
Outposts*

Lowell's Station Letter sent to the American Board of
Commissioners for Foreign Missions gives a brief description of the two outposts of his mission. As we are going with
him in his journal to the one twenty miles west with a meet-
inghouse which accommodates from seven hundred to a thousand people, we shall take here only his bird's-eye view of the
one east. It is fourteen miles away,

an exceedingly rich and beautiful spot. A stream of water falls
from an almost perpendicular height of four or five thousand
feet to a crystal lake whence it issues and proceeds to the sea.

Halawa

The valley contains from four hundred to five hundred inhabitants who live on the eastern part of the north side, so that
nearly all the inhabitants meet at one or another outpost where
we shall preach alternate Sabbaths. We hope by this means to
carry the gospel as it were to the door of every man on the

Island. This can not be done without great labour on our part as both places are very difficult of access.

Presumably as there were two at the station each in turn went to an outpost or stayed to preach in the Kaluaaha Church.

Both Mr. Hitchcock and Lowell sign the Station Letter and together witnessing the physical misery they have insufficient medical knowledge to help, they plead with the Board for

books most adapted to our immediate use. We have none in our library but Buchan. A dispensatory is one that we cannot as well see dispensed with.

Lowell learned by experience what has been revealed to so many others, that the necessary practice of medicine is a powerful means of calling the people to the missionary. The matter of knowledge or ignorance of medicine was in many sad ways brought home to Lowell repeatedly throughout his life.

January 6th. Returned today about half past ten a.m. A brief outline of my journey, reception, etc. Left home Saturday morning about half past eight a.m. in company with Lazarus and one of his servants, accompanied also by Hooker (a domestic). Having sailed about six miles, Lazarus proposed to stop and get some breakfast. We landed and went about half a mile on foot while the boys took charge of the canoe. As we were passing a certain house he called for the man who came in great haste to ascertain the wants and demands of his *konohiki* and chief. He was commanded to bring two calabashes of poi to the school house forthwith, which was but a few rods ahead. The next articles called for were fresh fish, fresh water, salt, etc. All of which were procured as soon as it was practicable. And in less than twenty minutes his honour had a feast prepared. But to behold the ceremony at the table! Some eight or ten natives gathered around and each took a fish which was in the last pangs of dying and the first compliment was to bite his head off at one mouthful. No part was permitted to escape without, except the eyeball. Two or three successive mouthfuls finished the fish, head, brains, entrails and all. Poi was their other principal

A Breakfast Declined

dish. Well, this bountiful and glutinous repast being over (of which I was invited to partake but very modestly declined, having breakfasted at the usual hour) we proceeded on our journey and arrived "Malalo loa" (away down) about one o'clock p.m.

A
Hookupu

We had been in the neat and elegant native house built on purpose for our accomodation but a few minutes when a woman presented me with a fowl and seven or eight large fish—soon after she was followed by another woman who brought six or eight large fish and three or four large potatoes. Lazarus took charge of those fish. But a few minutes more had elapsed when a man came with two fowls and he was soon followed by another with two bunches or "*opes*" of potatoes. Other individuals were bringing fish and poi to Lazarus. Directly another man presented me with two fowls and another fowl by another man, in all six fowls, and in all some forty or fifty fish, all of which were presented Saturday p.m. But one thing not to be forgotten amidst the whole is, Lazarus and his men and acquaintances feasted again and again that p.m. and evening. Indeed I was forcibly reminded of the scripture "Whose god is their belly and who mind earthly things." This scene I must not forget.

A Busy
Sabbath

Sabbath morning went to the house of worship, three miles distant and met a crowded audience—perhaps six hundred. Very attentive to the speaker. After morning service I attended the Sabbath school of some forty-five scholars. One man was perfectly blind but apparently as bright in his mental powers as any of the congregation. He had committed his verses by hearing others read them. Soon after the close of the Sunday school the people convened and we attended to the afternoon service. In all the meetings I prayed in native. The p.m. service closed about one o'clock. I then retired to a private house with Lazarus and some others from this part of the Island and partook of some refreshment served up in native style and eaten in native style likewise, i.e. I ate some fish cooked whole and a sweet potato, others ate raw fish and poi. A large number of natives gazed, wondered and admired while the "Houri" [*Haole* (Foreigner)] was eating with their own kinsmen after the flesh. Returned to our house, spent the night, but had very little rest owing to the everlasting chattering of the natives. Have resolved to tabu the house here after bedtime as it respects speaking.

At six this morning I set out on my return on horseback, accompanied by five or six natives, who by running much of the time, arrived here as soon as myself. Arrived here at half past ten a.m. It is probably about twenty miles—traveling in the crooked path. Today is monthly concert—also observed by us at this station as a day of fasting and prayer.

Lowell makes no comment as to whether Lazarus, left behind, also fasted!

Although Lowell records debilitating illness as again upon *Hospitality* Abigail about a week after recommencing her school labors, hospitality was not to be set aside, and he writes:

A Portuguese sailor having been quite sick for some time at Lazarus' and there being no prospect of his getting well there, we had compassion on him and brought him to our humble accomodation and have endeavored to take good care of him. He is much better and we hope he will soon be able to take care of himself and seek a habitation elsewhere.

Molokai, still sometimes called the Lonely Isle, but now *The* most inappropriately (always almost the center of the group *Lonely* and now daily visited by airplanes, and frequently by com- *Isle* fortable and swift steamers) had its loneliness, indeed, for our young bride and groom. The most painful part of it was the sense of separation caused by the lack of that greatest of heart-warmers, letters from home. Although the letters that Lowell did receive sometimes caused him "tender, heartrending emotions of bidding dearly loved friends adieu," those that Abigail *did not* receive from her family cost her much greater pain. Her grandchildren rise up and echo the rebuke in such a letter as this:

Molokai, November 11th. . . . The Hellespont arrived in due time, brought me no letters from family friends, five or six good letters from other friends, however. A month ago another ship arrived which sailed the last of April, five months after us. It brought me one letter from sister L. and one from brother L. and I assure you they were no small consolation to me. But why

so few? I received by the same ship seven or eight from friends
not connected with our family. Why so few from home? Do my
friends expect to hear when a ship is going to sail for the Sandwich Islands? Why a thousand ships sail that you know nothing
about. The only way is for you to send your letter to the missionary rooms and they will forward them the first opportunity.
And this you promised to do, and yet when a ship sailed five
months after us it brought us only two letters from home.
"Brethren these things ought not so to be." Excuse me if I
scold you a little for when you go 18000 miles from home you
will feel just as I do. Now will you not write once in three
months at least and deposit your letters at the Missionary
rooms. The most favorable opportunities occur in the fall, although there are others in the course of the year.

Abigail's "scoldings" seemed of little avail. In 1848 in a
letter of love and longing written to her mother she says:

It is now a little more than three years since the date of my
last letters from any one of my beloved family friends! No such
period has elapsed before and my mind is filled with most painful
emotions. Still as vessels homeward bound are leaving . . . I
take up my pen hoping that my dear friends still live and that
they will be disappointed and anxious even as we are if they did
not hear from us. Three years! How great the changes that may
have taken place!

Abigail's tender heart grieved, not only over her own losses
but for theirs, caused by her protracted illnesses or by the
loss of a letter long and painfully written, a narration covering months of events and activities in the mission, for sometimes a boat like the ill-fated *William Neilson,* a brig bound
for China, never arrived.

The Scene   With the close of the General Meeting of the missionaries
Shifts   in Honolulu in June and July, 1834, Kaluaaha, their first
home faded from the silver screen of Lowell's and Abigail's
life. By a new decision of the assembled brethren

we all separate, each to occupy a separate field.

. . . We have been assigned to Ewa (Oahu), as our field of
future labours. May the Lord give grace and wisdom and dis-

letter from
my Father

Brandon vt
July 19

Mr Lionel Jenney

Franklin Co   Greenfield

Mass

FACSIMILE OF LETTER FOLDED
FOR SEALING AS ENVELOPE

(see p. 309)

cretion. The King's favorite country seat is about three miles from the place pointed out for the station. He and his train are, or will probably be, a source of many trials to me.

Preaching there as a substitute minister, on a summer morning, Lowell found an audience of one hundred and fifty people, all of the former two thousand

that have not turned back to the Hewa (evil) . . . a precious few that as yet have escaped the awful whirlpool of intemperance . . . the door for lying, stealing . . . adultery etc., . . . offer materials to commence with. O for wisdom!

Lowell went to Molokai to fetch his household belongings and also preached in Lahaina and Wailuku on Maui. Various rather exciting events of physical discomfort and danger, on land and sea, afoot, horseback, in packet and canoe, were necessitated by such exigencies as missionaries must expect. A heart-warming in the parting from his Molokai flock caused him to write:

Some of them appear as near to me as any spiritual children in America.

b. EWA

On Lowell's return to Oahu, Abigail met him in improved health,

but her mind had been exceedingly tried by my long absence and a numerous train of sad events which had occurred in quick succession viz: the death of Mr. Douglas in a bullock pit on Hawaii; the awful murder of Captain Pausette and three of his company on some unknown barbarous island—the downfall of the Princess—and the arrival of an English man of war and her executing two natives who some two or three years ago murdered a Captain . . . while out at sea.

Delicate, indeed, was the situation of the Sandwich Island kingdom rocked as floating bales of value, a prey to pirate nations, rather than as summits of the highest mountains on the globe, established on rocks of justice and self-determination!

A
Tragedy

The Mr. Douglas mentioned in the paragraph above was a young botanist whose name still persists in the true nomenclature of our most commonly imported building timber, familiarly known as "Nor'west," the Douglas fir. He and his horse accidentally (today there are rumors of foul play) fell into a lava pit where had already fallen an angry bull which gored the invaders to death.

Had Kipling already written it, Lowell surely would constantly have been quoting his description of "the world so new and all," for, having dealt with elementals on Molokai in physical as well as spiritual and educational matters, it was to begin all over again in the new situation at Ewa. "Line upon line and precept upon precept" was Lowell's patient doctrine throughout life, and "here a little and there a little" was daily applied to his tasks as mason, carpenter, and instructor of a people whose lack of perseverance was a sore trial. One wonders how a New Englander with such apparent

Adobe

alacrity took up the making of adobe bricks and the timber construction pertinent to it. It was easy to accept the Hawaiian roof of thatch, using what was obtainable, *ti* leaf where *pili* grass was not to be had.

Leaving Abigail in Honolulu for her to establish her health before entering the new field, Lowell writes:

September 23rd, 1834. . . . Today we have raised the roof of my house. One week ago there was no adobe laid, nor but a few stones in the foundation. If the roof could be covered as soon, I should hope to soon associate with my wife in a comfortable home. But the natives do work when they please.

Visit from
Judd
Family

Sept. 26th. Day before yesterday I went to Honolulu and also sent a double canoe; returned today and Dr. Judd's family with me. They are on their way to Waialua. Abba remains still at Honolulu, now in the family of Mr. Chamberlain. . . . The Doctor came in Auhea's double canoe well manned—but on arriving here he found no food. The men went to Waipio and obtained food, etc. . . . Mrs. Judd was exceedingly delighted with Pearl River and its banks and also our building spot, etc. . . . She relished the water here very much.

John Ii

The high chief John Ii was one of the staunchest friends of

the mission. Residing on the fair lands of Waipio, he was a neighbor, and Lowell writes of him:

This evening, October 8th, John Ii has called and promised to put on the roof of the cook house. He thinks in the course of four weeks it will be done. The Lord is good and kind in causing the rulers of the land to aid us in obtaining comfortable habitation.

At the end of a weary week the enumerations of the daily tasks accomplished conclude:

Friday laboured nearly all day about the fireplace and oven foundation; laid one or two tiers all round the house and some three or four on the end back of the fireplace. Saturday, have laid dobes all day—some three or four tiers all round the house, raised the fireplace so high that I have hung the crane etc. Feel considerably exhausted this evening. May the Lord forgive whatever has been amiss and prepare me for the holy duties of tomorrow.

The Hanging of the Crane

Lowell's native help was paid sometimes in yards of cloth, sometimes in orders on the mission depository in Honolulu.

The only road to Honolulu was a rough and steep bridle trail which in an emergency could be covered by a horse in two hours, a trail long gone and forgotten by those who glide over the subdued hills and transformed gulches in powerful and comfortable motor cars. The only ride Lowell describes was on an unbroken and most unruly horse, the missionary journeys usually being made by canoe and at night to avoid the heat of the day. Worn by loneliness and by the anxieties because of Abigail's frailty and by the sometimes hurried journeys to her, Lowell wrote:

Bridle Trail and Canoe

November 15th, 1834. . . . This morning at half past twelve o'clock Abba and myself left the mission families at Honolulu and took up our anchor—and on a double canoe we came to this place, Waiawa, in four hours. Had a good time, good moon, favorable breeze etc. . . . Abba was considerably fatigued owing to loss of sleep, excitement, etc. . . . but feels comfortable this evening. All our friends and even the physicians thought it rather imprudent for Abba to leave Honolulu. I hope and trust they will one day discover their misjudgement on the subject. I had journeyed from this place to Honolulu and back about twenty times since general meeting—some six hundred miles. And I felt that if practicable she must come home. The house was in a suitable state to be occupied and I was in a frame of mind not to be denied the society of my companion any longer. She finds the climate, the water, taro etc. to agree with her much better than at Honolulu.

Nov. 25th. . . . Abba has been remarkably smart for her since she came from Honolulu. She has not performed much manual labour but has been able to oversee her business, give direction, etc. . . . We have been favored with considerable many presents since her arrival viz: some seven or eight fowls, four turkeys, one hog, fish, oysters, potatoes, taro, cabbage, wood etc.

Oysters   The good soil and water at Ewa made it possible to raise every kind of vegetable grown in the Islands. Oysters are mentioned again in a note from Abigail to Mrs. Chamberlain in which she is sorry not to be able to send any. How they originated and in such numbers as to give Pearl River (or Harbor) its name, we should like to know.

There was a pleasant comity of this world's goods between the missionary families in the different districts, as well as between natives and foreigners. The missionaries never traded with the natives, but took money for books only and paid for service, house building, or hire of canoe men, in cloth. Some of the local notes are as telling of daily living as the journals. A number of notes sent Mrs. Chamberlain, wife of the mission dispenser in Honolulu, are extant. Here are a few quotations, dated at intervals from October, 1834, to the following summer:

Red Earth   Dear Sister, can you or your husband procure for us two or three or four door mats, such as you use, otherwise I do not know but you will hear that we are irrecoverably lost in the dirt. We begin to have considerable of rain and the earth cleaves to the feet more here than I have ever observed anywhere else. Also our mats are of a character that will not bear washing and we are thronged with natives. I need not tell you that we are more filthy than we like to be. . . . We have had a high tide all day during this week thus far, consequently we have not sent for our cow. Hope to tomorrow.

We are very comfortably situated here in most respects. I have so little strength and native help that my house does not yet look in good order. We have now obtained a man and woman and I hope to get regulated after a while. Hemolele will return to Honolulu tomorrow. She has been of great service to us. I love her almost as a sister. She has had a good influence over the people here. The people are in a distressing state in this place. Backward in everything but sin. I do long to be able to do something for them.

The climate here is delightful. . . . Our cow gives us milk enough for daily use, if we do not use a great deal, and by saving it, enough to mix our bread, but we can make no butter. We have salted some pork which is our standby, and we have some fowls so lean as not to cook themselves. I find I cannot eat much strong meat, and bread and molasses has not a great deal of nourishment for a feeble body. I cannot go into my cook room to prepare delicate food for want of strength, and moreover my stomach has suffered considerable derangement for want of suitable food. . . . All these things induce me to ask Mr. Chamberlain for a cow that will soon give milk, that we can make butter. Have hesitated much about asking this favor, and should not did I not feel really the need of it. I do not wish any of you to part with another cow you are now milking.

An Invalid's Bread and Molasses

January 13th, '35. . . . We have a large single canoe which my husband thinks will accommodate your family very comfortably. We can hire two men to bring and return you for twelve yards of cloth, and we think that the benefit you will derive from a little change of air, scenery and relief from care will be more valuable to you than the worth of cloth. . . . We should like to send for you Friday night, and have you leave Honolulu Saturday morning at five o'clock, as it will then be high tide and a pleasant part of the day to come. . . . We shall be glad to see you, and have you tarry with us as long as you can be contented. . . . You can be as *kaawale* [free] here, for instructing your children on the Sabbath as at home.

Twelve Yards of Cloth

February 12th, '35. . . . I should like one of the shawls you spoke of, if they are not all disposed of. I have almost daily use for a common shawl at this season. I had a little green flannel blanket which I used to wear about my shoulders, but I lost it while you was here. Did it get mislaid into your basket? . . . Much obliged for the dried fruit, hope you did not rob yourself. Has there any come into the depository? Presume we shall have some if there has. . . . Our box from America was mostly filled with garments designed for natives—we judge that the best way of disposing of them. Mostly little girls frocks . . . a large parcel of letters, some excellent new books. Lowell's box from Heath contained a bed quilt and a pattern for a pair of pantaloons.

. . . I thank you for the butter. I thank you also for letting me know that it was from Kauai so that I may not only thank you for the trouble of sending it, but also, and more especially our kind sister who made the luxury for me. . . . We are greatly pleased with the prospect of a cow; thank you for offering one. . . . I have a favor to ask of Mr. Chamberlain when he makes the division of supplies received for the mission that he will in the Ewa bundle put in a pattern for at least one good dark frock for me. I understand both light and dark calicoes have been received. . . . I do want one good dark dress.

The only one I have had since I left America I procured of Mrs. Rice and it fades badly when washed, although I have been very choice of it; as my dresses have been mostly light color. . . . Are there any fans in the depository? I should be extremely glad of two or three. . . . If there are not enough perhaps Mr. Chamberlain will bear me in mind when he procures some. . . . Have had a pleasant visit from our brethren and sisters, Deill and Parker. . . . We send a few eggs in the jar. Please divide them between yourself and sister Tinker.

. . . Arrived at "sweet home" after a sail of four hours. A scorching sun and headache all the way, otherwise a comfortable passage. Find Ewa still here, although there is scarcely a man on the ground. All still laboring at the Salt Works. We found the bread, pie, etc. very acceptable. I felt again much obliged to you for them.

August '35, My dear Sister, Many thanks for your kind note, collar etc. . . . The collar I suppose was from one of my sisters as I had heard something about it before. It came in one of Miss Hitchcock's boxes. . . . I am able to do a little more for the people than before General Meeting. Have established a meeting for mothers to meet on Wednesday—only once a fortnight as I have a weekly meeting on Friday for all the females. . . . I feel an increasing interest in missionary labors, and only wish for health to be extensively engaged in them.

Females on Friday

And now the butter, if not the bread, comes back across the waters.

Do you want any butter for shortening? I have more than I shall use in some time, which I received from Kauai in the divisions before General Meeting. You know it does not grow any better by age and I suppose we shall have now and then a division from Kauai this year as last, so that if you are in want of any let me know and I will send you some. . . . Write a line when you are able. I know your hands are full, but trust you find your strength equal to your day.

Butter

To be equal to her day was all Abigail asked for herself, and, in spite of grievous "afflictions" and great lack of physical strength during many years, her prayer seems to have been answered.

By this time Abigail seems to have desisted from her journal letters. Lowell's journal of June, 1835, notes that Abigail received from her sister Mrs. Root, a shawl, some flannel, etc. These articles were evidently the response to Abigail's request for the same written from the chilly atmosphere of Molokai in November, 1833, when she stated that her New England outfit contained no cloak or warm gown. More than a year and a half to wait for a wrap! From this time on we have not more than a letter, or perhaps two, a year from her pen, as Abigail's duties increased with her gain in health and strength. It is probable that she wrote few if any more letters than are extant.

A Shawl at Last

Matters of flannel, great needs for small shawls, discussions of butter, fowl, and eggs were by no means the meat and drink of Abigail's spirit. That her faith was triumphant we have much evidence, but even the salubriousness of the climate of Ewa and a now nearer reach of medical help did not

Hither and Yon

keep her from repeated and debilitating attacks of illness that at times threatened great seriousness, calling Lowell in haste and anxiety long distances to her bedside. Not only had he his necessary building operations in hand, but could write on a Sabbath eve:

A Busy Day

Am quite fatigued with the labors of the day. Have attended six public meetings and talked upon an average of half an hour in each besides the other exercises. Morning prayer meeting, Sabbath school of children at eight, sermon at ten a.m., Bible class at twelve, preaching at four p.m., and an evening exercise. Abba has been rather feeble today and has not been out at all. Besides the religious exercises I have bled three persons and administered medicine to some eight or ten. This is doing with my might what my hands find to do. May the Lord add his blessing. Text a.m. Matthew 16; 26, "What is a man profited" etc. An increase of hearers of late.

Just after leaving Abigail on a Saturday evening about sundown a messenger overtook Lowell with word that Abigail was acutely ill and wished her husband to return. One feels for poor Lowell as he exclaims:

Anxiety

Having rode some twenty miles in the heat of the day over a very bad road and having preached four times I felt very much exhausted and that it was not my duty to attempt to retrace my steps that night.

Trusting to the providence of God and the presence in his house of a brother missionary, also the probability that Dr. Judd would be summoned, Lowell kept up his courage and next morning preached a sermon to

some seven or eight hundred assembled, then excused myself and returned post haste.

Mutual Love

The Lord sustained both the suffering wife and the distraught husband and Abigail could write:

The missionary husband and wife are all the world to each other. A separation is felt in all its agony. Well may it be said that when such friends part, 'tis the survivor dies. . . . Among other good effects which I hope have grown out of our trials sympathy for others has certainly been one. . . . The same hand that afflicts knows how to comfort. . . . Your faith decides that all is right. . . . Eternity will ere long make plain to us those things which now appear mysterious. . . . May your consolations greatly exceed your sorrows. . . . My health is not so good as when I saw you last. . . . I write little. . . . My hand trembles so. I fear you will hardly be able to make out the words. Do write me soon and tell me how you feel in view of God's dealings with you.

Little thinking it would be his last year at Ewa, a situation most pleasing to Lowell and holding opportunities of a field practically unworked, the young man seems to have put forth all his might in a variety of expressions of the zeal which filled him. On July 31, 1835, Lowell records:

We have been taking the census of Ewa and Waianae this month, noting a decrease in the previous three years of five hundred ninety-two at Ewa and two hundred fourteen at Waianae, the 1835 totals of the two districts being respectively three thousand four hundred twenty-three and one thousand six hundred fifty-four. These all belong to my parish, and are scattered over about twenty miles of sea coast. Here is work enough for a man to do especially if his companion does not enjoy firm health. Cannot the Board furnish a much needed teacher and wife? *His Parish*

It was a long-distance call and perhaps a deaf ear at the end! Lowell was grieved at the falling off in religious attendance. It would appear that the gay life of the young king and his sister who had a country home a few miles away drew the people after them in their manner of indulgences. Lowell cries from his heart:

When their light is converted into darkness, how great is that darkness!

Lowell's mention of census taking recalls the fact that there is extant in at least one district of our Islands a huge terrace of loose stones said to have been laid up at a census taking. A most impressive inventory, but one not easily to be checked over! One can picture the throngs bearing each his *Census Taking*

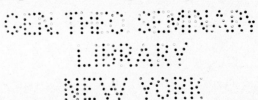

stone as a monument to his existence. This probably was a bait to the cheerful observance of command—as the litany has it, "Incline our hearts to keep this law!" Such a forgivable vanity doubtless affected also the contribution box of the early Hawaiian churches, when a feeble man would find some compassionate one to carry his stick of timber for him until at the end of the journey he himself could throw it on the pile. Much later on, when money came into circulation,

The Joys of Vain-glory

the members of the congregation carried their offerings up the church aisle to the receptacle, first dividing their gifts in portions so as to have the pleasure of repeated trips, and rejoicing the more if squeaky shoes, perhaps loaned from one to another for the happy occasion, made music for the ears of the contributor as he the more readily attracted attention. This matter of attracting attention calls to mind the fact that when in the early days articles of attire were hard to obtain, but the idea of fashion had already laid its heavy hand (does not Wordsworth describe custom as "heavy as frost and deep almost as life"?) on the simple-minded islander, a man would squeak his way up the aisle in proudly acquired footgear, regardless of any omissions in the rest of his dress, and drop the "loud-speakers" out of the window for some other member of the family to usher in to services.

On Abigail's birthday, December 4, 1835, Lowell exclaims:

Abigail's Birthday

Twenty-six years old. How rapidly we are advancing to old age.

And strangely enough, that seems not to have been a joke, although all his life Lowell loved a little joke, for on the following New Year's Day he who was to remain hourly ready for fifty-five years more observes:

Many will fall in death the present year. Perhaps it is the year for me to close my probation. May I stand ready at any day or hour's notice.

A Tabu

At about this time the chiefs published a *tabu* which put an end to the public disturbance of

perpetual hulas, drumming and dancing accompanied by howl-

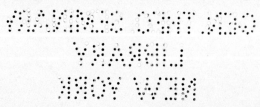

ings and intonations apparently unearthly and inhuman, drinking, fighting, burning houses and the like. Yesterday three idolators were conducted to the fort—who have resided within two or three miles of us in the past year.

Idolatry was supposed to be a thing of the past, but old faiths do not die too easily. Lowell on his way to Waianae was surprised to see a small stone idol standing by the roadside and dressed in *tapa*. Its requirement in worship seemed to be a contribution of *tapa* from each passer by. But Lowell plucks up heart when he remembers that the congregation, depleted two hundred or less the previous year, has more than trebled.

In spite of difficulties with day laborers who wearied him with complaints about their food, try as he did to please them, Lowell finished building his home, cookhouse and study.

Dwelling Completed

January 4, 1836. Yesterday was one of the most interesting Sabbaths I ever witnessed. . . . Brother Bingham and Brother Emerson were present and we organized a church of eighteen members, six by letter of recommendation from the Honolulu church and twelve upon examination. There were a number of church members present from Honolulu and Waialua. Whole number of communicants were fifty. A precious season indeed. Everything was performed decently and in order. The candidates appeared exceedingly well. They appear very near to me. I regard them all except two or three as instrumentally brought into the Kingdom by the joint labors of Abba and myself. May I have wisdom and grace sufficient to lead them for immortal glory. Mrs. Bingham and her three little children were present on the occasion. They came and returned on my canoe.

Jan. 17, Sabbath. Today have baptized seven children, four were the offspring of those who presented them and three were adopted children. I seem to hold a new relation to some of these people of late from what I did a few months ago. Pastor of a little flock. Very great is my love towards them. At present they seem to walk together in love and harmony. May the Lord of the Vineyard grant us his benediction, his guidance and his protection at all times.

. . . A brighter day has dawned. The time to build the

Lord's house has come. If these Islanders are not soon converted to God the blood of their souls will be on the professed followers of Christ.

A few weeks later the people were

Meeting-house . . . considerably engaged about building a house for the Lord —most of the men are scattered upon the mountains getting timber for the meeting house.

Immediately contributions for the church building began to be made, not only by the residents of Ewa but from the people in Waialua. The gifts were sometimes in money, but sometimes in live stock, wood, *poi*, mats, and *tapa*. The burden of disposing of heterogeneous contributions lay upon the young pastor. He would speak of it thus:

The Where-withal The people seem quite spirited in contributing to build a meeting house for the Lord. Six goats, forty bunches of bananas, five hundred fifty heads of taro, fowls, ducks, etc., to the amount of $27.56 have been handed in by different individuals. Four canoes have been despatched this evening with the articles for the Honolulu market.

Next day. I took an early leave of Abba this morning and arrived at Honolulu about eight o'clock. . . . Disposed of the products, etc. and obtained nails of various sizes and one more box of glass. Returned this evening . . . considerably fatigued.

A Glowing Heart Lowell's heart was glowing with the apparent spiritual health not only of his immediate church but of the population of the countryside. He was preaching to attentive congregations of several hundreds and the *Hoike* (quarterly examination of schools) occurring at this time also was most encouraging.

A gradual advance—no rushing mighty wind and then a barren waste. Slow and sure thus far has been the progress— what we have gained seems to be firm footing.

Lowell and Abigail were ready to move into the new house which the slow native plasterers and Lowell himself as painter were just finishing when, alas, the young wife was confined to her bed. The ministrations of Dr. Judd from far-off Honolulu were replaced by those of Dr. Rook (father of the child who was to be Queen Emma). He had moved his family down to Halawa, whence by daily canoe he could visit the invalid.

Poor Lowell! On June 24, 1836, during the General Meeting in Honolulu, he records in his journal:

Today the brethren have unanimously voted that it is our duty to leave Ewa and come to Honolulu to teach school. Mr. Bishop and his wife have been temporarily removed to Ewa. Probably will remain there for a considerable time. Our hearts ache and bleed to think of leaving Ewa, but the providence of God seems to direct us to do so. May he guide us in teaching the youth of Honolulu, in preparing a company of men for the high school, for great usefulness to this mission and for the kingdom of heaven.

Cast Down but Not Dismayed

c. KAWAIAHAO

Lowell writes July 7, 1836:

Our meeting dissolved today. . . . I am now wishing to enter upon the labors assigned me without delay.

July 8th. Notice. Honolulu School Keeping! ! I have commenced a school in Dr. Judd's school house. Thirty-five lads this morning. Eleven do not know their letters. Two assistant teachers, one male and one female.

12th. Preached at Ewa day before yesterday. Yesterday and today have been packing our things and removing them to the house of Waiau to await the arrival of Mr. Bishop, etc. Very tired this evening.

14th. Today the girls together in the school house *makai*, fifty-nine in number and as noisy and ungovernable as you please. The boys are bad enough but the girls are several degrees more noisy than the boys. The present plan is to keep up both schools both a.m. and p.m. I fear that all the good apparently gained will be lost again from the fact that the native teachers have no government.

Lowell as Schoolmaster

The pupils in this school were to "pour in to the number of four hundred," although not more than two hundred twenty-five continued regularly. Lowell confessed to the distant

Board that the first term made the greatest tax on soul and body, faith and patience in dealing with the children of this "New Sodom." Corporal punishment was necessary, was successful, and was approved by the native parents. No scholar left school because of correction. Moreover, the second term found order.

This morning Abba and I have had a pleasant ride in Jones' gig. Abba is apparently gaining rapidly. Yesterday Mr. Parker arrived from the Columbia River—on his way to the United States. He has been on an exploring tour among the Indians. Finds them more ready to hear the gospel than he expected.

Site for Punahou School

16th. Saturday. This day a number of the brethren have been up to Punahou to seek out the best site for a boarding school. Brother and Sister Bingham, Brother and Sister Judd, Brother Chamberlain, Tinker and myself and also Mr. Parker recently from the Columbia River. The site fixed upon was a few rods N.W. of the present dwelling house which now stands there. We dined, having three knives and three forks among us all. Our missionary attainments today seemed unnecessary, though we did pretty well. Mr. Parker is an interesting man. Abba rode out again this morning. Hope and trust she is gaining.

July 24th. Sabbath. This morning at eight o'clock I met with some three hundred fifty youths in the meeting house—an interesting congregation. At two p.m. met with them again in the school house, perhaps two hundred present. The children have behaved rather better than I expected they would.

July 27th. Today my school of girls numbers one hundred twenty-four. The children have behaved rather better than at first. Hope to be able to teach them some important things during the present term. I get exceedingly fatigued every night, the schools draw upon my very vitals. May the Lord grant me his rich blessing during the year in convicting the children unto himself.

Theft

August 10th. Some three or four of the girls in the first class have been found guilty of theft in the bindery. I left the house for a few minutes to get some advice how I should treat the case and on returning found the school in a perfect uproar notwithstanding there were four native assistant teachers in the house, so perfectly incompetent are they to govern others.

On the eighteenth, in the absence from the Station of Brothers Bingham and Tinker, Lowell wrote of abundant labors, having in addition to his schools, all the preaching of the station, etc. He and Abigail about this time moved into the house formerly occupied by Dr. Judd.

25th. Today the king and his train has come from Maui, where he has been residing for some months. A number of small native vessels accompanied him. There has been much firing of cannon both at the fort and on fort hill [Punchbowl]. *Arrival of King*

29th. Today I have inquired of every scholar whether he or she smokes tobacco. Some thirty-two girls and some twenty-five boys replied that they do smoke. The girls made no attempt to justify themselves, but the boys attempted to advocate the use of it. The great argument with them all was that it warmed the mouth and the *opu* (stomach) after eating. A real knockdown argument here in this torrid zone! !

September 4th, 1836. Sabbath. An increase in the congregation of youth today. The sacrament of the Lord's Supper . . . great congregation . . . long and tedious exercises. One person formerly suspended, restored; and one excommunicated.

Today for the first time I took the choir of singers into the meeting house. They sung pretty well all things considered.

September 9th. Yesterday the United States ship of war "Peacock" came to anchor outside and today she has come inside. This p.m. I have been off on board in company with Mr. Bingham and Kekuanaoa, the governor of the fort. Was introduced to Captain Stribling and Commodore Kennedy, liked their appearance well. *The Peacock*

September 10th. Have been with Commodore Kennedy *Ma* (meaning, and party) and the residents and Brothers Bingham and Dimond to see the chiefs today. An interesting time. Our people at Ewa *launa* (favor) us very much. They come up in companies to see us and this p.m. a number of the children have come bringing each a small present.

12th, Monday. Yesterday English services were held on board the "Peacock" man-of-war. Mr. Deill preached.

15th. Today Commodore Kennedy, Captain Guinnes and Mr. Bingham called into my school of girls. The Commodore appeared quite pleased with the appearances.

*Mr.
Whelen*

17th. Mr. Whelen, the Commodore's secretary, has concluded to lodge with us a few nights while in port. He is a very pleasant and agreeable man and hopefully pious. He went out a merchant to China, but the climate not agreeing with him he is on his return home and the commodore's former secretary being removed, Mr. Whelen takes his place on his return. The residents are making many parties these days.

Parties

"The residents" seems to be the term applied to the foreigners not missionaries. Sympathy between them and the missionaries was more or less according to circumstances. Their parties that furnished elaborate refreshments without grace before meat, and especially those that included wine drinking or dancing were under the ban. And when ladies who had partaken of the Lord's sacrament indulged in these worldly pleasures it was a matter of great distress to the minds of the unworldly pastors.

October 9th. The "Peacock" has left today. Well, they have gone, sailed too on the Sabbath. This is all of a piece with Commodore Kennedy's other conduct whilst here. I hope Captain Stribling is a good man, and also Mr. Whelen. Alas for the rest of them.

*Must
Abigail Go
Home?*

Sunday, October 2nd, 1836. Four years ago Abba and I united our interests in matrimony. They have been four years of toil and anxiety and pleasure too for it is always a pleasure to me to be doing good. Abba has been ill for nearly three years, though able to do more or less. There is very little prospect that she will ever enjoy firm health again, while she resides at these Islands. Dr. Ruschenberger, a skilful physician on board the U.S. man of war, advises that she return to a cold climate for a season. May the great head of missions guide in this thing.

*Arrival of
Roman
Catholic
Priest*

Have conducted four public religious services today—two with the children and two in Brother Bingham's congregation and attended the English service this evening at the seaman's chapel. A Roman Catholic priest has just arrived, and report says that two or three more will be here ere long.

During my morning discourse, which was founded upon Second Timothy, 3; 16, I alluded to the sentiments and practices of Roman Catholics. . . . I moreover stated that a Roman Catholic priest had just come to this place and that it was my *manao* it would be *pono* (good, right) for him to return in the same vessel in which he came. Now whether it was wise in me to advance that idea in public or not, it is the sentiment of my inmost soul.

Lowell's sentiment was that of a good many other "inmost souls," and there were to come many sorry days of clashing in religious matters.

The genial Mr. Whelen wrote to Abigail as the U.S.S. *Peacock* stood "Off Monterrey" at the end of October, 1836:

It gives me great pleasure . . . to commence . . . a correspondence, which it will at all times give me great pleasure to continue, and I hope frequently to hear that your health is improving and that your labours among the natives at Oahu are blessed of God in the conversion of many souls. I shall always recur to the month passed with you as one of happiness and profit and trust that the opportunity I there enjoyed of meeting again with *Christian* friends will not pass unimproved. . . . The town of Monterrey is . . . on a beautiful acclivity and well calculated for a large city were there any means of procuring an adequate supply of water. . . . The surrounding country is hilly and covered with large oak and pine trees. . . . Beef, fish, potatoes and mutton are abundant. . . . Game also is abundant and many of our officers procure it daily. Since the destruction of the Spanish Missions, the population and prosperity of the neighborhood has decreased considerably, and there was at the time of our departure, an insurrection daily expected. . . . I regret exceedingly that I was not able to find any of the rock weed at this Port, no one had seen it here—I may however meet with it on the coast of South America. There is a Kelp . . . apparently of the same nature but it is too bulky for exhibition.

A Picture of "Monterrey"

Abigail was evidently on one of her hunts for natural objects of interest.

I have learned that the Catholic Missionaries who were expelled from Oahu are now in Monterrey and intend returning

Popery

there, on their way to the Gambier Islands. . . . I have seen
and I must confess with regret Mr. B——'s letter to Dr.
Ruschenberger with regard to them. His description of popery
might answer for two centuries back, but will not for the present age.

Please remember me to him and to Mrs. B. and to . . . all
of which I shall remember with kindness. I am very desirous that
some short and plain work on Political economy should be
translated for the use of the Chiefs, as I am persuaded that
little can be done to benefit them materially, without a great
change in the present policy of the Government. There is
nothing wanting but this change, to give each native a comfortable living and enable him to extend to others on the islands
of this vast ocean the blessings which they now enjoy from
the Gospel. . . . Very sincerely in Christ's affect'n, Edw. S.
Whelen.

Visitors

Acquaintance from time to time during her long life in the
Islands with visitors in other walks of life, people of refinement, culture, and breadth of vision were as wellsprings in a
desert to Abigail. Would she could have had more of that
stimulus in the early years when her activities were cramped
by feebleness of body and her eager mind too often groped
for what was not there.

An Island
Trip

October 20, 1836, found Lowell and Abigail with Mr.
Parker embarked on Hopili's chartered vessel for a short
tour of Molokai and Maui. The voyaging was uncomfortable
and, to Abigail, somewhat frightening; but after distress of
mind and body came a week-end with the friends at their first
station, Kaluaaha, and, again, anchor dropped in Wailuku
Harbor (Kahului), the voyagers received an especial welcome. It was considered "providential" that they had just
come in time to be of use at the protracted meeting planned
for the first of November.

The
Protracted
Meeting

The "protracted meeting" was the technique of missions
brought from New England. Perhaps in our day it seems like
some prophylactic inoculation causing an inflamed conscience, a fever of revival and, if effectual, producing immu-
nity against an ingrowing, selfish, lustful life and establishing

a wholesome godfearing and righteous substitute. Revivals
are now looked at rather askance, are they not, as though we
must beware of an emotional lead in this age of reason. Yet
turning to nature, we see the benefits of her changes of mood.
Perhaps there is in human life as close a rhythm and harmony as in other forces of nature and the awakening of the
spirit to the things of the spirit are as seasonal and much to
be desired as the coming of the spring of the year or the
"unwonted rains" after a period of drought.

Apparently, Lowell was one of the most zealous of the
brethren, deeply sympathizing with Father Lyons of Waimea, the Hawaiian hymnologist, in his way of working with
consequent sweeping conversions. Lowell belabored himself   *Fervor*
and his Honolulu brethren for not having greater faith and
so producing greater results. At times when he had listened
to a discourse from some brother or other his journal would
comment, "Very much engaged," or, "Not very much engaged," referring, one supposes to power and eloquence, or
at least a convincing manner. How much the sometime lack
of zeal could be accounted for by overwork, too long or hard
riding, a sleepless canoe journey or rough channel crossing,
the dear Lord must have known and weighed in the balance.

The "revolution backward" which made a vivid impression
on Lowell when he began his labors at Ewa and Waianae was
but the dark hour before the dawn. The depression of 1834
and 1835 dispersed as a cloud and the conch shell calling to
sunrise prayer, or worship at later hours of the Sabbath
brought numbers constantly increasing in 1836, 1837, and
1838.

In 1833 Lowell and Brother Hitchcock had cried aloud
from Kaluaaha to the Home Board for medical books "most
adapted to our immediate needs." Their medical library consisted of one book and the young men were in great distress
witnessing physical ills they could not help. How their spirits
must have chafed that even the promptest response to their
request must be a year or more in reaching their hands. Now,
in 1836, from his solitary post at Ewa, Lowell cries afar to
Boston:

Let all who go on mission possess at least some general

knowledge of medicine previous to their leaving the halls of
science.

He adds a plea for a copy of *Henry's Commentary on the
Bible*, with the apology:

I feel the need of that work very much and think I may be
enough more useful to meet this expense.

At the end of the year he is bold enough to write the Board
a description of the mission organized in Honolulu as: one
doctor, one editor, one translator; no one to teach school.
Why? The missionary mothers had "numerous offspring" or
"enjoyed feeble health" or both—making station schools
"little else but a name." Therefore the local board of the
Islands had unanimously voted it the duty of some clergyman to leave his church and engage exclusively in teaching
the youth of this great village containing a population of
nine thousand souls. There was need, declared Lowell, of
Forty twenty more clergymen and of forty schoolmasters; "the na-
School- tion is sinking without them." He told the Board that he had
masters been advised to return home for his wife's health but being
unwilling to do so had been transferred by the local board to
Honolulu where she might be near the mission doctor. But
even as he wrote, his prayers to men and to God were being
answered by the great reinforcement of missionaries already
on their long voyage around the Horn.

Abigail, always a student even if illness prevented her
favorite work of teaching, requested a work on conchology
and also *Lavoisne's Atlas.* Before they reached her she had
become the private tutor of the king's three-year-old heir,
Alexander Liholiho.

Working In the protracted meeting, held on Maui during Lowell's
His Way unexpected visit just mentioned, he took a large share,
preaching sometimes at three places in an afternoon to congregations of a thousand attendants. Among the texts quoted
in this long series of discourses given by Green, Armstrong,
and others, Lowell's seem to be more tender and inviting and
less dismal and denunciatory than some of the others.

Home On returning to Honolulu, school teaching and examina-
Duties tions of schools, reading and thinking on the disturbing sub-

jects of Catholicism and Unitarianism, eagerness over the determination of a native convert to go as a foreign missionary, sorrowful partings with missionaries returning to America, physical breakdowns of brethren, the death of an unconverted princess, endurance of "abuse cast upon the mission," desertion by unfaithful servants, practical work with others—missionaries and "residents," physical labor "on the *pali* to help repair the road" (with resulting injury to his finger), filled the days to the end of January, 1837.

The year 1836 ended, as we have already surmised, on a minor note in Lowell's heart. Some weeks previous he and Abigail had called on the Princess Harieta who was very ill. Having more concern for her soul than her body, they conversed with her about it and felt that she too had a little concern for her eternal welfare. At that time they had a short interview with the King, over whom their hearts yearned. But the last day of the year, worn with anxiety over the serious illness of a brother missionary, who with his family had been with them preparing to embark for the United States and questioning recovery and return, Lowell, with what heartbreak we may be unable to measure, announces calamity thus: *The Princess*

> The Princess Harieta died yesterday about noon. I fear she has gone to hell.

On New Year's Day Lowell draws a long breath, squares his shoulders to renewed burdens and writes:

> How important it is that I enter this new year with new resolutions to serve God. The fact that some five thousand of the Sandwich Islanders have died the past year is enough to make one tremble. The fact that six hundred million heathen will pass into eternity in thirty years is an appalling thought and ought to rouse all my energies to serve God. The providence of God has moved Abba and myself from place to place since our arrival at the Islands. Where we shall be removed the present year I cannot tell. May the Lord guide and direct in all our subsequent labours, trials and enjoyments. And oh that he would bless the children under my instruction and bring them to unfeigned repentance. A number of protracted meetings are *New Year's Resolution*

in contemplation, one at Honolulu *nei* [this, of place or time],
one at Ewa, and one at Waialua. May the way be abundantly
prepared for the rich blessings of grace to be poured down upon
us. Among the blessings which call for devout acknowledgments
to Almighty God at this time is the firm health that I still enjoy
and the comfortable health of my dear Abba.

Then began a protracted meeting in Honolulu with three
thousand attendants at the sunrise service. Next morning a
thousand more attended the meeting, which was addressed by
the friendly high chief John Ii. The king, who had been
much sobered by the death of his sister Harieta, and other
Royal chiefs attended this meeting. The following evening before
Wedding the service the king was married to a long-time favorite and
brought her and other chiefs to the service. Two days later
Lowell records:

Very small congregation, for the King has ordered all the
people to make preparation for the funeral of Harieta, his
sister.

Royal February 4th, 1837. At two p.m. the procession formed at
Funeral the house of the King—a band of music—the King's guard,
perhaps two hundred, and the missionaries—the chiefs—the
foreign residents and numerous friends composed the procession. The corpse was drawn on a covered cart and large *Kahilis*
[feathered standards marking royalty] were carried on each
side—all in the highest splendor and pomp imaginable. A
miserable climax of the protracted meeting. Mr. Bingham addressed the audience on the occasion—very hoarse—very few
heard him.

Evening—I preached—text "Come unto me all ye that
labour and are heavy laden." Very small audience, just as was
to be expected after such a scene as had taken place during the
day. Minute guns were fired from the fort and from the hill
from two o'clock till sundown!

Dedication Despite Lowell's depression and fear of the effect of this
of Ewa splendid occasion upon the hearts of the people, the work
Church went on and was especially encouraging among the children,
sixty of them accompanying Lowell as he went from the
Honolulu protracted meeting to one at Ewa. There it was his

joy to preach the sermon of dedication in the church for which he had labored. Although Mr. Bishop had been stationed there in his place, Lowell had kept an eye on the work of building, declaring, as the structure was reared, that the adobes were the finest he had ever seen although the carpenter work needed some rebate from the contractors for carelessness. It was, he said,

an elegant church building, ninety feet long, forty two feet wide with a verandah all around it,—plastered inside and out, a good pulpit, etc., etc. The house will contain from ten to twelve hundred people. On the Sabbath probably not less than sixteen hundred persons were present, the verandah was full all around the building. The usual number of attendants during the meeting was about one thousand. A number of hopeful conversions occurred. . . . On the whole I think it the most interesting meeting that I have attended on this Island.

A fortnight later Lowell was off again for a protracted meeting at Waialua, taking Abigail as far as Ewa for a brief visit—going and returning "outside the reef" and finding the trip enjoyable. Still a fortnight later Lowell attended a protracted meeting at Kaneohe for a few days, Brother Bingham taking his place there when he returned to his school duties at Kawaiahao. The Kaneohe Church was filled to overflowing, a "ranai" being built for them outside. *Sowing beside All Waters*

In Honolulu, the people were quite engaged about building a temple for the Lord. The King has subscribed three thousand dollars, Kinau, four hundred dollars. Other chiefs some forty, some twenty-five, some twenty, fifteen, ten, five, four, three, two and one. In all to the amount of more than five thousand dollars. *A Temple for the Lord*

April tenth, Lowell's journal breaks forth almost into song:

American news. Thirty-two missionaries. Last Saturday I went to Kaneohe to spend the Sabbath with Br. Parker. The Spirit of God is moving in a marvellous manner upon the minds of quite a number of people there. The work has appeared to be

quite as powerful since the regular protracted meeting as during the meeting. Solemn and interesting time there yesterday.
On my way home I received a note from Abba informing me that
a reinforcement of missionaries had arrived from America, . . .
fifteen pairs and two single ladies, nine for school teachers, two
physicians, and three preachers and one assistant of Brother C.
Bless the Lord O my soul for this seventh and great reinforcement to this mission. They have had a blessed time on board—
the captain, second mate and a number of the crew hopefully
converted. They find us all engaged in revivals on this Island.

*The
Seventh
Reinforce-
ment*

This seventh reinforcement, April, 1837, like the seventh
wave of the ocean, scored a high-tide mark in the story of the
Hawaiian mission. At about the same time, July, 1837, the
Catholic Fathers, once turned away, were established, and
the very clash of ideas the shouting and the tumult of the
Son of God going forth to war in human breasts, in com-
munities, is it not like the embroiling of the sea when the big
waves stir up so great a cloud of sand as to obscure the
depths and temporarily to forbid a clear reflection of the
heavens? Even so it is in the order of the Universe. Who can
be sure of reading history aright?

*Father
Bachelot's
Algaroba*

A picturesque symbol of the time is the planting by Father
Bachelot, on the Catholic Mission grounds, near the later site
of the Cathedral of Our Lady of Peace, of the first algaroba
tree. What a missionary in the vegetable kingdom it became,
this mesquite of desert lands coming to break up shallow soil,
the scant covering of old coral reefs, or arid plains which
knew water only when winter freshets tore their way through
gullies like the arroyos of Southern California. Living in spite
of blasts of salt spray in Kona storms that burn the leaves
from the thorny twigs, when receiving any care and attention
it grows swiftly into noble structures with graceful limbs and
lacy foliage, offering firewood, honey from its flowers and
fodder from its pods. What great benefactions it has be-
stowed for ninety years! Now its frailty of root and its inevitable fall before the century mark are held against it and
hundreds of algarobas are being replaced by other tree families. But its beauty and usefulness will long outlive its popu-

larity. After many years a Protestant missionary, and son of
a Protestant missionary to Hawaii, finding Father Bachelot's grave on a distant isle of the South Seas, planted upon
it a coconut tree—a tribute from one brother to another.

We must return from this divergence and many thoughts
leading us far afield. We are back again in 1837, rejoicing in
the arrival of the *Mary Frazier*. On the following Sabbath
Lowell confides to his journal:

Today Captain Sumner and his Second Officer and four of the
sailors have at their own request been received by Brother Bingham into the native church. A strange thing indeed!

The assignment of the newly arrived missionaries was as
follows:

New Assignment of Missionaries

On Kauai—Dr. and Mrs. Thomas Lafon: Koloa.
  Mr. and Mrs. Edward Johnson: Waioli.
  Mr. and Mrs. Edwin Locke: Waialua.
On Oahu—Mr. and Mrs. Amos Starr Cooke: Honolulu.
  Mr. and Mrs. S. N. Castle: Honolulu.
  Miss Marcia M. Smith: Punahou.
On Molokai—Mr. and Mrs. Bethuel Munn: Kaluaaha.
On Maui—Mr. and Mrs. Mark Ives: Hana.
  Miss Lucia G. Smith: Lahainaluna.
  Mr. and Mrs. D. T. Conde: Hana.
  Mr. and Mrs. Charles McDonald: Lahaina.
On Hawaii—Mr. and Mrs. Isaac Bliss: Kohala.
  Mr. and Mrs. Edward Bailey: Kohala.
  Dr. and Mrs. S. L. Andrews: Kailua.
  Mr. and Mrs. Abner Wilcox: Hilo.
  Mr. and Mrs. O. H. Van Duzee: Kaawaloa.
  Mr. and Mrs. H. O. Knapp: Waimea.

The Board also decided that Mr. and Mrs. Bishop should
remain at Ewa, Oahu, and Lowell and Abigail in Honolulu.

Since the reinforcement brought nine school teachers it
was reasonable that Lowell, an ordained minister, should
again take a mission station and the Board so decided, but
its location was a matter of considerable debate and prayer
and Brother Bingham appointed "nine of his most judicious
men to think on the subject." The council for a time was

King and Councilors Debate

divided whether it should be in the village or *mauka*. Governor Kekuanaoa "begged to express his *manao* that it should be in the village," and the decision was for it in the district Kaumakapili. Two weeks later Lowell's journal states:

I have this day made a bargain with Louis Morstein to do the carpenter work of our new dwelling house about to be built at the other end of this village. He engages to do the whole house for four hundred eighty-six dollars, i.e. the work specified by me in writing, a copy of which is not only in his possession but in my own also. I hope to move down there in the course of a few months. Today a proposition has been made to the people to aid in building a school house for me. Something, I think, will be done by them.

Work Old and New A few days later he had native carpenters at work on the window frames and sashes for the native schoolhouse. Before resigning as schoolmaster at Kawaiahao Lowell

. . . continued to superintend those schools till the quarterly examination in October, when two hundred fifty-five of my pupils were present and appeared well.

Mrs. Amos Cooke, in her paper read at the jubilee of this seventh reinforcement in 1887, wrote of Lowell's having

. . . charge of the schools when we arrived. Mr. Cooke and myself commenced attending his school the second week after our arrival, and were gratified to find that we could take a part. We could teach classes in reading, writing and arithmetic. It assisted us in learning native character and especially in getting the language. It was our private opinion that we made greater progress than our pupils did.

Lowell wrote in July of his

. . . school with the new brethren and sisters in the native language. . . . They appear to have made considerable of a commencement on the passage. . . . A spirited examination of schools today. My own school numbered two hundred twenty-two. Brother and Sister Cooke are getting along well. Much encouraged to proceed, still I hope ere long to get another school in operation down in the village.

Drawn by F.A. Olmsted

C. T. Sanford. 1841.

Lith of Endicott N.Y.

KAUMAKAPILI CHURCH WITH FIRST THATCHED ROOF

How glad we are for Lowell's encouragement and support. His own acquisition of the language had been hard as regards pronunciation although he had written (in only four days) and delivered his first sermon in Hawaiian within four months of his arrival.

Life is a complex matter in one generation or another, on our great continents or on lonely isles of the sea. At this juncture school teaching, house building, and the thousand demands of a practical missionary's life are bound up with matters of Catholicism versus Protestantism, dissipation of the island rulers, matters of intoxication, etc., even national and international concerns. English and French men-of-war take a hand in advising the king and reports have it that the royal guns on Punchbowl, the slight defense of the little kingdom, are secretly spiked, the port offered blockade, the lives of the missionaries threatened, etc. True or false, just or unjust, the reports, acts, and motives, the waters were troubled and the little band of missionaries had need of large faith. Humbly and trustfully

Complications

. . . the brethren and sisters met in Brother Bingham's room to pray for this nation and for the King. O that he might let intoxicating liquors alone during this visit and consultation with foreign representatives of war! August 12th, 1837. Overturn and overturn these days. Brother Lorrin Andrews has been providentially detained here until this time since general meeting and yesterday the chiefs gave him a unanimous call to leave the High School and become their teacher in politics and this and that branch of science, pertaining to the welfare of the nation. It appears that he has had some warning of their movements and he says he has had very little sleep for several nights. Last evening he called a meeting of the brethren of this station and laid the subject before us. The Chiefs will give him a salary of six hundred dollars and furnish him a good house, pasture for a cow and a spot to plant potatoes, etc. We were all of one mind on the subject, viz. that he can do more good in this sphere than at the High School, for though the pupils might be taught the various branches of politics, yet they can do nothing when they leave school because the government is directly opposed to an enlightened policy. Such is the present crisis of affairs that

Political School for Chiefs

there must and very soon will be a revolution in the government, and we think to teach the chiefs what to do is the wisest course we can take. They have selected Brother Andrews to instruct them and we think he is the man for that post.

Abigail's Invitation

But O what will become of the seminary is the great inquiry today? They have been sounding Abba to see if she will not consent to go to Wailuku or Waioli and supply the place of one who is qualified to go to the High School. But she gives them no encouragement. The Lord guide us in this matter.

August 23rd. The brethren of Oahu convened at Honolulu day before yesterday to talk over our affairs as affected by the last general letter of the Board. We have agreed to take salaries, five hundred fifty dollars annually for family and travelling expenses, as the Board has suggested and have advised where and when not to go on with buildings, etc., etc.

Planting a Friendship

September 9th. Having been obliged to look after my buildings, workmen, etc., the past week I have not been in school. Brother and Sister Cooke have taken the burden upon themselves. . . . They have advanced rapidly in acquiring the language.

This coöperation with Brother and Sister Cooke must have been particularly congenial, for Mrs. Cooke, when Juliette Montague, and our Abigail Tenney were friends and fellow schoolmistresses in the New England villages of Amherst and Sunderland. It was a happy reunion for the two young women and it would have been still happier could they have realized then that their friendship was to be passed on and on to great-great-granddaughters!

Funeral of Manini

November 1st, 1837. Have this day been called to officiate at the funeral of Manini a Spaniard who has been upon these Islands for thirty or more years. A large concourse of both natives and foreign residents attended. I offered a prayer in English at the house. The corpse was then carried to the native meeting house and there I preached in the native language.

Grass and Mangoes

Manini was the native pronunciation of Marin, and the Hawaiians gave it as *manienie,* to the Bermuda grass which was but one of many valuable plants brought to the Islands by this foreigner. It is said that the first mango trees were planted by him, now called the Hawaiian mango in distinction from many grafted varieties, and that they are still standing in Pauoa Valley; also that Vineyard Street takes its name from his planting of grapes.

November 8th. A very strange phenomenon in the sea last night. The tide arose and fell some twelve or fourteen times between seven o'clock and midnight and when the tide went out it was some five or six feet lower than at low water mark. Several of the ships in port rested on the ground and many of the fish in the stream and edge of the sea died. November 20th. Letters from Hilo inform us that the phenomenon above alluded to was far more dreadful there than it was here. The tide arose fifteen feet above high water mark, destroyed the houses on the beach and eleven persons were drowned, swept off all the canoes in the harbour, besides a vast deal of other damage.

A Tidal Wave

d. KAUMAKAPILI

Shortly before moving to Kaumakapili, a district of twelve or thirteen thousand inhabitants, Lowell wrote the home Board:

Now I must leave this interesting field to commence anew. . . . The new field is quite uninviting in some respects. In the immediate neighborhood are eight or ten grog shops frequented by abandoned sailors, disreputable foreigners and disreputable natives. Of all the heathen that I ever saw the white faced heathen are the most abandoned and hopeless. The Sandwich Island Gazette has been trying to prove this mission an entire failure.

December 19th, 1837. We have this day moved into our new house at the new station, Kaumakapili, and this p.m. we had a meeting in the school house, . . . Brother Bingham the preacher. I should judge that six hundred were in the house and about four hundred out in the yard. Brother Bingham's text was Acts 10; 33. . . . A good and faithful discourse . . . four main points dwelt upon—repentance, faith, love and benevolence or assistance to the teacher. Our prospects at present are quite flattering but what the Lord intends to do with us, or by

Flattering Prospects

us is at present hidden from us. But why should I distrust him who has been faithful so long? Nay, let me rather believe that the mountains can be removed into the sea, that children can be raised up from the stones of the street, and that he can make use of clay and spittle to open blind eyes, and lead men to Christ the fountain of all good. The people are many of them very kind and bring us a great many vegetables, fowls, etc.

Requests   In the Station Letter a month previous, Abigail, with improving health, after her years in solitary stations finding

. . . calls from her sisters and morning rides in a carriage . . . more beneficial than medicine,

anticipated her wants in housekeeping with a request of Boston for a good, substantial cast-iron furnace (by which she might mean a little stove; but no, for she used a fireplace with crane and irons, and oven in the wall), but, O extravagant woman! she asks for a two-quart saucepan! Lowell applies for a man's saddle, as one here would cost thirty-five or forty dollars. We hope the request was granted and the saddle was at least half-way comfortable, for many weary miles on protracted-meeting jaunts lay in the years to come.

A Tender   December 24th, Sabbath eve. The scenes of this day at this
Shepherd   new station have been quite interesting. In the morning at eight o'clock with the children. One hundred present, thirty of whom had attended my school at the other station and seventy new ones, and at nine a.m. the house was filled and as many as four hundred out of doors—in all one thousand—about the same number both a.m. and p.m. Very much the biggest p.m. meeting heretofore. My bowels yearn over them. I have endeavored to be faithful to them today.

Slander   My enemies have been circulating an abominable falsehood this last week about me. Why I cannot tell, unless it is to maim me at the very outset. The story is that I have committed adultery with a native woman, kept the child in our family for three or four years and now being likely to be detected I have murdered the child! Adultery and murder the charge of some of my whitefaced neighbors. If this is the bud, what must be the blossom and fruit of their slander? The Lord forgive them and lead them to repentance.

Great cause for thanksgiving to God for the improved state of Abba's health. She has laboured quite hard during the past week in moving and arranging our things. Yesterday both the domestic women being sick, she baked alone—a thing that she has not done before since her health failed. The climate is far better than at the other station. Good air, good water and abundance of the good things of the land. May the Lord grant his benediction and then we shall be blessed indeed. *Thanks-giving*

Here is inserted a selection from Lowell's address at the dedication of the second Kaumakapili Church on the original premises, now the corner of Beretania and Smith Streets. This second church was a two-story building of red brick that, from the ardent urging of King Kalakaua to the people that as they had two hands, eyes, ears, etc., they should raise enough money to give their church two steeples, had the same until an accidental fire in the neighborhood leaping to one of the spires, shed its firebrands, destroying the church and all of the then Chinatown. At the dedication mentioned, the local press recorded Lowell's reading of a historical sketch *The New Station*

. . . with a force and fervor that were astonishing considering his great age and the fact that only a few months ago he met with a severe accident. He said, in part,

"The native grass houses were very numerous at that time and we found it very difficult to secure a suitable lot for the mission family and another for the school house.

"In those days the land all belonged nominally to the king and high chiefs. Most of the land in this neighborhood belonged to Paki, one of the high chiefs. But like the centurion in the gospel who said to one man go and he goeth and to another man come and he cometh; so this high chief commanded two or three families to vacate and he would furnish them houses in some other locality. In this way, a little oblong square, about one-fourth of an acre was obtained for the mission premises and another for the school house yard. *A Precious Half-Acre*

"Our first work was to build a dwelling house and a large school house. I think it was some time in November when we were

ready to commence operations in this part of town, in the good
providence of God, this was just at the commencement of the
great celebrated revival which continued three years, and when
the chiefs and people all over the Islands were easily persuaded
to meet often for prayer and praise to God and to listen to the
reading and preaching of the Gospel.

*The
School-
house*

"We used to meet in the school house on the Sabbath and for
early morning prayer meetings. But we soon found that the
school house did not accomodate one half of the congregation;
and we built a large *lanai* in the front yard and covered it with
rushes to keep off the sun and strewed the ground with grass
and rushes for them to sit upon, a la Hawaii.

*The
Pulpit*

"My pulpit was the door sill, with half of my congregation in
the house and half outside. I was then in the prime of life and
found it very easy to preach.

*Organiza-
tion of
Church*

"On April 1st, 1838, Rev. H. Bingham assisted me in organiz-
ing a church; twenty-two persons were received by letter from
the Kawaiahao church, two from Ewa and one from Kauai and
forty-nine were received on profession of faith. This was the
commencement of Kaumakapili church fifty years ago.

*The Adobe
Meeting-
house*

"Soon after the organization of the church we resolved to
build a large adobe meeting house; the walls to be three feet
thick, one hundred twenty-five feet long and sixty feet wide
inside. Our first plan was to build it twenty feet high, with a
gallery on each side, but when the walls were put up fourteen or
fifteen feet high, the adobes began to crush about the doors and
windows and it was then obvious that it would not be safe to
put a heavy roof upon a two story adobe building.

"We then decided to raise the walls only twelve feet, dispense
with the galleries, ceil the audience room overhead with lath and
plaster; plaster the walls inside and out, build a verandah seven
feet around the house, and when thus finished the audience room
and its spacious verandah would accomodate twenty-five hundred persons who could hear the preacher. The cost of this
great structure was three thousand dollars the most of which
was raised by the church and congregation, leaving a debt of
only one hundred dollars.

"We were one year and four months in building that house of
worship and it was dedicated August 29th, 1839.

FIRST KAUMAKAPILI CHURCH
WITH LATER SHINGLED ROOF

SECOND KAUMAKAPILI CHURCH
OF BRICK WITH TWIN STEEPLES

"Sixteen glass windows and large panelled doors made it of very neat and pretty appearance, as an American visitor described it, and one cool and easy to speak in.

"For thirty years I was the officiating clergyman and pastor of the Kaumakapili church and congregation, and administered the ordinances of baptism and the Lord's supper to more than three thousand persons."

3. HARVESTING

Trying to enter adequately into a conception of what the years of the "Great Revival" meant to the workers in the field, we continue with Lowell's journal.

January 8th, 1838. . . . One week ago today i.e. the first day of January . . . commenced a protracted meeting in Mr. Bingham's house; [Church at Kawaiahao] . . . large congregation, probably 4000 the first day and on Tuesday it increased to 5000. Brothers Bishop and Emerson were there to assist us. It has been a good meeting and I think that a considerable number already give pleasing evidence of genuine repentance. One rum distiller and rum seller has abandoned his business, poured some twelve gallons of liquor upon the ground and another man has poured seven gallons upon the ground today. Several have burnt their cards and others have burnt their *pahu hulas* [drums]—others have abandoned their pipes and tobacco, and three drunkards have been to inform me that they have abandoned their abominable habits and practice. The Lord be praised for his goodness and loving kindness to this abandoned place.

I think that I shall hold two meetings per day this week and hope the blessed Spirit will shake this place to its center. Some ten or twelve hundred people present yesterday and my plain remarks seem to have been blessed. To God be all the glory. Jan. 17. A large number of scholars these days. One hundred forty four girls yesterday and one hundred one boys and one hundred fifty or two hundred who wish to learn to sing. But I must refuse the greater part perhaps. We are exceedingly straightened for want of a large place of worship. January

The Great Revival

22nd, 1838. . . . . Had a very sick night Saturday night and yesterday also. Was unable to preach at all. . . . Seized with a cholic pain. O how welcome rest after that short period of pain. What then must be heaven after a life of toil and pain. And O how dreadful is hell, an endless hell, where "the worm dieth not and the fire is not quenched."

Brother Lyons

Brother Lyons continues to write glorious news from Waimea. The Lord guide him and bless him abundantly. The subject has been agitated today whether I had not better go to Waimea and see wherein the state of things differs there from what it does here. But I have no wish to do so. The reason why we do not witness more of the blessed influences of the spirit here is our unbelief. Lord help our unbelief. I am expecting to go to Waialua this week to labor with Brother Emerson in a protracted meeting. O for a preparation of heart to go and take hold on divine strength and receive a rich blessing.

To Waialua and Back

February 6th, 1838. . . . . Protracted meeting. On Thursday the 25th of January Abba and I set off for Waialua on a double canoe went as far as Ewa and stayed the first night. Next day we left, I on horse back and Abba was carried on a rocking chair. A very pleasant jaunt. Found Mr. Emerson well etc. My sickness the Sabbath previous to our leaving had left me in a weak state and on arrival at Waialua I found it necessary to bleed and take physic. In two or three days felt better. Abba has been very smart while at Waialua. The Lord crown our labors with his blessing both among the adults and youth. Brothers Bishop and Parker were there to aid us. Yesterday (Monday) we returned to Ewa by land and today we came up on a double canoe on the outside. Arrived here about nine this a. m. Kinau *ma* [including attendants] have been at the meeting and Paki *ma* also and they have appeared well. Some fifteen or twenty of Kinau's boys profess to have given their hearts to the Lord during the meeting. Some fifteen or twenty other children and as many as one hundred adults. The Lord enable them all to make thorough work of repentance and consecrate them all, souls and bodies to his service.

On my return I found people very glad to see us. The schools are orderly and increased in numbers during my absence. I feel under new obligations to my Lord and Master for his loving kindness and tender mercies to me and mine during my absence.

I find that the government is making great alterations in the public streets. A very good thing.

February 8th, '38. . . . Am quite feeble today—pressure in my head. Have been bled and feel relieved. Some seventy or eighty men have commenced cultivating patches of ground for the Lord, to purchase a bell and build a meeting house. The Lord grant us his blessing.

February 17th. . . . Have devoted the past week to hearing the thoughts of the people. Between eight and nine hundred have told me their *manaos*. Some forty of whom I may propound for the church ere long. Some two hundred have come round for the first time the present week. Their thoughts are very dark and incorrect. Still I have convincing evidence that the Lord is moving upon this mass of human beings. O for faith to believe, for strength to labor for the eternal salvation of these immortal beings.

Glorious tidings from Hilo these days. The year of Jubilee for the Islands has come and ransomed sinners are returned home. Everlasting thanks to our glorious Lord and master. I am expecting to organize a church here ere long. A preparatory meeting for that purpose this evening.

Feb. 22. Ship Tractor from Boston arrived this a. m. bringing us a few letters. . . . Great are the embarrassments of the Board and they have reduced our whole expenses to $30.00 per year. . . . Mr. Richards is expected to return soon. He writes us that he was not received by the Board as our agent. The Lord have mercy on the American churches and the American Board and their missions. March 19th. . . . The good work goes on among us—though not with such astonishing power as on Hawaii. Hundreds are there hopefully converted in one protracted meeting. I have been examining interesting cases in this new field for two weeks and have marked down more than one hundred whom I shall probably propound before long.

Feb. 23. Commenced a protracted meeting with the youth of my school and those of Mr. and Mrs. Cooke's school last Monday and closed this p. m. About five hundred youths have attended meeting twice a day—solemn time and numbers have hopefully repented. Between one and two hundred have told me their thoughts who never were serious previous to the meeting. A great day this for Hawaii. Sow the seed and reap the harvest the same month, yea the same week. 26. Glorious news from Hawaii today. Br. Lyons letter dated February 19th informs us that he has admitted to the church since last General Meeting, Six hundred and that the number will probably swell to one thousand before the year closes!! The brethren at Hilo write us that they received to the church five hundred the first Sabbath in this month and that the power of God has been astonishing among them since that time.

Seed Time and Harvest

American news also today. Brother and Sister Richards have returned from the United States, passage of one hundred thirty odd days. They are as well as usual—in fine spirits. We have received a few letters and think there must be others on board. . . . One letter informs us that C. T. has left Rowe and gone to Barre and has now a congregation of from three to four hundred. Is it possible that with the aid of deacons and school masters he can look after so numerous a congregation? During the last three weeks more than fifteen hundred have told me their thoughts and profess to be serious, but where are any deacons and other helps? The Lord have mercy on the ministers in the United States.

A Gentle Sarcasm

March 29th. . . . The brethren on this Island have come today to hear Brother Richards' report and attend to other business that it may be deemed expedient to do. His report has been quite interesting—his reception by the Board and committee rather chilling. Missionaries not well received who have been in the field and indeed the Board have passed a law that missionaries must not leave the field without first obtaining leave from the Rooms! We missionaries do not feel very easy under this yoke and shall probably make an effort to break it off. We as an Island have voted to not hold a regular general meeting this year, but Island meetings and a delegates meeting.

The Yoke Galls

A few words concerning "ex post Facto" laws of Board concerning this mission already in the field. I am quite unhappy to have a law enacted by my patrons forbidding me to return to the land of my fathers. I know not that I shall ever think it my duty to return to America still it is undesirable that it should be a crime for us to run to and from that knowledge may be increased, our health be restored and we talk face to face with friends on things vital to the salvation of the heathen world. On the other hand it could be a blessed thing both for the churches at home and the heathen abroad if our fathers and friends of missions would come to visit us and see what we are doing and how "extravagant" we live. May we not find fault without a cause.

Here the journal records what we have already noted regarding the organization of the Kaumakapili Church. On this thrilling day in his life Lowell exclaims:

Organization of the Church

O, how much occasion for gratitude to God for his special blessing to this new parish, since we first came here. Here let me raise my Ebenezer, here let me take a high stand for God and renew my covenant to be his and only his forever.

April 8, 1838. Sabbath, A good time today. Riveted attention. Propounded one hundred and five persons for the church, three of whom are teachers in the school. Have daily evidence that the spirit of God is still in the midst of us.

April 16th. Have just returned from Kaneohe—protracted meeting. Abba was carried in a chair by natives, excepting a few rods on the steep part of the pari [pali]; there she walked both in descending and ascending. She got along very well. The meeting commenced last Monday evening and continued till this morning. Brother Bingham came over Thursday noon and stayed with us till Saturday noon and preached four times. Dr. Gulick preached once. Brother Parker and myself did the rest of the preaching four times a day, besides attending a meeting with the children daily at 8 a. m. and a church meeting daily at 1 p. m. The meeting has been exceedingly blessed—there has been far greater emotion than at any meeting that I ever attended before. Some five or six *konohiki* or head men, besides the principal chief of Kapali, Koolau have been hopefully converted during the meeting and also some thirty perhaps of the youths, and a large number of the congregation. Such has been the state of feeling that many of them have burst out in the midst of the sermon and given a brief account of their sins and penitence. I never saw it on this fashion before.

Over the Pali

Never on this Fashion

Hoike

19. *Hoike* of schools. Today we have held our first examination of schools. The children appeared admirably well, especially the girls. O what a change civilization and proper instruction does make.

*Garments
of Praise*

One hundred and seventy eight girls present, mostly clad in European style, i.e. they were well dressed and generally had bonnets and behaved admirably well. They have for the most part made good proficiency in their studies. One hundred fifty three boys present. They were more rude and have made less proficiency but on the whole I am very much gratified with the school. The whole number of scholars who have had their names enrolled during the term is four hundred and fifty. Some three hundred eighty adults presented themselves for a *hoike* today—though they have not had a school of late. I hope however to do something for them ere long.

Increasing labors made schools necessarily dependent on native teachers, a high-school graduate who had helped Lowell the previous year becoming principal and very popular. He had five assistants.

*Zion in
Travail*

April 29th. Protracted meeting . . . commenced last Tuesday. The meetings daily have been as follows. Praying and preaching at sunrise, children's meeting at eight o'clock preaching again at ten a.m. Church prayer meeting at one p.m. and preaching again at three thirty p.m. . . . Zion commenced her travailing pains Thursday noon and they continued to increase till Friday p.m. when she got a little relief but not much till Saturday morning. We then felt as if she had indeed brought forth—very many rose to interrupt the speaker and tell of their surrender to the Lord. The church have been in an agony of prayer for two or three days and I trust many have been converted during the meeting. . . .

I have set apart this week and next to talk with people—they are to come in small companies, with some church member. . . .

May 2, '38. Instead of one hundred fifty new ones coming to tell their thoughts this week four hundred twenty six have been here, who were *paakiki* [hard] until this meeting. I presume at least one hundred of them were struck under conviction Sabbath night and others on Monday and Tuesday of this week. God is in the midst of us of a truth, performing his own glorious work and to him be all the glory.

5. Have had a case of church discipline this p.m. Kalu is proved guilty of lying, and I have suspended him for the present.

Church Discipline

8. I am binding up sheaves again this week and expect to set them up next Sabbath for the church to look at. The Lord continue to send us the former and the latter rain till the elect are all gathered in. May 13th, 1838. Sabbath. Preached this a.m. from text "No servant can serve two masters" etc. . . . Large and attentive audience. The head man and his wife from Kahauiki were present for the first time since we commenced here. . . . They have been great despisers of the gospel and of Christians. Last Wednesday they called at my study and told me their thought.

Binding up the Sheaves

Last week I labored in the vineyard every day from sunrise till half past nine in the evening. At the morning meetings I endeavored to break up new fallow ground and mellow the soil and cast in the seed. At nine a.m. went daily with my sickle to reap down the waving harvest and bind up for the Lord's granery. Last evening I numbered up the sheaves and behold I had one hundred sixty two. At the close of the morning sermon today I stood them up before the church and congregation. The whole number now propounded to join this infant church the first Sabbath in June is three hundred forty eight. There are others to be gathered in during the present week—some seventy or eighty, perhaps.

Seventeen-Hour Day

May 20th. Sabbath evening. A great concourse of people today. I should judge there were two thousand, including the children and youths. . . . O what gratitude is due to the God of missions and the God of revivals for his great goodness to me and mine here at this new station. We have been here only five months and we are now counting about five hundred converts. . . .

Gratitude

June 3rd. Sabbath evening. This has been a pentecostal day with us; a glorious day indeed. The day itself has been very pleasant and the scenes of this day at this new and infant church are long to be remembered. I have this day admitted to the church four hundred thirty three persons and baptized four

Feeding the Multitude

hundred twenty nine of them; four of the youths had previously been baptized. Our school house being so small we could not be accommodated there, we took our position in the large verandah built in front of the school house. The people had brought in a large quantity of green grass and strewed all through the place and they were all requested to sit down upon the green grass, some fourteen in a row and mounting to thirty one rows. The candidates behaved with great propriety and generally were well dressed and O the change in this part of the village. Great indeed is the external change—the Lord grant that these dear lambs may live together in love and union and be a burning and shining light in this wicked place.

Ecstasy

The very mixture of metaphors creates for us the atmosphere which zealous Lowell breathed. For any brother as shining and burning a light as Lowell, it was a mercy that there was an exchange of brethren to help each other at protracted meetings; for inadvertently the vicissitudes of travel aided the physical as well as the spiritual life. Work and play were intermingled with good results as noted in the next entries of the journal.

Moonlight Canoeing

July 24th, 1838. Returned last evening from Kauai. Brother Tinker *ma*, Parker *ma* and myself *ma* chartered Kahekili's vessel—sailed from here on the fifth instant twenty eight hours passage to Koloa—had a pleasant time at Koloa—put up at Dr. Lafon's. Sailed from Koloa to Waimea in a canoe, and after a short but pleasant visit we embarked again on board a canoe to sail around the pari to Waioli. Delightful time. We were twelve hours going around the pari—moonlight etc. Found our friends well at Waioli—Brother Johnson however had gone to Honolulu. Very verdant and healthy place, much desired by many. I could like it much better if the mountains were two or three miles further off. I felt that my health improved much while there and so did Abba's. We spent some two or three days in a protracted meeting—came on to Waialua and spent the night at Debora's and Tuesday morning visited the falls, obtained some oranges and arrived at Koloa in the p.m. On Thursday evening we sailed for Honolulu and arrived here just four days from the time we left Koloa.

The Captain smuggled on board twenty nine passengers to our great amazement and on Saturday night we were very nearly capsized. This matter is to be looked into. We feel considerably exhausted with sea sickness, though we hope to recover entirely. *The Seamy Side of Travel*

July 27th. Have had a settlement with Hekili and he or the Captain is to pay me twenty nine dollars for the twenty nine persons smuggled on board, half in cash and half in *waiwai* [goods]. Thus ends this affair. *Wages of Sin*

August 4th, 1838. Have this day suspended from the church five persons for smoking tobacco and lying about it. The Lord preserve this church from returning again to their former vices and deeds of darkness.

5. Sabbath. Have this day propounded ninety one persons for the church. I get most convincing evidence that the Lord did a great work here last winter and spring, and that truth still takes hold of the hearts and consciences of many in this congregation. 12. Have this day propounded seventy seven persons for the church.

August 16th. . . . Have held a church meeting today and performed the painful ceremony of excommunicating Terehabela Kaawa from the church. O to see one of our praying brethren come into meeting with his chains on attended by officers, and looking as if he had lost all his friends—yea he had taken an harlot and forsaken his own beloved wife! The Lord sanctify this afflictive dispensation to this infant church. *A Brother in Chains*

September 2nd, 1838. Sabbath evening. An interesting day this—communion service—nearly all the members present. Some five or six suspended for bad conduct, three or four sick. Over two hundred stand propounded for admission hereafter. This church are children in knowledge and in practice and are frequently falling out by the way. They need great watchfulness on the part of the pastor and very much instruction. *But Children*

Lowell's Station Letter to the American Board of Commissioners for Foreign Missions records Abigail's health as good:

September 3, '38. She is nearly as smart as when we left the

United States! What shall we render unto the Lord for all his benefits unto us and our people the present year?

September 8th, 1838. Have this day heard of the death of two of the members of this church. Puhi died on Tuesday the fourth instant and Kanakaole, a lovely native girl, died on Wednesday the fifth. In her dying moments she wished her love *Death* to be given to us her teachers, to Mr. Bingham and to Mrs. *of the* Dimond. Then called for the covenant of this church, printed on *Righteous* a hand bill, and while reading it, fell asleep in the arms of her Saviour. "Blessed are the dead who die in the Lord."

September 22nd. Our people have been raising the dobe walls of our new meeting house [Kaumakapili] this week. . . . The foundation of the stone church [Kawaiahao] is also laid and some four or five courses laid around.

September 29th. "The Fly" an English man of war, Captain Eliot is in port. Captain Eliot is very friendly to us missionaries and so is Count Strelisky, a passenger of his, a Polish gentleman. Captain Eliot is an entirely different man from Captain B. and Lord R. He appears to take a deep interest in the well-being of this nation.

October 19th. Have this day returned from Waialua where I have been after the timbers for our meeting house. The big rafters are all on board the King's brig, except one that sunk to the bottom of the ocean.

Suspen- November 10th. Have this day excommunicated four persons *sions* from the church . . . two for intoxication and lying, one for adultery and one for lying and smoking tobacco. Suspended two also—one for drinking a glass of gin and trampling upon the Sabbath and another for smoking tobacco. Have restored today four persons formerly suspended. O, what a care to look after these ignorant church members. The Lord give wisdom and grace that every thing be done according to his mind and will.

Still November 17th. The weather for two or three weeks has been *Feudal* very unfavorable for our 'dobe meeting house. Some two or *Rule* three thousand dobes have been washed down which had been recently made and now I do not know when we can make and dry more. The people are obliged to work almost constantly for the chiefs. O for a revolution in this government!

December 6th, 1838. This day has been observed by us missionaries and people of Honolulu as a day of thanksgiving and praise to Almighty God. Something new this for this nation. The people turned out pretty well to meeting and they dined in small groups and in a few instances in large groups. We missionaries all dined at Dr. Judd's and supped at Brother Binghams'. *First Thanksgiving Day in Hawaii*

An interesting day—seemed like old times—thanksgiving in the United States. Very many are the mercies of God to this mission, and the year past no adult member has died and but one child that I know of, that is one of Dr. Baldwin's. Some of our number have been brought near the grave, but all are convalescent and most of them well again. As a mission we have been abundantly blessed in spiritual things. Several thousands have been hopefully converted. What shall we render unto the Lord for all his goodness unto us?

February 23rd, 1839. . . . Letters from the United States. . . . War between England and Russia. The Sandwich Island Gazette says that two French men of war are expected here ere long to call the King to an account for sending away the proscribed Catholics. *War between England and Russia*

March 18th, '39. A great deal of sickness among the natives for a few weeks past—the mumps and fevers. We give out at least forty portions of physic daily—chiefly emetic. Nearly all the cases recover when they call upon us in season. Very many prefer their old heathen doctors and they die off rapidly. *The New and the Old*

Lowell hears that Brother Lyons at Waimea, Hawaii, may have a wagon not in use and at once writes begging him to let him have it, or even its remains. (Lowell will have the transfer of property made on the mission accounts.) He must have the wagon if possible, for riding does his feeble wife more good than anything else. . . . Life was looking up for Lowell in his new station and he was doing his share to encourage Abigail on the road to health.

April 4, 1839. Kinau, the queen Regent died about twenty minutes past twelve o'clock today. I called in about twelve and sat a few minutes; the physician was called; the King and chiefs were all assembled. I stepped over to Brother Chamberlain's to *Death of Kinau* see Brother Clark and a messenger called saying that Kinau was very much worse. Brother Bingham and I went immediately but she had ceased to breathe.

Dark Providence

The providence of God seems rather dark in this case, and still it is; it must be for the best. I have been looking for a change, an overturn in this government. It is at hand most certainly. But whether it will be overturned for the better is more than I can say or guess at present.

Writing sometime later to the Board at home Lowell said:

The death of Kinau by palsy seemed to paralize the people. When a Chief dies lands pass into other hands consequently tenants may become penniless and the mourning of parents upon the death of a chief preys upon school attendance.

At the close of the General Meeting, 1839, Lowell records on June twentieth:

Ten Thousand New Church Members

Our brethren are returning again to their stations as they have opportunity. It appears from the reports of the different stations ten thousand seven hundred sixty three persons have been admitted to the churches during the past year and that fifteen thousand five hundred fifty one are now in regular standing. One hundred eighty one have died during the year. One hundred twenty one have been excommunicated, four thousand three hundred ninety nine children have been baptised the year past.

July 4th. Stupidity prevails at an alarming degree these days and weeks. The death of Kinau and the *hihia* [confusion] of the Chiefs causes the spiritual feelings to set back wonderfully. O that God would revive us again and save us from a spiritual calm and spiritual desolation.

France Takes a Hand

July 9th, 1839. War! War! A French man of war has come to anchor today and the Captain has informed the chiefs and the consuls that unless this nation will advance $20,000 and give them a site for a Catholic Chapel, and grant the Catholics and Frenchmen all the privilege that they do to Americans and Englishmen the town will be taken in forty eight hours. All the English and American residents except the missionaries are invited on Board the frigate while the scene takes place. . . . A truce till the King can come from Maui, *paha* [perhaps]. . . .

July 11th. This day we have observed as a day of fasting and prayer. Solemn day. I find it good to be tried, to have death at the door. But O, the horrors of war! There are some fears that the King may not come down from Maui. Should he not, hostilities may soon commence. And what will become of our poor wives none can tell. . . . The Lord take care of his servants whom he has so long blessed. . . .

A Solemn Day

July 13th. Our probation expired yesterday at 12 o'clock, but the King has not arrived and therefore the enemy conclude to delay the hostilities a day or two.

At 3:30 p.m. this day the war declared on the ninth terminated.

Hostilities have not taken place. Twenty-one guns were fired from the fort and as many from the frigate. The twenty thousand dollars were delivered and the papers signed by Kekuanaoa and Auhea, the King not having arrived. Thus "peace" is declared between France and the Sandwich Islands. Yes, a French revolution has taken place at the Sandwich Islands. They established the Catholic religion at the cannon's mouth. O what an act of injustice!

"French Revolution"

July 18th. O, distressing. . . . Another thing extorted at the cannon's mouth. The tabu duty upon the importation of wine and brandy is removed except for five per cent.

August 17th. Hard times—No money to be had scarcely at any price. Carpenter J. told me today that he had lent one hundred dollars for four months and was to have thirty dollars, i.e. ninety per cent, interest. What think you of these days, ye that have long been praying for such times? The prayers of some of the wicked are answered, judgments return upon their own pates.

Hard Times

On Thursday Abba and Mrs. Dimond set out for Ewa and Waialua, borne on men's shoulders. Our meeting house is nearly finished and we hope to dedicate it on the 29th. Bell house is up and the bell hung.

Last evening Madam Boki, Liliha, died very suddenly. . . . She had no warning—died while asleep. . . . The wailing last night and this day has been tremendous. . . .

Death of Liliha

October 14th, 1839. Brother Bingham commenced a protracted meeting but under very unfavorable auspices, there being many whale ships in port and also the American East India Squadron, viz. the frigate "Columbia" Commodore Read, and the sloop "John Adams" Captain Wyman. These with their officers and crews demand much of our time. Some of the officers are professedly pious.

November 4th. I was seized last Thursday with an attack of the colic which held me about eight hours. Left me very weak and feeble. I feel that I need relaxation after my incessant labours.

*Friends
at Court*

The squadron sailed this morning having accomplished much apparently in behalf of this mission. Their publications forthcoming will testify for themselves.

For those who have not known, or have forgotten, days before automobiles and the round-the-island highway, we give Lowell's description of his circuit made for that relaxation coveted in the last paragraph.

*A Holiday
for Health!*

November 12th, 1839. Last week on Tuesday I left home and set off, horseback, for a tour of Oahu, hoping to benefit my health thereby. Stayed the first night at Ewa and the two following nights at Waialua. There I found Miss Ogden and Martha Ann Chamberlain wishing to go on with me. Left Waialua eight a.m. on Friday—passed through Waimea and Waialee —here we rested a little. Then passed on to Kahuku, alighted and took our luncheon under some hau trees—then passed on through Laie and came to Hauula, where we despatched a messenger to go five miles to Kahana and request the head man to get us a breakfast. Arose at early dawn and proceeded on, through Punaluu and came to Kahana, found our breakfast ready. Here we stopped an hour, refreshed ourselves and horses, then proceeded on through Kaaawa. This is the boundary line between Brothers Emerson and Parker. Kualoa is the first district in Brother Parker's parish, here we obtained a canoe of natives and sailed to Kaneohe, Brother Parker's station. Brother and Sister Parker absent at Honolulu on account of ill health. His domestics however were there and provided for our wants. Sabbath day preached to his congregation my health being much improved by the jaunt. Monday morning we set off again to complete our tour and after leaving Kaneohe district, we ascended a pari and descended again to the other side and came into Kailua—called on Kahuna, a head man, who furnished us with cocoanut water and meat and then we proceeded on to Waimanalo, a most barren place and very few inhabitants on the sea shore where we travelled. Stopped at the house of a church member by the name of Lono. Refreshed and talked a while with the people, passed on and ascended the other pari which has been recently worked by culprits and is now very passable. From there on to Maunalua. It is lava, rocks, barrenness and desolation in the superlative degree. At Maunalua by the seaside we spent the night. Martha Ann Chamberlain, a *Riding* stout six year old, who rode before me all the way, became very *Double* much fatigued and she lay upon me like an inactive mass for several miles, which was quite a tax upon my feeble health. This morning the people assembled and I addressed them for fifteen or twenty minutes and after imploring the blessing of heaven upon them we moved slowly onward and arrived home at noon.

November 27th. My birthday. Thirty-seven years old. Thanks *"Going* to my Lord and Master for preserving goodness another year. *West"* O how rapidly I am beginning to descend the western hill. How many years have quickly gone, but they have been the best years of my life. Have gathered nearly a thousand people into the church and over one hundred fifty more stand propounded. My health is also quite good again now. What shall I render to the Lord for all his mercies to me and mine and this ill deserving people.

December 17th, 1839. The Catholic priests . . . pronounce *"Wives and* the Protestant missionaries false teachers because they have *Panta-* wives and wear pantaloons instead of gowns: they say that all *loons"* of us missionaries are living in adultery—that as priests we have no right to be married. Moreover that as soon as their bishop and priests shall arrive, we Protestant missionaries shall all be ashamed and leave the field. . . . The Lord grant that I may not be driven from this field. If however He may see it best for me to lay down my life here by the edge of the sword . . . may I be ready for the event and may the event be overruled for the furtherance of Christ's cause in these Islands.

In 1840 the mission on the little dots in the great expanse of sea is looking away to the needs of the continent and

. . . six enterprising native men have volunteered to go as missionaries to the Rocky Mountains in answer to a call for one pair of native helpers. A contribution will be taken to provide the outfit of the pair selected.

A Pleasure Trip

July 8th, 1840. Brief notice of voyage to Hawaii, visit and tour upon that Island, etc.

Abba and I embarked on board the brig "Clementine" Captain Walker, for Hawaii this morning at eleven o'clock, with a favourable breeze. Light winds and calms alternately all the passage to Kawaihae, at which place we dropped anchor Saturday noon the 11th. We were quite seasick for forty-eight hours, after which we began to relish a little food. At two p.m. on Saturday went on shore and called at Captain Beckley's and immediately made preparations for going to Waimea the p.m. Some twelve miles from the shore. Kawaihae is a hot, rocky barren and very disagreeable place. No vegetation and nothing to induce one to live there that I can see, except that it is a good harbor and it is a good bay for fishing. There are two large Heiaus, heathen temples or altars there and a sulphur spring, which is a good bathing place. I employed five men to carry Abba and our baggage to Waimea and Mrs. Young favored me with her horse. We set off about three p.m. and arrived at the missionary station half past seven evening. Found Brother and Sister Lyons well—their little daughter Fidelia sick. . . . Curtis not very rugged. Some three or four miles before arriving at the station the climate became quite cold and we felt the need of cloaks and mittens and a good fire was very acceptable. It rains almost constantly here of late, though we were much favored this eve there being no rain. Brother and Sister L. have a comfortable, framed house finished off, with chambers.

Civilization Necessary Proof of Christianity

July 12th, 1840. Sabbath. Preached for Brother Lyons today and took Mrs. Lyons' school both a.m. and p.m. Children rather interesting—comfortable school house, but a miserable meeting house and the people poorly clad. They have a stone church under way, the walls are up one hundred twenty by fifty feet. Very little at this station which looks like civilization. Civilization and Christianity must go hand in hand in order that any permanent good may be accomplished.

Monday, 13th. The weather is rainy and cold and the roads on to Hilo are so bad that we think it inexpedient for Abba to proceed on the journey.

In a letter of this date Abigail wrote Mrs. Bingham:

I left Honolulu with the most confident expectation of visiting the whole country round about, going to Hilo to the volcano, and the new one and finding out many things that had not been known before. *Now think of my mortification in not being allowed to do any of these things!* The travelling has been represented to us as so exceedingly bad and fatiguing, the rains so constant, added to the total lack of accomodations by the way, that my careful husband was quite appalled and could not bring himself to consent to my pursuing the journey any farther. It was a very great disappointment to me, to us both. . . .

Abigail's Disappointment

Lowell resumes:

. . . I have sent on a messenger to Hilo to request the brethren to send me a canoe to Laupahoehoe. Mauna Kea is in full view at this station and some snow visible on the top. Can see also Mauna Loa and Hualalai.

The Roughest of Coasts!

July 15th. Set off this morning from Waimea for Hilo on horseback with two natives to carry my clothes, and food, etc. . . . Good roads for three miles and then four miles of exceedingly bad road, wet and soft and the horse and footmen slipped in knee deep and sometimes the horse went in nearly to his belly. As we advanced the road grew better and when we turned off to the East to Hamakua the road was hard; some small paries— occasionally a stream of water. The general face of the country is a gradual ascent and sometimes a rapid ascent from the sea to the mountain, a distance of several miles. Considerable of the country appears to be good soil, but very few inhabitants on the road which I travelled. Arrived about half past four at the residence of a graduate from the High School by the name of Solomon. He entertained us kindly and gave us lodgings. He is trying the experiment of a boarding school. Found a company of boys here on their way to the boarding school at Hilo.

Horseback

On Foot

July 16th. Solomon called the neighbors together at sunrise and I preached to them a short discourse—breakfasted and set off in company with the boys on foot, it being difficult to proceed further with my horse. Pari after pari and some of them very steep and difficult of ascent or descent. At half past eleven we came to a cold spring of water at the foot of a high precipice and we stopped and dined. How wise of Abba not to have come this road. No possibility of being carried up or down these paries except by one stout native who could take her in his arms as he would a child. . . . Passed on over paris and stones and arrived at Laupahoehoe at half past two p.m. The pari which descended into this place is the worst of all yet in our course.

Lava,
Rain, and
a Sermon

And O what a place! As full of lava and sharp stones as you can well imagine. I shall probably never forget the impression made on my mind at Laupahoehoe! Soon after our arrival there it commenced raining and rained till nearly night. The people assembled however and I preached them a sermon. Two men had arrived from Hilo with a canoe to take me the remaining thirty miles by water. Brothers Coan and Lyman wrote me by the men stating that their arms, hearts and doors were open to receive me and regretting that Abba was not with me. At dark the prospect of going in the morning was quite forbidding, it being rainy and wind ahead.

July 17th. At one o'clock the canoe men aroused us and said that if I was not afraid of the rain we had better set off for Hilo. The wind was ahead, though light and it was quite dark and they must row all the way. Being then ignorant of the dangers of this place and not knowing the distance, I ventured

A Night
of It

to set off with them at two, having taken some refreshment and committed ourselves to the Lord. The sea was not rough—light head wind and rain abundant—good canoe and three men to row and a spare paddle which I used some myself. Passed along under an iron bound coast and every few rods a stream of water was pouring down into the ocean. Men rowed well for two or three hours. Daylight appeared at four o'clock and then we began to distinguish objects on shore. Kahakai was very loquacious and I was obliged to check him frequently. Having arrived within about eight miles of Hilo, the currents changed and it was a very unpleasant sea for an hour; the sea was all chopped

up and in perfect agitation. This was succeeded by large and
heavy swells and soon after we came into the bay and the raging
of the waters abated. We came in sight of Hilo about nine
o'clock and arrived there at ten o'clock having been eight hours
on the water. Found the families all well and very happy to see
me. But O, how disappointed in this place! From accounts I had
expected that the country ascended rapidly from the sea to the
mission houses and onward to the mountains. But my impression
was very incorrect. The ascent is very little from the shore to
the mission houses, which are from forty to sixty rods distance,
perhaps. All the country off through Puna appears low, like
the wooded lands in America. In Hilo the land is more elevated
and mountainous and fertile than in Puna. How great the contrast between the mission premises here and at Honolulu. Here
vegetation is so luxuriant that you can hardly get about, while
at Honolulu there is almost none at all. Here trees and shrub-   *Dense*
bery almost cover up the houses, walks and fences, and it is with   *Vegetation*
much difficulty that they can keep down the grass and weeds. At   *—Barren*
Honolulu it is with great difficulty we can make anything grow.   *Honolulu!*

All three of the families have good houses with chambers
finished off. Everything is comfortable and inviting. Fine bathing houses. Stopped with Brother and Sister Coan.

July 18th. Good night's rest, breakfasted with Brother and
Sister Wilcox, explored their garden, ate an abundance of good
fat figs and pineapples. Visited Mr. Pitman. He is trading pretty
largely with the natives in *pia* [Hawaiian starch]. Visited also
the Chinaman's—their sugar works, saw their molasses stored
in old canoes, and it is said to have a fine taste in consequence of   *Sugar*
the number of rats in it. Dined at Brother Lyman's—visited his   *Works*
school house—chambers where the boys sleep and their dining
hall. All their walks are paved with pebbles—ti leaf fences. . . .
Rain in abundance. Attended a church meeting and preached
this p.m., about three hundred present—pretty good attendance. No schools in operation just now except the Sabbath
school, the brethren and sisters having just returned from
general meeting.

19th, Sabbath eve. Attended the Sabbath school and Bible
class at nine o'clock. They appeared pretty well. Preached at
ten o'clock from John 3; 19. Being pretty rainy not very full

house—pretty good attention. At two p.m., preached again, from Isaiah 48; 22. Rains powerfully this eve. Could Abba be here during this visit should enjoy it much more.

20th. Monday. At one p.m. set off on foot in company with Brother Wilcox and seven natives for the new volcano. Travelled till half past six over fine lava, coarse lava, and solid rock lava —seldom saw a house. Passed through a piece of woods four miles wide resembling the low woodlands of New England, excepting it is almost impossible to penetrate these woods except where a road has been made. Slept at Keao.

Lava
Lava
Lava
July 21st, 1840. Arose after dawn and after imploring divine blessing we proceeded on our way. Stopped at half past seven and breakfasted at Makuu. Pleasant weather, but O the lava, lava, lava! How can the inhabitants live in Puna? At half past nine a.m. came in sight of the three new sand hills formed by the hot lava coming in contact with the ocean. They are supposed to be nearly three hundred feet high. They stand in a right line near the waters edge like so many cones. Our men being bare-

Ti
Sandals
foot they all fell to making themselves sandals out of the *ti* leaf. But O, the country through which we have just passed, and oh, what plantations of decomposing lava. Holes are dug into it and potatoes and taro and bananas etc., planted, where I should

A
Mystery
no more think they would grow than in the very granite itself. And still they say they get pretty good crops. Having rested and shod the company, we passed on and came up with the black lava which but a few days ago was a liquid flowing mass. Now behold, it lies broken up and tumbled to pieces and in every ugly shape imaginable. I should think it some ten or twelve feet deep

Lava Sand
on an average. We were first struck with the peculiarity of the sand, it being obviously of the same nature with the lava. We attempted to go on to the lava and pass over it to the sand hills, but found it exceedingly difficult, the lava having broken up and tumbled in so many directions, and moreover it was in many places quite hot. We however succeeded in reaching the sand hills, ascended them and here took a broad survey of the great surface over which this lava had spread. We judged the lava to be from one half to three fourths of a mile wide down at the sea and some acres of land have been made by the lava rushing into the sea. The trees on each side of this great lava tract are ap-

parently dead for at least half a mile and the sand thrown back
into the woods is several feet deep near the sea and grows less
and less for six or eight miles from the sea. Plantations of taro
and potatoes are buried up with this sand. Passing off from this
burning lava upon the neighboring sand, we ate a melon which
seemed very delicious—then passed on up several miles, stopped
and dined. And here some four miles from the sea the sand is
two inches thick. The appearance of this great territory is not
unlike that of a great burnt piece of new land in New England,
. . . here and there a tree unschorched. So here . . . the hot
lava flowed down against the trees and set them on fire, but the *Lava Trees*
top of the lava cooled before the tree was burnt off and it then
fell upon the top of the cooled lava and there it lies.

Towards night we loaded two men with specimens of new lava,
ready to return to Hilo in the morning. Spent the night at
Makahanaloa.

Anxious if possible to see the source of the new volcano,
Brother W. and I took each of us a man, a little food and water,
resolving to spend the day, if there was a probability of accomplishing our object. We passed up through a woods some four
or five miles—bad road—and raining quite hard and behold we
came forth upon a new world of it, several miles in extent each
way. We then despaired at once of finding its source that day,
for it was impossible to travel over the new lava. At a distance
we saw several large smokes—two miles—three miles and some *A River*
four or five miles distant. We travelled some distance upon the *of Fire*
lava till we came to the bed of a great stream or that which resembled a river of ice broken up and tumbled into every possible
position. This was meandering—several rods wide and its banks
from ten to twenty feet high. Having gazed upon this wonderful
phenomenon of God's works for half or three quarters of an
hour and eating a pineapple and taking a good refreshing
draught of water, we returned to Makahanaloa. Arrived there
again about ten o'clock a.m. and after resting a few minutes,
we set off for the old volcano. At noon stopped at Makuaunui
and dined at the friends of Nuimaka. Then we passed on in a
heavy rain over acres of lava with a little shrubbery—here and
there a small tree and a large quantity of *oheloes*. Passed
through one long and bad piece of woods—raining in torrents,

muddy and in every sense bad. Persevered till sundown and arrived at the upper village of Olaa. Here we found a good native house with a good fire, dried all our clothes, refreshed ourselves with our food and retired to rest. Found I had chafed off the skin in several places on my feet and my shins were quite sore.

July 23rd, Thursday. Arose at an early hour and proceeded on to the old volcano. Misty and rainy all the a.m. Arrived at the volcano at half past twelve noon. Found a small hut with one side, roof and the two ends thrown up by former visitors to keep off the wind and rain. Dined and rested till two o'clock p.m. and then Brother Wilcox and I and four natives descended the crater to the black ledge. On approaching the brink, "Oh," said Brother W. "what a change!!! Some two or three months ago when I was here the whole crater was level with the present black ledge and now behold half of it is sunk down some three hundred feet. Then there was a great deal of action, now the fires and smokes are nearly all extinct. Then there were fifteen or twenty lakes of liquid lava boiling and spouting, now only one small lake in action. Then there was a most splendid sulphur bank— now it has entirely disappeared." There are still sulphur banks, but the sulphur is so mixed up with dirt that it is very poor. This crater is said to be from eight to ten miles in circumference. Found very little difficulty in descending to the black ledge and the fires being nearly extinct we apprehended little or nothing while walking over it. Found some very delicate specimens of lava but could not handle them without their falling to pieces. The weather was fine all the p.m. and we travelled several miles to and fro over this wonderful phenomenon of nature. At dark ascended again and slept in the hut before mentioned a few rods from the edge of the crater. Cold, piercing wind but clear all night. Had we not been well supplied with clothes we must have suffered. The following was my night clothes, undervest, shirt, stockings, drawers, two pairs pantaloons, vest, woolen jacket, box coat, bed quilt. Lay with my head all covered with my bed quilt. Rested pretty well.

The Deep Pit

July 24th, 1840. At dawn had a clear and splendid view of Mauna Loa and Mauna Kea. Started immediately for Hilo, hoping to reach there by night, though it is probably forty miles. Men came on bravely till ten o'clock and after that they began

Splendid View

to grow weary. My right leg complained most bitterly and I began to fear that I should not be able to travel all day. But we arrived at Olaa, half the distince to Hilo, at twelve o'clock. Rested, dined and told the men they might fall behind and take their own time, but Brother W. and I should try to go to Hilo before we slept. We passed on and having travelled three or four miles two of the men came up with us and soon a third and shortly after the fourth and so on, so that we all reached Hilo at dark. The latter part of our journey it rained very hard and oh the sharp lava as we came into the village of Hilo—it did seem that I must cripple down and stop. On arriving and taking off my shoes and stockings, found the skin worn off in five places on one foot and six places on the other, and with all my ankles and shins did ache most prodigiously. But after bathing felt better and after supper a native *lomied* [massaged] my feet and ankle bones and they received some strength and ease. On retiring to rest bathed my feet and ankles with laudanum and soon fell to sleep. *Aches and Pains*

25th. Saturday. Comfortable this morning though rather lame. Evening. Have been packing up my specimens of lava in a barrel. All three of the families supped this evening at the table of Brother and Sister Wilcox. No tea or coffee—each guest furnished with a tumbler of cold water. This is as it should be. Lodged at Brother Lyman's. *Plain Living High Thinking*

26th. Sabbath. I attended the Bible class at nine and preached to the congregation at ten o'clock. Brother Coan, at two o'clock, preached an hour and ten minutes, not from the desk, but walking about among the people. Trials are coming upon him in the church—smoking tobacco seems to be the most prominent thing just now. *Peripatetic Preaching*

27th. Monday. This p.m. have been with Brother and Sister Lyman to visit the waterfall one and a half miles off. Pleasant time. The fall of water is about one hundred feet and to one who has never seen Niagara Falls it should be a great sight.

This suggests that Lowell must have made an excursion thither himself when a student at Auburn, New York.

This eve. a cold water party at Brother Coan's. Great harmony and brotherly love apparently prevail among all the fami- *Brotherly Love* lies at this station. Have bid all farewell expecting to leave for Laupahoehoe during the night.

Another Night Ride

July 28th, 1840. Left Hilo at half past twelve, midnight—a mountain breeze for one and one half hours then a squall from the sea—took in sail and rowed till sunrise. About three o'clock a tremendous great breaker came in from the sea and threatened to engulph us, but providentially it spent itself before it reached our canoe. At sunrise raised the sail and came on well till half past seven when the sea breeze struck us and we were in straightened circumstances for a few minutes, but by dropping the sail we obtained relief. We had then three miles to row in a very agitated sea—came along pretty dry till just as we entered the harbour a roller came up behind us and dashed against the side . . . and filled the canoe about half full. But we were in two feet of water and thankful to bid adieu to this dangerous sea with only one spout from Neptune. I breakfasted, wrote a note to the brethren at Hilo and then set off on foot. Having travelled from ten to twelve miles on foot, the horse that had been sent from Waimea for me came up, the native having descended the wrong road. Being quite lame was glad to get a horse though I have become so much of a pedestrian that I did not care much about a horse in ascending the mountain. It is several miles from the sea to the woods and then eight or ten miles of woods to Ned's the beef catcher. These woods are heavily timbered, principally with *lehua* and *koa*. Ned not at home—off catching beef. We

Straw-berries

stopped, put out the horse and I went to picking strawberries which abounded there. Gathered about three quarts in half an hour.

"In Ambush"

29th. Wednesday. A wretched night this. The fleas have waged war with my poor weary body all night. Lying in ambush I could but endure till daylight when I got a fair view of them and I then gave them each a broadside and came off victor. We

Fled the Scene of Action

hastened from the scene of action, lest a new reinforcement be despatched to our annoyance. Came on some five or six miles and then breakfasted—while at breakfast my horse took fright, broke his halter and made for Waimea. We followed him some four miles but he was so cunning that we could not catch him, so I had the great annoyance of having a horse with a saddle on a few rods ahead all day and I limping along behind with lame feet and ankle bones, and then had the privilege of paying for the horse into the bargain. Dry, barren country—few or no inhabitants, road lying along at the foot of Mauna Kea. Good cart road most of the way. Some five or six miles before we reached Waimea we came into the perpetual clouds of mist and rain which hang over that place and it rained hard and we became soaked through. Reached Waimea at five p.m. Found Abba and Brother Lyons well, etc. It rains and blows here like a perpetual storm. *Tantalus!*

30th. Thursday. Resting today. Have heard that the "Clementine" sails next Monday for Honolulu and that there will be no other opportunity probably for a long time. *Resting*

July 31st, 1840. Friday. Left Waimea for Kohala—Abba being borne on men's shoulders. The day has been fine—men kind—road half the way very stony and bad. We find Brother and Sister Bliss well and we are exceedingly disappointed . . . in this station. Supposed it was in a wilderness but there is no woods in four miles of the station. It is a plain, open country gradually ascending to the mountains. Delightful spot about two miles from the sea and ten miles from a harbour for vessels. Brother Bliss has a neat adobe house. He appears to be rather *akamai* [apt] in fitting up things—a kind of Jack of all trades, though I think rather *hemahema* [lame] as a missionary teacher. He is about building a framed house. His meeting house is a miserable thing, just ready to fall. *Kohala*

August 1st. Saturday. Preached to the church and attended a funeral of a church member today.

August 2nd. Sabbath. Preached twice for Brother Bliss today. Full house in the morning—lot of rattle head children. Fine field for usefulness. Exceedingly pleased with our visit.

3rd. Monday. Beautiful morning. Set off at nine a.m. for Kawaihae and arrived there just before sundown. Hard day's travail—rough roads, etc. But alas no vessel here. The "Clementine" has not yet returned from Kona. Take up lodgings in Brother Lyons' house. *To Kawaihae*

4th. Tuesday. Widow Young takes pity on us and invites us into one of her houses and gives us the use of her cook house, pantry, cupboard and its contents while we stay here. Very hot today. At ten o'clock the fishermen returned and she sent us two *Aku* large fish, *aku*. The people assembled at the sound of the horn and I preached a sermon.

5th. Wednesday. No vessel today—another present of two fish, taro and potatoes. Preached again this eve.

Heiau

6th. Thursday. Visited the *Heiau* [temple] this morning—it is a huge pile of stones covering more area than our meeting house. At eleven o'clock sail ho! "Clementine" has hove in sight. She anchored at one p.m. Called immediately on Esquire French and engaged our passage to Honolulu. Vessel will sail Saturday eve. Had we known beforehand of this long detention we might have stayed longer at Kohala or gone even to Kona and back

Shells

again. But we have now an opportunity of collecting a few shells found in this bay. Have collected eighteen of one kind and fifty of another and two or three of a third.

August 8th. Saturday. They are putting their beef on board today, and we expect to go on board at sundown.

10th. Monday. The "Clementine" took her anchor at eleven o'clock Saturday night and moved a little out of the harbor that night. Yesterday morning she took the trades and came on bravely and we came to anchor after thirty-six and one half

Home Again

hours. . . . But we have arrived home, to our own dear home, and right glad we are. . . . People express great joy at our return. Very few cases of *hihia* have occurred during our absence. Some few have been drinking to excess and two or three have been smoking tobacco. The Lord give wisdom for time to come.

4. HEAT AND BURDEN OF THE DAY

Movements of Missionaries

On our arrival we learn that Brother Bingham *ma* sailed on board the Flora on the third instant. Mrs. Thurston and family, Caroline Armstrong etc. have gone as passengers. Brother Armstrong and family have come to take Brother Bingham's place and look after his church and congregation. Brother Parker has taken a voyage to California for his health. Intemperance rages in the streets at a fearful rate.

Persecution for Righteousness' Sake

Once again Lowell is to suffer persecution at the hands of his fellow townsfolk—groundless slanders not from the mouths of the vile, but from his fellow countrymen in their misinterpretation of one of his sermons given in English at the Seaman's Chapel.

September 5th, 1840. Mark this period. A very unhappy state of feeling in this village and especially among my brethren at Honolulu *nei* in consequence of one particular expression in my sermon last Sabbath evening. . . . My text was Matthew 7, 12. "All things whatsoever ye would that men should do to you, do ye even so to them, for this is the law and the Prophets." In illustrating the text I was unfortunate in one case by saying. If A, is vile enough to lend his wife to B. it does not follow that B. shall do the same to A. for this is contrary to the law and the prophets, which say "Thou shalt not commit adultery." For this some of the unpenitent residents have taken umbrage and propose to publish a note in the Polynesian disapproving of my taste etc. And the consequence is that one or two members of the church have prepared a notice as an exchange, which states that the Episcopal service will be read twice a day hereafter till other arrangements can be made. Which is the same thing as saying that the doors of the pulpit of the Seaman's chapel are closed against me! This is more than I expected from those who will do as they would that others should do to them. I can bear to have the wicked speak and publish evil of me for doing my best in the service of the Lord, but to have my brethren shut up the doors of the sanctuary and thus join with the wicked world, this is too much! The Lord pardon them for this thing. Not that I wish to preach in that chapel. No, it has ever been among my greatest trials to be called upon to preach to such a fastidious audience, especially when my labors among the people have been so great. I trust however, that God will over rule this affair to his own glory.

"Forgive Them"

September 5th, 1840. The Polynesian has come out today but the Notice that I mentioned yesterday as expected out today has not made its appearance. Some of the parties concerned began to think that they had assumed a responsibility too great to bear and they took the notice out.

September 6th. . . . Sabbath. . . . Communion with us today—a great concourse of people . . . house crowded to overflowing. . . . Today I have propounded one hundred and four who have stood firm thus far in this tempest of evil. . . .

September 13th. . . . Sabbath. Today I have exchanged with Brother Armstrong . . . a thing I never did with Brother Bingham though I expressed a desire so to do. Brother Arm-

Given the Pulpit of Kawaihao

Leis in Church

strong is doing good in that church and congregation. Not one fourth the leis to be seen there today that there usually has been. . . .

For many years leis continued to be associated in the minds of foreigners with ancient heathen worship. Today missionary great-granddaughters appear in church bare-headed, bare armed, and adorned with leis as a part of their charming costumes.

Dealing with Criminals

The next paragraph shows methods of dealing with criminals which seems a far cry from our methods, practice, and social philosophy. We note also that three years later Lowell records without comment, the punishment of a sailor who had stabbed a native as "fifty dollars and one hundred lashes."

October 20th, 1840. A memorable day this and a dreadful day also to two wicked natives, Kamanawa and Lono. . . . They were hung this morning at 11 o'clock for the crime of murdering Kamanawa's wife. They gave her awa and other drugs and thus took away her life in two or three hours. But what is most distressing in their case is they exhibited no satisfactory evidence of penitence before God for their sin. On the day of trial, Lono confessed that he had killed Keawehawaii, the former captain of the Keikaika and his former wife and that he had assisted and instructed Kamanawa in murdering his wife, Kamokuiki. But today he declares that he was guilty of murder

On the Scaffold

but that he did not intend to murder etc. Poor wretched beings, I fear they have both died with a lie in their right hand and that they have gone to receive at the hands of the Lord according to the deeds done here in their bodies. Brother Armstrong and I both went up on the stage, and Brother Armstrong offered a prayer. An immense concourse of people collected in the streets, I should presume from twelve to fifteen thousand. The stage was erected on the top of the fort on the mauka side facing the street that passes up to Pearce and Bevans establishment. The people were comparatively still, only one burst of noise and that at some distance and of short continuance. A terrible scene! May another never occur at these Islands.

The next day brings an abrupt change of subject.

21. A brig from Columbia River. Doctor and Mrs. Blank, passengers to America. Sad tales about their character and conduct. They or rather he, has been expelled from their church. The real bone of contention is not very obvious—though it appears that he is dissatisfied with the "Superintendary." It is also reported that he has taken improper liberties in kissing *Kissing* some one or more of the sisters. Let me and mine take warning and never fall into this snare of the Devil.

October of this year records once again a grand *hoike* of schools, this time the pupils numbering nearly seven hundred and representing all the schools from Moanalua to Maunalua *Hoike* (the Two-Seas to the Two Mountains, over the *pali*). The "superficial" examination, followed by speeches from visiting and interested naval officers, was succeeded by a procession led by a band of music and Brother Cooke and the young chiefs through the village to the Kaumakapili Church where "pigs and turkeys and pies and melons were served to the great company which included a goodly number of ladies and gentlemen."

Lowell's hope for a "good and lasting effect . . . upon parents and children" calls to mind his many descriptions of similar events. He is always displeased with any unthoroughness of test, and any misplacement of emphasis, but always patient and hoping for the best. There must so often have been intense weariness in well doing. Upon his birthday in November he wrote:

Preached on board the Vincennes. . . . A number of the officers and men were present from the Peacock and also a number of residents from the shore. In all two hundred or more present. Had a good degree of freedom and hope I gave no offence and hope too that good may grow out of the sermon. Was sorry to have all the people from shore go down to take a lunch after sermon, and some of them doubtless to take wine.

News of the death of Abigail's favorite sister, Louisa, received at this time undoubtedly urged the following sentiment:

Another anniversary of my rapid life, thirty eight years old.

With Fifty
Years Yet
To Go
. . . On perusing the Heralds and newspapers and periodicals we find that a large number of our friends and acquaintances are dying off and going to their long home. So many of my friends having gone home I feel almost impatient to go too. The Lord give me patience and perseverance and a willingness to labor and toil and bear the burden and heat of the day and at length to go like a shock of corn fully ripe.

How wonderfully his expressed desire was fulfilled in his death more than fifty years later! Yet he could not believe it would be, for twice in the next few months he wrote:

O what a short year . . . twelve months passed away like a dream. Well, I am fast approaching the hour of my dissolution. My missionary work will soon be done. Let me then be at peace with God and man and be already ready. . . . Nothing but a desire to win souls to Christ and train them for him keeps me from desiring to be absent from the body now and present with the Lord.

Shortly after this Lowell was seized with a violent attack of asthma and for three nights almost suffocated. The poor man was but beginning a recurrent trial of the flesh that if painful for his family to witness, was as much more terrible for him to endure. This persisted at times to his extreme old age.

Entertain
Strangers
The needs of hospitality increased with the times—guest families coming to lodge sometimes for weeks together. In March, 1841, Lowell writes:

. . . Commenced to build a house to entertain strangers i.e. have torn down the horse and wagon house and are about to rebuild them in another place and build a room so that we can lodge a family overnight when necessary.

October 22nd, 1841. Last evening had a social party consisting of the King, Kekauliohi, the Governor Kekuanaoa, Captain Aulick of the United States Ship Yorktown, a man of war, Consul Brinsmade, Dr. Wood and family, Brother and Sister Armstrong, Dr. Judd and wife, fourteen in all. Very pleasant interview. How desirable to exert a good influence over the powers that be. . . . My prayer is God save the King and all his chiefs and this wayward, fickle minded people.

Lowell's worries were farther reaching than the boundaries of his group of islands. His ears seemed at times to ring with the prophetic injunction, "Cry aloud and spare not." Perhaps the parent board in Boston sometimes felt him to be reaching beyond his sphere, or perhaps they muttered some churchly condemnation, or perhaps they just considered him a spunky child when he called across five thousand miles: *Cry Aloud and Spare Not*

. . . Perhaps our rules of church discipline are more rigid than those of American and English churches. Biblically, intoxication is a disciplinary offence. We hear of rum-selling deacons and rum-drinking laymen at home and we wish very much to hear that such men are removed from the church of Christ.

Considering the general feeling toward Catholics in this Protestant Mission, it is good to find Lowell requesting from Boston, "such books as set forth Catholic sentiments and beliefs." More light and fuller, dear Lowell, we must have!

Marking progress in material comforts, Lowell's entry for December 17, 1841, is headed:

Notice! Have this evening paid Mr. Brinsmade a doubloon ($16.00) to purchase us a lamp, proof against the wind, to suspend in our middle room. He expects to embark on board the Joseph Peabody for the coast tomorrow to go to the United States overland (isthmus of Panama) and hopes to return here again in about twelve months from this time. *A Wind-Proof Lamp*

Did our dear family enjoy the light of anticipation all of a year?

December 18th. . . . the Peabody was towed out of the harbor, there being no wind either for or against her. She leaves apparently with great reluctance.

December 24th. . . . I sent Brother Emerson $20.00 in cash towards building his meeting house. Only $13.62 of it has been paid in and I trust the people to pay me the rest ere long. I also sent sixty three yards of bleached cotton at two cents per yard *Bearing One Another's Burden*

which amounts to $13.00. Five dollars and sixty two cents of
this have been paid for by the natives in sugar bags, firewood,
eggs, mats, etc. and the remaining $7.37 is our present to that
building.

April 1st, 1842. . . . . The good work of the Lord goes on
with increasing interest among the people of my congregation.
Many who have since been abandoned to their sins ever since
the introduction of the gospel into these Islands are now turning unto the Lord for the first time. They say that they have
despised all religion until now—they have been atheists and
infidels in the highest sense of the terms—that when a man died,
he dies like a brute. One sorcerer is among the number, who says
that he has prayed many people to death and has taken much
property from his poor neighbors by his smuggling and deceiv-
ing them. He now pronounces it all a work of lies, deception
and high handed wickedness. The people are not so boisterous
and enthusiastic this year as in 1838 and 1839, but the work
appears to take a firmer hold of their ears and consciences. How
changed the scene now from last year. 1841 was a trying, sift-
ing time with us; head wind and a boisterous sea, some thirty or
forty Jonas overboard to the mercy of the raging elements in
order to save ourselves from an entire wreck. But thanks to God
the scene is greatly changed for the better at present. We now
have a fine trade, have found thirty of the men cast overboard,

*Our Sails
Spread*

we are spreading all our sails to the winds and our little bark
moves on finely. To change the figure—the Lord has heard the
cry of his people and is visiting us this winter and spring with
a copious shower of divine grace. The spiritual rain commenced
in December and the spring tide together with the rivulets from
the mountains are causing the river to rise and swell and over-
flow its banks and now on the Sabbath people are beginning to
cry out that the way is too straight. Two Hundred fifty six
now stand propounded for admission to the church. These have
expressed hopes for one, two, three and four years. Hard and
obstinate cases, persons who now profess repentance for the
first time, are daily occurring. My whole time is devoted to the
people in preaching, lecturing, exhorting, public and private
conversation, etc. My soul doth magnify the Lord for the timely
visitation from on High. Brother Richards arrived from Maui

two or three days ago and brings intelligence that the King has signed a pledge of total abstinence from all inebriating liquors. The Lord grant that he may abide by his pledge.

A few days later the weary Lowell began a

Voyage and Tour to and on Maui. . . . Sailed . . . on board the whale ship Francis Henrietta, Captain Raynard, for Lahaina. . . . Arrived at Lahaina in five days and one and three fourths hours.

This trip is made by steamer today in not more than six hours and by plane in one hour.

I suffered considerable seasickness for three days and nights. My appetite then returned and the remainder of the voyage was comparatively pleasant. I forgot to take along a few nicknacks *Forgotten* for seasickness, such as crackers, soda powders, tamarinds, *Tamarinds* lemon syrup, chicken soup, etc. Our voyage was uncommonly long having calms and gales in quick succession. The foretop sail was badly rent one night and the main yard sprung, so that we made a new one while we lay becalmed two days. The fourth day we had a pretty severe mumuku which lasted half an hour off Kawaihae. A real fishing excursion this, having seen three *A Real* finbacked whales, one shark, a school of porpoises, and several *Fishing* flying fish. I prefer on the whole to be a fisher of men. Although *Trip* the passage has been rather long, yet on the whole pleasant, chiefly because of the passengers, viz: Brethren Richards, Armstrong, Dimond and also Mr. Robinson the ship carpenter and Mr. Butler the famous pilot. The Captain is not a pious man though he treated us politely. It is about five and half years since I was at this island. (Abba was with me at that time in company with Mr. and Mrs. Parker). Supped and lodged at the house of Brother Richards. Sabbath a.m. preached in English to the seamen and in the p.m. to Mr. B's. congregation of natives. In the evening held a meeting with some of my church members who are at Lahaina. Some of them appear well; others have fallen into sin and are going the broad road.

April 12th. Wailuku. Examination of the Female Seminary today. The girls appear admirably well as respects their behavior in school, at the dinner table, singing, etc.

13. Set off for Hana on horseback with Brother Armstrong. . . . Left our horses at Kalawaia. . . . Passed on about two miles over hills and palis . . . lodged at Makaiwa.

Hana

14. At 1 a.m. took passage in a canoe around the palis and arrived about two and a half miles from Mr. Conde's at sunrise. They were all very happy to see us. Mr. and Mrs. Conde have a good stone house, four rooms on the ground and two chambers all finished off. They have an excellent climate and a fine beautiful country. Mr. and Mrs. Rice are their associates and they all appear to be very happy in each other, very much attached to their station and would not exchange it for Honolulu or Lahaina.

Canoe, Horse, and Whaler

After a few days of visiting and preaching on that side of Maui, canoe, horse, and then a whale ship returned Lowell to the joy of home, wife, and infant son in Honolulu.

July 21, 1842, gives us an entry of especial interest.

Dedication of the Stone Church at Kawaiahao

At 3 o'clock this p.m. the King (come down from the Capital on Maui for the purpose), chiefs and people and considerable many residents being assembled in the new stone church, we proceeded to the solemn work of dedicating the house to the Lord. After the introductory prayer and singing, Mr. Armstrong read an account of the work and expense of building the house. It was commenced in the spring of 1837 and has been five years and nine days in building, and reckoning the *paahao* [prison] labor of the natives and the gratuitous labor of the church members and others at about six cents per day, the whole cost of the building as now completed is supposed to amount to $30,000. Of this sum the King has contributed $4200.00. The King came forward to the pulpit with a written document in his hand, stating that he willed and consecrated this house to the worship of Jehovah according as they had been taught by the American Missionaries and that he never wished it to pass into the hands of men of another faith. He dwelt at some length on this point and appeared exceedingly well on the occasion. The five divisions of the church were each next called upon to state what their object had been in building the house. Each *luna* [overseer] declared with an audible voice that they had built

FIRST PHOTOGRAPH OF KAWAIAHAO CHURCH, 1857

CHAMBERLAIN CORAL HOUSE

the house for the Lord and their people all responded to the
same.

I was then called upon to offer the dedicatory prayer. Mr.
Armstrong preached the sermon and Mr. Bishop made the
concluding prayer. The singing was good and the performances
all passed off well. I remark here that the corner stones of that
church and of this dobe church were laid upon the same day—
this house was one year in building and that five years. This
house cost $3000.00; and that $30,000.00, so that the odds
make the difference. Our house is very convenient, humble and
respectable and I feel very thankful for it. There is a very unpleasant echo and reverberation of sound in that church and
many complain that they cannot hear. I truly sympathise with
them in their disappointment in this respect.

This year had brought a smaller attendance than usual of *Released*
brethren from the other islands at the General Meeting. *Mission-*
Great changes were coming in the mission in the withdrawal *aries*
from it of several of the missionaries. The character of need
in the community was inevitably changing with the passage
of more than twenty years since the arrival of foreign settlers. But with the weight of all the unsaved souls upon his
heart and conscience, it was agony to Lowell to see one missionary after another loosen his connection with the parent
Board in America, and become detached first for positions
in the Government and later in undertakings of personal concern or business. In one letter to the Board—his was for
years the position of official scribe—he felt

. . . constrained by a sense of duty to speak on the subject of
reasons given by the missionaries leaving the Board.
    First;—Dissatisfaction with common stock system and other
regulations,
    Second and third;—Aid received by Board from slave holders
                    Streaks of blood in barrels of flour,
    Fourth;—Education of Children [But what about Puna-
hou?]
    Fifth;—A man has private rights.

All this, Lowell declares, causes distress to the remaining
missionaries. And Lowell, for one, poured out the grief of

his broken heart in many pages now yellowed by time and hushed in the silent bookstacks of the American Board of Commissioners for Foreign Missions rooms in Boston. Were Lowell to read subsequent history he must see in how many cases the years proved the wisdom and value of this severance, and what good was accomplished by these men in specialized service in the Government, in education, political economy, stability, and general advancement in civilization.

Local Support of Missionaries

One subject that had been agitating the minds of the missionaries in the field as it had also been agitating the minds of the Board at home was the matter of support of the local missions by the church members. December 18, 1842, Lowell preached on the text, "They who preach the gospel should live of the gospel," and commented on the occasion as follows:

The house was well filled and they gave riveted attention to my remarks for almost an hour. I hope and trust that they will do considerable for us during the year 1843. I have occasion to enumerate some of their deeds of benevolence from the last five years, such as the building of our church $3000.00, bell house and bell $200.00, building a public bridge $150.00, contribution for Waialua church $80.00, contribution for Kaneohe church $80.00, for Molokai church $80.00, rethatching the station school house (a present, this, to the government) $50.00, contributions for the furniture and table of the Lord, bread and wine, etc. $180.00. Total $3820.00. My proposition to the church this a.m. was that each male pay 25 cents cash and each female pay 12½ cents cash towards our support in 1843 and in addition to this that each contribute once during the year in wood or timber, or fowls, eggs, potatoes, onions, sugar bags or mats; and that we turn them to as good an account as we can. All this will not probably meet all our consumption wants, but will count towards our support as far as it goes.

October and November bring a variety of subjects in the journal entries. Several Methodist missionary families arrive from the Columbia River, "most or all bound for the United States." Reverend and Mrs. S. C. Damon arrived to work in the Seaman's Bethel. A brig arriving from Tahiti

. . . brings tiding that the French . . . have taken the Society Islands. . . .

California Taken from the Mexicans

November 15th. . . . Sail Ho! a brig from the Coast of California. She has fled to this port to escape from the Americans who she says have taken California from the Mexicans. Well what next? Who can tell what a day or two may bring forth? Wars and rumors of wars, turning and overturning and by and by the Lord will reign from pole to pole and from east to west.

November 18th. Rioters in the village . . . the avowed object . . . to break down a law requiring all sailors to return to their ships at 8 o'clock at night. The Governor is rallying all his officers, sheriff, constables, soldiers, etc., and arming them with guns, swords and dirks. The drum has been beating on the fort all this p.m. Must there be blood shed this night?

A Village Riot

November 19th. Fine morning—all is well—peace and quiet during the night. The troublesome Captain . . . yielded the point. And about 8 o'clock in the evening the gun fired from the fort and nearly all the ship bells in the harbor responded. The war is over and the militia discharged and sent home.

Here we enter upon one of the most dramatic scenes of Hawaiian history. As the vivid story bears its own sequel in its hand, we will make no preface or comment. There is an unwonted break in Lowell's faithful and almost daily record of immediate events. But after about seven weeks without an entry, Lowell's journal tells us on February 13, 1843:

International Drama

An American man of war, the Boston, Captain Long has come to anchor today. A timely visit this, for the English are threatening to do great things and perhaps the arrival will check their malice and rage a little.

How little Lowell could dream that her namesake *Boston,* fifty years later, would play another major part on the miniature stage of Hawaii's destiny!

February 14th. Today I have visited both of the ships of war in the harbor, accompanied by several of the missionaries of this village. Lord Paulett was very polite to us—though he had previously insulted the American Consul, the French Consul, and several of the most respectable American merchants in this place. They called upon him but he refused to extend to them any civilities. Consequently the state of feeling in the village is very indignant towards his Lordship and most of the English residents.

February 17th. The King has arrived this p.m. from Maui and the Governor has received him in high style. All his soldiers dressed in uniform met him at the wharf with a band of Music. As the King's vessel came into the harbor on passing the Boston, Captain Long fired him a salute of twenty one guns. But the Englishman remained as sullen as a tiger. The American residents all paid their respects to the King, so that he knew who his friends were.

18. Last evening Lord Paulett demanded a private interview with the King. The King said he must have his interpreter. Lord Paulett then made out his demands and informed the King that if they were not complied with before 4 p.m. today he should bombard the village. This morning at sunrise they towed an English brig outside, as a refuge for the English ladies and all this a.m. the English have been carrying their most valuable articles some on board ship and some out into the country. An abominable and insulting sham just to bring the King to terms. Well they have succeeded in causing the King to yield and at 2 this p.m. a forced salute was fired from the fort. This is peace with a vengeance! ! We all thought that the French war, by Captain Laplace was insufferable. But alas the English have shown out more of old Adam than the French. The Lord reward them according to their deeds.

Lord Paulett's Hand Wins

February 25th. Mark this day! ! At 3 o'clock this p.m. the King gave up his kingdom into the hands of the English, Lord George Paulett acting agent. A sad time in some respects and *oluolu* [favorable] in some respects. The manner in which the English have conducted the week past is outrageous beyond description. Making demand after demand with no legal foundation until the poor King was jaded and vexed nearly to death and then submitted to their barbarous and piratical demands. Still it may be well for them in the end. The American residents are greatly incensed. . . .

March 10th, 1843. The recent political revolution weighs upon my mind with the weight of a mountain. The very thought of the course pursued by the English to get possession of the Islands is sickening and disgusting in the extreme. Their throats were like an open sepulchre and like the grave which cries give, give, give, and never says it is enough. So were their demands until they got the whole. To see this government apparently in health and strength seized and buried alive, is truly heartrending. Still the Lord may have permitted this, heartrending as it is, to prevent a still greater calamity, viz: falling into the hands of the French. A native vessel, the Hoikaika, is expected to sail for the coast tomorrow to be despatched for the United States and England. Mr. Marshall goes to take charge of the American and Mr. Simpson the English. Looking at the right and wrong of this unhappy affair I confess everything is all confusion. Political rights and national rights are all so different from those of Christ that I may disagree with some of my neighbors on these points. There are those who contend that might is right, extortion is right, oppression is right, violation of treaties is right.

March 15th. . . . Today I attended the funeral of Kahakili, one of the high chiefs. The English officers with their band of music were present and marched to the tomb. Only one of the old chiefs left, Governor Adams. O how sad to see the nation thus afflicted and bereaved! To see the foreigners enviously exulting to get the chiefs out of the way that they may have free course and live as they list! *Death of High Chief*

April 25th, 1843. *Ea!* [What!] Look at this! Lord Paulett has annulled the law against adultery and turned all that class out of prison. Now we begin to foresee what is coming. He has violated his assertion in his proclamation, i.e. to abide by the existing laws. *Hawaiian Law Annulled*

May 8th. Mr. Bishop has written a memorial to the Honorable Commissioners requesting them to establish the law again and they have hit him a hard rap on the knuckles and told him to attend to his own business and they will attend to theirs.

Yesterday the two congregations in the village met at the stone church and talked on the subject of the nullified law. Armstrong, Gulick, Ives, Aaroa, one of the singers, John Ii, and one of the Luna Kanawai [Judges] and myself made remarks. Good I hope will be the result.

May 30th. The political state of things has hung over our minds like a threatening cloud, but thanks to Almighty God we have recently heard good tidings from the United States and England. We now hope that the English flag may soon be taken down and the Hawaiian restored to its place. We have heard also that a host of Roman Catholics, priests, nuns, relics, etc. etc. are on their way to these Islands. Trials are before us. The Lord give wisdom and grace equal to our day.

Plucking up the Tares

June 4th, 1843. Sabbath. I have been overhauling some of the church of late to see what ravages Lord Paulett's revolution has made among us, and in the first three *apanas* [districts] we have suspended about twenty persons for rum and awa drinking, gambling, *puhi baka* [smoking tobacco] etc. Have held a communion with these three *apanas* this p.m. and if we can succeed in plucking up some of the tares in some of the remaining *apanas* we may observe the ordinance of the Lords supper with them next Sabbath.

June 18th. Sabbath. This is the third Sabbath that we have been holding communion with different parts of this large church. The whole number now suspended is about ninety, eighty of whom have probably gone astray since Lord Paulett's revolution and annullification of the good and wholesome laws of this nation. A great many church members are sick and are

The Shadow of Death

going to the grave. Not less than twenty deaths in this church have come to my knowledge within a month, a part of whom died however more than a month ago. O with what rapid strides this church and people are going down to the grave. They can not long exist as a nation!

July 10th. Dreadful state of morals among the people. It seems as if the devil had come down in great wrath and that the people were full of his infernal spirit. This morning K. at Pauoa has hung herself—was caught in adultery last night and has acted as judge, jury and hangman in her own case and gone post haste to receive the wages of her iniquity. She was a member of this church. I am prepared to hear almost anything from either foreigners or native church members.

July 19th. Hoike of schools. . . . The number of scholars has diminished at least half—*aloha ino* [exceedingly loving or sympathetic] for the rising generation. How distressing it must

be for a physician to see the plague sweeping off the people and
he can do nothing to stay its awful ravages. So with the watch-
man for souls to see the civil arm enter the land and demolish
the christian landmarks and infuse an influence into the minds
of the people more fatal to the soul than the smallpox to the
body.

Lowell closes a paragraph, which in vehement language
paints horror upon horror of licentiousness in the village,
with these words:

The Lord rebuke this son of Belial, put a hook into his nose
and lead him to the place whence he came.

July 26th. Sail Ho! Man of War

A frigate—English! Well, what next! She proves to be the
Dublin, Admiral Thomas—a peace maker. O how timely his
arrival! The King has just issued his protest against Lord Paulett *ma* and Commodore Karney of the American frigate Constellation has issued his protest against Paulett *ma* and the
ferment is high. O if Admiral Thomas has come to adjust
matters in righteousness then this insufferable Lord George
Paulett's reign will soon expire.

Enter
Admiral
Thomas

July 28th. Good, good tidings today! Report says that the
Admiral has virtually restored the Islands again to the King
and extinguished the British commission and next Monday the
English flag is to be taken down and the Hawaiian raised again
. . . and Lord George is to salute it and also the other English
ships of war now in port. The Lord reigns, let the earth rejoice.
On arriving the Admiral did not go to Lord George to ask him
why he had done thus and so, but sent immediately to have an
interview with the King and it is reported that he has scarcely
noticed Paulett since his arrival. I think that Paulett and his
advisers must feel rather cheap in this day of righteous retribu-
tion. The triumph of the wicked is short. But oh, the ravages
that sin has made among the people for the last five months and
four days. It seems to me like an age, but fire makes rapid work
among tinder, stubble, dry grass and often times in the woods.
How much easier to tear down than to build up, to pollute than
to sanctify, to remove wholesome laws and barriers against vice

and let the people rush into every species of sin than to call them back again into the paths of righteousness.

July 30th. Sabbath. Text Romans 12; 15, "Rejoice with those who rejoice and weep with them who weep." The awful blight and curse which Lord George has cast upon the moral state of things is so appalling that I find it exceedingly difficult to dwell much upon the first half of the text. My large congregation is diminished more than half and between one and two hundred church members have become involved in sin and are under church discipline, etc, etc., and the awful leaven of licentiousness is going through the whole length and breadth of the land. How can a father who has lost an eighth of his children rejoice, though four who remain may be in tolerable health and the other four lie at the point of death? And though this vile sea monster has a hook in his nose and will probably be soon taken from us, (in this I rejoice) yet how can I rejoice over scores of church members deeply involved in guilt, many of whom will probably never reform again? God's arm however is not shortened that he cannot save—let me then hope for the best.

Restora-
tion Day

July 31st. Mark this day! A great and memorable day this for King Kamehameha and the Sandwich Island nation. Rear Admiral Thomas, Commander of H.B.M. ship "Dublin" has today publicly restored the Islands again to the King. We all now clearly perceive that Paulett has been acting without authority and that the Devil has been his guide. . . . But a more complete overthrow never took place since Adam was turned out of Paradise than that Paulett has experienced this day. I remember that Haman was hung on the gallows he built for Mordecai, Pharaoh was drowned in the Red Sea and Judas hung himself. Captain Lord George Paulett without any authority affected to destroy a sovereignty and create another sovereignty, but . . . the house, or kingdom, which this Jack built is thrown down flat, there is not left one stone upon another.

This morning July 31st, a little before ten o'clock, Admiral Thomas accompanied by several officers and the marines from the "Dublin" "Caresfort" and "Hazzard" (three English ships of war now in port) marched upon the plain, the place appointed, to unfurl the Hawaiian flag. At ten o'clock the King and the chiefs and the King's soldiers arrived on the plain—immediately the Hawaiian flag was unfurled, the English flag at the fort was hauled down and the Hawaiian raised there—instantly a large Hawaiian flag appeared on Fort hill. Firing commenced. The artillery from the "Caresfort," "Dublin," "Hazzard," Fort, Fort hill, etc., etc., the "Constellation" (an American) and several American whalers.

All the marines passed around twice in review before the King and Admiral. Considerable maneuvering of the artillery and marines, firing, dismounting and remounting the field pieces—these exercises lasted about one and one half hours. A large concourse of people—some eight or ten thousand perhaps.

On returning I followed the King to his apartments and there witnessed an affecting scene, viz., the rebel soldiers (one hundred forty). During the reign of Lord George Paulett these men swore allegiance to Queen Victoria and thus became the enemies of their King. The Governor had forbid their going upon the plain to witness the exercises there and on their return sent down to the fort and called them up to the King's house where they three times saluted the Hawaiian flag and then took a solemn oath of allegiance to Kamehameha III and after that the King allowed them to come into his presence.

At one o'clock p.m. a religious meeting for thanksgiving etc., was held in the stone church when the King addressed the audience saying: "Where are you, common people? The life of these Islands has been restored to me as I had hoped it would be—I therefore wish you all to know and acknowledge me as King. The old laws are to be revived and transgressors will be punished. This is my thought that you acknowledge me king." Doctor Judd then read the Admiral's communication wherein he restored the Islands to Kamehameha III. John Ii then entered the desk and made an address, expressing the joy which was felt at the restoration of the Islands, etc. He then read a document from the King in which it was stated that the prisoners are set free from Hilo to Niihau and that the people are to have ten holidays and after that the business of the kingdom is to commence. I was then called upon to offer a prayer, after which the congregation dispersed.

At three p.m. the King went off to dine with Admiral Thomas

Ceremonies in the Stone Church

on board the "Dublin." As he passed through the harbour the "Caresfort" and "Hazzard" each saluted him with twenty-one guns and having arrived outside between the "Dublin" (English) and the "Constellation" (American) they each saluted him with twenty-one guns after which the King went on board the "Dublin" to dine. During all these exciting scenes as well as during his five months' captivity the King drunk nothing intoxicating, water only.

August 1st, 1843. Today the king and chiefs have held a feast up Nuuanu Valley and returned this p.m. in state, conducted by a band of music and followed by a large train.

August 2nd. The King and some of his chiefs have dined on board the U.S. ship "Constellation," (Commodore Kearney).

August 3rd. The King has today made a feast for all his friends, natives, residents and men of war—up Nuuanu Valley. I was present. There was an immense concourse of people. The scene was very grand and imposing. The table on the ground spread with leaves was one hundred eighty feet long and loaded with an immense quantity of food—pigs, turkies, flowls, ducks, bread, potatoes, taro, luau, etc., etc. On the sides of the table were the English flag, the French flag, the American and Hawaiian flags, and over the King and Commodore and Admiral was the royal flag with the King's crown in it. A large collection of gentlemen and ladies from the village—among whom were several of the missionaries and a large number of the officers and midshipmen from the ships of war. How happy and joyful everyone appears—cheerful countenances, hearty shake of the hand. How much better is freedom than captivity. Brother Hall has written an anthem on the occasion styled the

"RESTORATION ANTHEM

"Hail to our rightful King!
We joyful honors bring
This day to thee.
Long live your Majesty
Long reign this dynasty
And for posterity
The sceptre be.

"Hail to the worthy name!
    Worthy his country's fame,
        Thomas the brave!
    Long shall thy virtues be
    Shrined in our memory,
    Who came to set us free,
        Quick o'er the wave.

"Praise to our heavenly King
    To thee our thanks we bring
        Worthy of all;
    Lord we thine honors raise!
    Loud is our song of praise!
    Shine on our future days,
        Sovereign of all."

                    (Tune God save the King)

On the other hand how sad and heart-piercing every move-
ment of the kind must be to Lord George Paulett. Every salute
to the King must be a most deadly thrust to him.

Lowell recorded later that

the Admiral kept Lord P. saluting and paying obeisance for two
or three weeks whenever His Majesty had occasion to pass
through the harbour to and from ships of war. Sometimes instead of firing twenty-one guns he would man his yards and
order his band of music to play "God save the King." The
British Commission has taken French leave—*aloha ino* [pro-
found sympathy] for a man in his predicament.

August 4th, 1843. About sundown last evening the frigate
United States, Commodore Jones and Captain Armstrong, came
to anchor and this morning the American sloop of war, Cyane,
Captain Stribling, came to anchor. O what a fleet, four frigates
and two sloops of war, viz: the Constellation and the United
States (American frigates) Cyane, (American sloop) Dublin
and Caresfort (English frigates) and Hazzard, (English
sloop). One would think that the Sandwich Islands are beginning to look up in the world or in other words other nations
are beginning to look at the Sandwich Islands. The Cyane has

brought intelligence from the United States of America and England—good news from a far country in reference to these Islands. Mr. Brown, a commissioner from the United States to these islands is on his way hither—a teetotaler.

Depression of Spirit   For months following the events last recorded Lowell seems to be under a cloud of gloom. While he clutches at hope as his church members return to the fold, new members inquire the way, many couples seek the institution of marriage and he contrasts the situation as "Not so during the days of the reign of fornication," he mourns over the return to the United States *via* Hawaii of worn, broken, and discouraged missionaries from the Columbia River and laments the hardships of missionary work in the Northwest. He grieves over the report of

an English whale ship . . . cut off at Strong's Island, all the men massacred and most of the property taken out of the ship then scuttled by the natives.

He is distressed over the death of a young white girl (living in the family of a missionary) whose post-mortem indicated that hers was

. . . an obstinate case . . . her early departure much in the light of suicide . . . her sickness caused by tight lacing and her end . . . in consequence of starvation.

Deaths of brother missionaries, also of little children of the mission, and backsliding of church members, "licentiousness" among foreigners—all wring Lowell's heart. At the end of the year 1843 he denounces uncompromisingly the dethronement of the Queen of the Society Islands

Queen Pomare   . . . in short order, all her prayers and entreaties to the contrary notwithstanding. Public robbers—in the nineteenth century. In 1839 they robbed the treasury of the Sandwich Islands Government to the amount of $20,000.00 and in 1843 they have robbed Pomare, the Queen of the Society Islands of her throne and kingdom. The Lord rebuke them!

Returning from a protracted meeting on Kauai in March, 1844, Lowell recognizes his condition thus:

My health has not been good since my return . . . want of
appetite and general weakness, with some cholic pains. A great
depression of spirits too much of the time owing in part to ill
health and in part to the state of our schools and the worldly
mindedness of the church members. . . . The poor teachers are
in a sad predicament—a wonder they have not long since abandoned their schools. . . . The Government are owing the school
teachers of these two parishes about $350.00. All other persons
are promptly paid . . . but Government School teachers must
go begging or live on the wind.

A portion of this church are rapidly imbibing the spirit of
their rulers. . . . If the rulers (church members) may chew and
smoke tobacco and attend balls . . . why can not they do the
same. . . . If a dollar may fill the eye of a chief, why may not a
shilling fill the eye of the kanaka? Hence eternity with all its
pleasing and dreadful realities is hid from their minds . . . and
hence too *palaka—launa ole mai—apiki—alunu* [indifference—
unfriendliness—deception—covetousness] and what not. These
are some of the first ripe fruits of the . . . day which has just
dawned upon us. . . . Tidings this evening that there has been
a riot at Lahaina. Rum the cause. Sailors threatened to take the *Liquor*
life of the King . . . hence a mob, stones thrown and many injured both natives and sailors. This is also out of the fruits of
the new kingdom. . . . Strange doings of late! Seven licensed
grogshops (Six in Honolulu and one at Lahaina) have recently *License*
been sold at auction to the highest bidder . . . the whole . . .
for more than $3000.00 . . . independent of the earnest peti-
tion of natives, residents, and ship masters that such an abominable thing might not take place. . . . Two of the police officers
have fallen into intemperance this week [April] and been ban-
ished from the presence of the Government as rebels. This is
among the first ripe fruits of the license law for 1844.

. . . The distressing intelligence . . . that Mrs. Dole is
dead. . . . She has been ill . . . for some time. Last Tuesday
she gave birth to a son, and now she lies a corpse!

Under this cloud of darkness Lowell could not know the *Birth of*
remarkable future that lay before that babe, Sanford Bal- *Sanford*
lard Dole. How Lowell's heart would have leaped, how he *Ballard*
would have blessed God, could he have foreseen that the puny *Dole*

babe, whose life was saved at the breast of a missionary sharing the sustenance for her own child, should one day be
President of the Provisional Government succeeding the overthrow of the Monarchy in 1893, then President of the Re-
public of Hawaii, and, upon the annexation of the Islands
in 1898, the first Governor of the Territory of Hawaii. For
twelve crucial years Sanford Ballard Dole, beloved of native
and foreigner alike, was to be Admiral of this "the fairest
fleet of islands."

All this Lowell could not dream and he wrote wearily, regarding the deaths of two near and dear members of the
home people.

*Lowell
Longs
To Be
at Rest*

. . . Never have I felt so cheerful and happy at the death of
friends as at this time. For some months I have often wished
that the time for me to go home to my Savior had come. But I
must wait a little till some more worthy and better prepared go
first.

*Lowell
Disturbs
His Towns-
men*

Once again, in 1845, Lowell's preaching disturbs some of
his fellow townsmen and the King and Queen, Governor and
High Chiefs with Foreign Ministers of government are

. . . all seated . . . in front of my stand to hear my explanation . . . the next Sabbath. The grand object unquestionably
was to *hoopai* [punish] me. I preached from the same text again
and held them about an hour and I have heard since that they
regarded the sermon as sound, scriptural, orthodox, etc. There
is an effort making of late to saddle and bridle the church and
set the government astride, church and state!

Gorham D. Gilman of Boston, a sometime resident of
Honolulu, wrote of Lowell thus:

. . . Bold and fearless preacher, without respect to persons,
condemning and reproving wickedness in high places as well as
in low one—and seeking to discharge what he deems his whole
duty. In the course of his preaching—remarks from the pulpit
were deemed of a personal nature by an important citizen who
demanded a repetition of the sermon and an apology. He had
the pleasure to hear the whole sermon as before, obnoxious part

and all. . . . He is much liked by his people and enjoys their full confidence.

This same month, April, 1845, we learn from Lowell that:

. . . An epidemic has come over this village during the last forty eight hours and I presume that not less than five hundred have called on me for salts since yesterday noon, twenty hours ago. It is a kind of influenza, coughing, sneezing, headache, dizziness, etc. The impression has emanated from the powers that be that a good portion of salts will relieve the sick, and hence the rush to me for salts. I have heard as yet of only one death. . . . The epidemic has become so prevalent that we . . . had the house of the Lord open and the bell rung at the usual hour in the morning simply to announce . . . that all exercises . . . were postponed till such time as we might be recovered as a people from the influenza. . . . After making a few remarks about the nature and treatment of the disease among us I dismissed the congregation.

Five Hundred Patients

That night Lowell himself was stricken and then Abigail and then the new baby daughter, Emma Louisa born the previous June fourth, and, in spite of all her parents' fears in this and other illnesses, destined to live to be the support and comfort of their old age. "The Domesticks" also were all sick and the disease, abating a little, broke out afresh causing in two months some sixty deaths in Lowell's church—two hundred from the village at large having died in the first four weeks of the epidemic.

. . . How dismal and disheartening to go to the house of the Lord and see only about two hundred where formerly there were fifteen hundred and sometimes two thousand. . . . Almost the entire population are sick. Clouds and darkness are round about this people—the nation is rapidly passing into the hands of foreigners and the natives are rapidly passing into Eternity.

In November, 1845, in a letter to his brother-in-law, Lionel Tenney, principal of a female seminary at Marietta, Ohio, Lowell writes:

We all report ourselves in usual health at this date. I do not mean this that I am as well as when I left the United States— nor as well as I was during the years 1838–9, 40, 41 etc. Those were the years of God's gracious visitation from on High— years of revivals—protracted meetings and other extra labor daily from early dawn till nine o'clock at night; preaching, teaching, exhorting and talking with the people. Verily it was good, yea a blessed privilege to be here.

But I can by no means perform such an amount of labor now. Two sermons on the Sabbath, with a Sabbath School, is my regular task now—Monthly concert—a singing school Tuesday and Thursday afternoons, a church meeting every Saturday p. m.—daily administering medicines to the sick—visiting the sick—attending funerals, and looking after wayward church members, and also looking after my family, makes up the amount of one week with another. And perhaps that is as much as you expect your healthy, robust ministers in your cold and bracing climate to do.

This letter does not mention to his relatives such odd jobs as his journal of nearly equal date contained:

Odd Jobs

I and my family set off this day for Waialua . . . and arrived home . . . having been absent nine days. Was full of sympathy for them in reference to their meeting house—came home and started a subscription paper aiming to raise $200.00. . . . I shipped on board the schooner Victoria $156.00 worth of lumber, nails, glass etc. for that meeting house and . . . went over with carpenters to frame and raise the roof. The third day after our arrival Mr. Sweet, the boss carpenter was taken sick, and in nine days he died. The other carpenters put up the roof with my superintendence.

*A Visit
Home?*

Further perusing the letter of Lowell to Lionel, we quote:

You have very kindly suggested the idea of our returning home to visit our friends, refresh our weary bodies, address the churches on the subject of missions, etc. etc. Such a suggestion finds us contemplating this important subject. I shall be obliged to spin a long yarn to give you a clue to the circumstances which have been transpiring the past year, to bring us to talk and reflect on this subject.

The United States, Great Britain and France have declared this nation independent, as you have heard long ere this. But this independence we think will be of short duration. The policy pursued by the King's ministers has hitherto been such as to give pretty general dissatisfaction. . . .

Lowell Digests the Political Situation

Reverend Mr. Richards, formerly a member of this mission, and Haalilio, the King's former secretary were sent on a special embassy by the King of the Islands—to Washington, London and Paris. Having accomplished their mission, Haalilio died, soon after their embarkation from Boston to return to these Islands, with the consumption.

. . . Our schools which are nominally supported by Government have suffered for the want of the means of support, and consequently the teachers have become very inefficient. They are about to be reorganized again under the Superintendence of Rev. Mr. Richards, the recently appointed minister of Instruction and it is hoped they will revive and flourish again for a short time at least.

Politics run high with you in the United States occasionally and carry all before them. Such excitement I regard as very destructive to vital godliness, and the less we professing Christians have to do with them the better. This little community has been greatly excited on political subjects for some time past. But we hope there will be less in time to come. The Government have published a paper in which they of course have always justified their own proceedings and there being no other paper in which the residents could express opinions of a different character, they have recently obtained a printing press and operators for printing and have issued three or four papers by the name "The Sandwich Islands News." It is conducted by an association of gentlemen, and thus far we have been quite pleased with it.

Island Politics

Here Lowell's spirit of Americanism flows in a forceful stream. Let there be liberty of thought, liberty of the press! And he was quite as strongly Hawaiian, too, for we note grief in his voice as he exclaims, in this same letter:

This nation is rapidly passing into the hands of foreigners.

The Kings' ministers are all naturalized foreigners—and the lands are rapidly passing into the hands of such and others who take the oath of allegiance. Aliens also are establishing themselves in this country, leasing lands, and cultivating the soil and their herds and flocks are becoming very numerous etc. etc.

In spite of all his gravity, the real Lowell smiles, albeit grimly, in the next paragraph.

Some fears are entertained these days by masters of ships homeward bound on account of the rumors of war between the United States and Mexico. Mexican privateers may be out seeking whom they may devour. Should the "Angela" be seized with her mail, then you will understand why this letter, the newspapers and box of canes have never come to hand, and will charge the same to the war department.

The Reverend Mr. Bingham, one of the pioneers of this Mission, who returned with Mrs. Bingham to the United States some six years ago, to recruit their health, have taken a dismission from the American Board, and of course from this mission also. Mr. Whitney another of the pioneers has died here in
the field. The American Board do not intend to increase the number of missionaries in this field, and it is quite doubtful in my mind whether they will even keep our number good. The brightest and best days of this mission are probably numbered. Still we are hoping for more season's of refreshment from the presence of the Lord.

Thus does Lowell binding up the sheaves feel the burden of the wheat and the tares together. Oppressed by the weight of them, the responsibility, the lack of perfect grain, with eyes cast down in weariness and frequent discouragement, who shall blame him if he at times loses sight of the shock of full corn he hoped to be, and was, after nearly half a hundred years more?

III

FIRES IN THE FALL

1. ABIGAIL'S HEARTH

THE element of fire means increasingly more to us as life advances. Wars, absences, lonelinesses remind us of home fires kept burning. Griefs, disappointments, misunderstandings are trials "so as by fire"; the fiery furnace of suffering glows in memory as a character beacon. The loss of a home by fire taxes fortitude so to put it out that it consume not contentment in living. Sometimes its painful blaze lights the way to more stately mansions of the soul. To those who know the change of seasons of the temperate zone, the fires in the fall along the roadside, transforming the litter in the aftermath of summer, not only warm the memory and stimulate the imagination by their remembered odor, but signify the necessary readjustments made not only in house- and city-keeping, but in mind-and-spirit-keeping if life is not to be clogged by the futile and the worthless, though once gay, trappings of the past. Fires such as all of these belonged to our Lowell and Abigail.

We who are of Nordic blood connect sentimental and spiritual values of human conversation and cheer with the traditional fireside. A still earlier energy in our cells connects us with the mingled delight and discomfort of the camp fire. Even we in this subtropic land cherish fire as a suggestion of intimacy and beauty.

With all of this by way of apology, let us gather at Abigail's hearth. It is high time, for through the period of harvest and the heat and burden of the day we have seen and heard little of Abigail even though we have felt her presence. Really to find her we must go back through the years from 1845, where we left Lowell weary in the field, to 1837, and, indeed, into the cookhouse where she is at work—the cookhouse set a little apart from the rest of the dwelling—an old custom still surviving in other tropic lands, Sumatra, for instance—but practically abandoned in our islands.

Kaumaka-
pili

We are on the Kaumakapili premises, not to be found now
unless an old-timer point it out. The children who frequent
the Beretania Street Playground, on the street of that name
—a memory of Britain's hand in our history—and Smith
Street—named for Lowell—play where Abigail's little ones
played, and rest on the grass that once covered the sleeping
place of five of her seven. It is but a short walk to the bank of
Nuuanu stream, but it is hidden by Chinatown's open-faced
stores instead of low-roofed native huts. Macadamized streets
with corners, lights, sidewalks, and shop signs replace irregular, dusty lanes. Where once were handcarts, today are automobiles. No telephone poles and wires then offended the
skyline, but neither were there trees in the desert village that
could not coax the plant growth coddled by the daily showers
of the valleys, *mauka*. From this spot plunged down the then
steep "Commercial Hill," taking its name from the Commercial Hotel, the glorified one of the many "grog shops" that
found business in the neighborhood. Kukui Street at the foot
of the hill suggests the pleasant shade of trees that probably
bordered the stream crossing the beautiful Nuuanu Valley.
Taro patches lay along the hollow until the once steep Judd
Hill, the other side Pauoa Stream, must be laboriously
climbed afoot or horseback.

Without radios, telephones, steam whistles, street cars, fire
motors, ambulances, and trucks, the hum of human voices, intensified by boisterous sounds from the grog shops or household wailings, must have had little interruption save by the
occasional ringing of the church bell in its thatched belfry,
calling to services in the large thatched church.

Domes-
ticity

The New England energy of our Abigail was irked by the
sight of an Hawaiian helper sitting down to fry taro, and
even to the end of her life except when prostrated upon her
couch she had some part in the preparation of the frugal
meals. How the taste remains of her meat and potato hash
made with a little milk! How fragrant still, the cookies just
from the oven. How golden and brown the johnny-cake!
Brown sugar was not so well washed as now, but seemed much
sweeter and was always used unless at a "Company" repast

strawberries might make a novel entrance with white sugar
as high compliment!

Emma, the surviving daughter of Lowell and Abigail, at
the age of twenty-five, decided to write her memoirs! Her decision did not hold beyond a few pages, but from them we
glean the following:

Our town house stood opposite the large thatched church my
father had built at Kaumakapili. At first we spent only the
summer months at Nuuanu Cottage, built in 1843, which later *Emma's*
became our permanent home. The town house had a basement *Memory*
partly below ground and the rooms in the basement were *Picture*
reached by steps cut into the ground and paved with stones. *of the*
Most of the rooms were used for storing various things, but one *Home at*
was finished off with windows that came above the level of the *Kaumaka-*
ground and admitted light and air. The walls were plastered *pili*
and whitened. There were many shelves on two sides that
reached nearly to the ceiling. Some of these were filled with
books and some with bottles of medicine. There was a long bench
on the third side and a table covered with books, pens, ink and a
lot of writing paper on the fourth. Upstairs on the first floor
were a neat parlor, bedroom, dining room, pantry and kitchen.
In the kitchen wall was a funny little door and into that door
used to go the bread when it was moulded into tins, sometimes a
pie and a loaf of cake when mixed, and after awhile the door
would be opened and the bread, cake and pie would come out
ready to eat, but oh so hot. When I grew older I knew that place
behind the door was called an oven, but for a great many years
I did not understand what made it so hot.

Fortunately for the education of the children of today
who, with their electric buttons, must learn even of kerosene
and wood stoves from books and pictures, there are extant in
the carefully cherished houses of the Mission at Kawaiahao
two old fireplaces with their cranes, black pots, and ovens in
the stone walls.

Another room in the home at Kaumakapili that is vivid in
Emma's memory is the bedroom, for

. . . in the bedroom, on a lounge lay, day after day, my mother.
. . . Mother had beautiful shining eyes and red spots on her

cheeks and to me she was the most beautiful person in the world. She could tell lovely stories.

Hospitality   Abigail loved company and graciously dispensed hospitality to the end of her days. She minded not her lack of this world's goods nor the meager fare and accommodations she had to offer, but showed her fineness of feeling in offering gladly what she had in her "modest home" to a true "gentleman or lady."

A visiting chaplain described an evening in her Kaumakapili home as one of high intercourse on matters including several branches of natural science. Some of the guests were linguists, all, cultured and thoughtful. Interesting shells were discussed, Abigail showing her rare orange cowry. She showed, also, impressions of plants which she had taken. How she would have revelled in modern color and motion photography! With all politeness, Abigail might be subjected to difficulty in suppressing mirth on such an occasion as this. Royal guests were being entertained at tea, the King and Premier, themselves. Said Abigail:

Twenty or thirty retainers stood without the door to protect the royal person of their sovereign. One of the royal highnesses, who has a wardrobe groaning with finery, took the occasion to come in a calico frock with diamonds in her ears! and kept her immense person enveloped in a huge cloak all the evening.

Guests might be royal, or poor and needy, strangers, or broken down friends of old times. One brother missionary died, not only in this hospitable home, but in Lowell's arms, leaving to his care the financial arrangements for the bereft wife and children. A family from another island might occupy the spare room in the tiny yard for weeks at a time, while the delicate hostess must cater to their needs with always indifferent help.

Over and over again Abigail's energy had been in excess of her wisdom and physical fitness, and she had experienced those frustrations of nature, the fall of unripe fruit, the debilitating and dangerous enemy of maternity—miscarriage.

It was for this reason the happy home at Ewa had been

abandoned, that Abigail might have the watchful care of the
mission doctor who resided in Honolulu.

Even with medical care she has been taxed with bearing, *The Empty*
but not rewarded with rearing, children. Have we, in the *Cradle*
plastered house at Kaumakapili, caught sight of a wooden
cradle? It has been in the storeroom, among things not in use.
The hand has reached for the cradle but the cradle has refused to rock. Twice in his letters to the Board in Boston,
Lowell has recorded, in 1839 and in 1840, the birth of a
stillborn son, and then has cheerfully described Abigail's taking up the burden of living and being more of a helpmeet to
him in mission work than ever, but at what cost to herself
words do not tell. One week after Lowell's return from his
mission tour in April, 1842, he and Abigail were a third time
mourning the death of an only child. But the childless father
nearing forty could say:

. . . Precious boy, we mourn thine absence. Thou wilt not
return to us but we shall soon go to thee . . .

thus emphasizing the thought of coveted departure in his
paraphrase of David.

Only one year later, while grieving over the fate of his
adopted land as he sees it and mourning over the flock of his
chosen pasture, Lowell records the birth and death of a
daughter, adding:

These repeated providences of God are dark and unintelli-
gible to me, i. e. I do not know what particular sin, or sins, they
are destined to correct. I think there are but few parents more
fond of children than we are, and perhaps this is the very thing
that cannot safely be indulged. Doubtless the Lord has good
reasons for plucking all the flowers in our garden. . . . The
fourth time I am constrained to say "The Lord gave and the
Lord hath taken away and blessed be his holy name!!!"

Abigail never submitted passively to her successive terrible *Triumph*
disappointments. While her arms were empty of the burdens *of Spirit*
she longed to bear and when the cookhouse might not ring to
her springing step, the couch of a semi-invalid could be to
Abigail, as the log to the famous Mark Hopkins, a place of

power in the educational world. In Abigail's case, we find it also the starting point of an industry. Her body might be inert but her hands and mind were busy and happy with the dusky-faced sisters who came to her home. *The Friend* of July, 1843, in a short article entitled, "Yankee Ingenuity, Missionary Instruction, and Hawaiian Industry Combined," and running as follows, pays tribute to Abigail who

The First Sugar Bag . . . now fours years ago . . . instructed a native woman to make *the first sugar bag*. Since that time not less than 65,000 bags have been made and sold for $6,500.00 (or ten cents each). A very handsome sum for native female industry. It is but justice to remark that most of this labor has been performed by females connected with the Kaumakapili Church in Honolulu. During the first year the females contributed about $400.00 toward the erection of their house of worship. The natives in other parts of the islands are following their example.

N. B. The quantity of bags required of the Koloa plantation for the current year will exceed fifteen thousand.

It is not for our interest at this point to carry on the figures to show the present-day enormous quantities of jute bags from India that long since replaced the woven *lauhala* bags made after Abigail's pattern and instruction. Rather we turn back a page to a rare experience that came to Abigail during the year at Kawaiahao after leaving beloved Ewa. All unconscious of its beauty, Abigail herself has drawn a picture of this "royal" opportunity! Quoting her words:

A Royal Child Some time after we had become accustomed to our new life Her Royal Highness Kinau, then Regent of the realm, brought to me her little son, Alexander Liholiho, and requested me to receive him as a daily pupil. He was but three and a half years old, but was a very bright and intelligent child. The arrangement was that he should come to me every morning with his nurse and spend the whole day, returning home at night. Then followed months of delightful work with this sweet little Prince. I gave him his first knowledge of the English language, and I taught him "the sweet story of old." The dear child grasped knowledge with avidity and delight. He learned rapidly to speak the English language, and we had six happy and profitable months together. At the end of that time Her Royal Highness expressed herself so pleased with his progress that she proposed to us to adopt the child for our own after the custom of the country, and offered to resign him to our sole care and guidance. But the little Prince had already been named as heir to the throne and it was rightly judged that any new arrangement would involve trouble in the court and country. So we had to restore the dear child to his natural guardians, and the establishment of the Royal School a few months afterwards provided him with all the educational advantages he required. But our hearts followed him with tender love through all his years as prince and king, and he called us "father and mother" for many a day.

This last is a comforting thought for the King as well as for his teachers, since Kinau, his good Queen-Mother, passed away in 1839.

Abigail's intense interest in children flowers in many sentiments expressed by herself at different times. For example:

Love of children is the strongest passion of my nature, and teaching is my normal condition. . . . It was a glad day for me when I gathered my first group of Hawaiian boys and girls about me, and met the little dusky faces raised to mine, as wide awake and eager as were the children in the far away home land.

Love of Children

She would agree with the psalmist that "children are an heritage of the Lord" and "happy is the man that hath his quiver full of them." But, oh, when the arrows are spent and the quiver is empty! One realizes that Abigail, who as a child wept from loneliness when only five or six were at home, must have had a peculiar capacity for suffering for her dead children, yet no rebellious murmur seems to have escaped her. Yearning for her own, she wrote her eldest brother in 1845:

I hear of "Bro. John A.'s promising daughters" and "our smart nephew Frederic" quite often. Still it would afford me much more pleasure if some of those smart and promising children would report themselves to me. I want to know what they are doing from year to year, how much they attend school, and with what books they are conversant, and a thousand other things. We have had five little children—but one only is spared to us. She is a fine healthy little girl almost 18 months old. She is just weaned. She is quite forward—talks a good deal—is ever busy. She is doing her best to help me write this letter—to which end she has not ceased to interrupt me about twice a minute from its commencement. Her name is Emma Louisa and she bears some resemblance to our dear little sister Arethusa. . . . I think the letter would have been better written, but for my little Emma's attempts at assistance. She has been in my lap pulling the sheets about, to her liking. You will think her not well brought up.

Here is a record of nearly that date written by Emma herself in later years.

In one corner of our pleasant yard was a small white enclosure filled with large bushes of pink and white four o'clocks. This was a daily resort. When a little over two years old I was made to understand that beneath the flowers lay the bodies of three little brothers and one little sister, whose spirits were transplanted to fairer gardens ere I first drew breath. The next day I spent my visit to the flowers in digging with my little hands in the dirt and finally going heartbroken and weary to mother with the information that I had been digging and digging and could not find them. . . . Three months after I was

awakened one night to find a bright light in the room. There was more or less disturbance and upon acquainting my parents with the fact of my wakefulness, Father took me out of my little trundle bed and placed me in Mother's bed. There I saw a small black head and a little bundle of flannel which I was informed was a little sister. Only the promise of a longer visit "the first thing in the morning" induced me to return to my trundle bed. That early visit was faithfully made and I can remember the little thrill I experienced that it was *our baby to keep always*. I had forgotten the little enclosure of four o'clocks.

There was an addition to our house soon after in the form of a large commodious bedroom or nursery. I chiefly recall the taking possession part, the intense interest accompanying the placing of my bed and bureau in the new room, the accomodation for playthings etc.

Then followed a long period of happy times. The little sister was on her feet and we were little girls together. The twin dolls —their wardrobe so amply supplied by Mother—the plays— going a visiting—keeping house under umbrellas in different corners of the room—disciplining our dolls—riding in the little cart—all come thronging thick and fast. I cannot remember any quarrels with that little sister—she at least was amiable— generous to a fault. But Baby Ellen's feet soon joined the others under the four o'clocks.

This baby sister seemed near and dear to Emma through- out her life span of seventy-six years. In her young ladyhood she wrote a poem to Ellen, full of longing for the compan- ionship she missed. In her journal, begun in the Nuuanu cottage home at six years of age, of which much more anon, she repeatedly tells of visits to the little graves that were still down at the old home in Kaumakapili. For instance:

. . . September 15th, 1850. This morning we rode to town. *Little* Mama and I carried some fresh flowers to lay on the little *Green Beds* graves of my dear little brothers and sisters. . . . December 10th. This is the day on which my sweet little sister Ellen died. She has been gone from us two years. They have been years of sorrow to us and of Joy to her. We loved her very much and if we did not hope to meet her again in Heaven our hearts would break. I wish I may be as gentle and lovely as she was.

Following the lead of little Emma we have run several years ahead of our story. But the subjects of her thought intimate much that had consumed the vitality of Abigail. The repeated illnesses and resulting debility of her first five years in the Islands had made her physicians warn her that she probably could not bear a living child.

But on July 2, 1841, Lowell recorded:

The birth of a son. . . . Fair prospect that both the mother and child will do well. The Lord has been better to us than our fears on this occasion. Doubtless the Lord had good and wise reasons for bereaving us of our first and second sons and we hope and pray that he is giving us the third in mercy and loving kindness. We now sustain a new relation in life, that of parents.

May we be faithful to our trust and both dedicate and train up this child for the Lord Jesus Christ.

Little Lowell   Four months and a half later Abigail wrote delightedly of the stout, healthy happy baby—jumping, kicking, and laughing by her side. But in August, 1842, she wrote her family:

More than three months have passed during which time I have been trying to summon fortitude to tell you my tale of woe. . . . It seems strange sometimes that in all this wide world, death could not have found a victim among the abandoned, the nuisances to society but that he must enter our dwelling and take our one only little darling treasure who can be so illy spared. . . . But hush every murmur. Death was commissioned by one infinitely wise and good. . . . I can never describe to you the glow that lit up that little animated face. . . . Strangers would mark him from among a number. . . . Every one said "What a picture of health!" But at the same time they said "What a heavenly expression his eyes have" and then would caution me not to love him too fondly. . . . I take pleasure in recalling the exercises of my mind on his account, the night of his birth. He was given to my joyful heart at nine o'clock in the evening. I never closed my eyes in sleep all that night. I devoted the time to prayer for my new born babe. . . . The covenant established between God and believing parents suddenly opened to my view, with a vividness and freshness of a first impression. It was as if I had never heard of it before. . . . I laid my precious child in the arms of my Redeemer . . . and peace, such as I had felt many years ago when I yielded my own heart to him, took possession of my soul. . . . When praying for him I used almost always to find myself calling him *Thy little child* instead of *my little child*. . . . I tried to hold him with a loose hand to feel that he was only a lent blessing. But alas! my heart is strangely prone to excess in its affections. . . . O I was too happy.

After giving her parents many examples of little Lowell's intelligence, sensitiveness, and discrimination she added:

. . . He was very fond of cheerful music but mournful or plaintive tunes would make the tears stream down his little cheeks, as if his little sensitive heart would break. We used to be obliged to carry him out of meeting when such tunes were sung. While I carefully guarded his little nerves from all sudden shocks, I at the same time endeavored to strengthen them by gradually accustoming him to things that were at first unpleasant, for I know how many such things he must meet in life if he lived. It really seemed as if he understood my wishes . . . for by the time he was six months old, he evidently made an effort to overcome his feelings. It used to affect me very much to observe him when listening to music, while his eyes were full of tears, and his lip and chin quivering, make an effort to force a laugh, and in this way regain his self-possession. One of our physicians of much practice, told me he never heard of a similar case—and thought it most extraordinary.

Having cut six teeth and begun to walk and talk before he was ten months old, although seemingly well and strong, he sickened and died in three days, many other little children both native and foreign dying about the same time.

The next year after little Lowell's passing brought a day which, as we already know, recorded the birth and death of a first daughter. Would the cradle never rock?

The passing of these little children, cared for to the best of existing knowledge, also the testimony of an old sampler on which a hundred years ago a little girl cross-stitched the many births and deaths of her brothers and sisters in their New England home, points the long road we have come from large proportions of infant mortality. Still we must cry, with the singer of *In Memoriam*, "Let knowledge grow from more to more!"

Infant Mortality

A glad year, the next, was coming. Little Emma Louisa, destined in health and joy long to outlive her parents, their constant comfort and joy, was to be born on June the fourth, 1844, at half-past seven in the morning.

Memorable day! There have been some rather alarming symptoms about the babe. Still we think she has a pretty fair prospect of surviving. We have been bereaved so many times that we hold this precious new gift with a loose hand—we know not the hour when it may be called for again. The Lord be

praised for his goodness thus far. . . . For the last two or
three weeks Abba has been gathering strength for this day. May
we not forget our mercies and obligations for favours received
whether they be removed immediately or otherwise. Mrs. Thurston and Mrs. Wood were with us. Dr. Wood the physician.

Oh, the never to be forgotten kindnesses of all pioneer
women for each other! But oh, the thankfulness due from
women today for the aseptic surgery, the clinical care before
and after childbirth, and the ameliorating circumstances of
delivery, that ignorance, and even false modesty, prevented
in earlier days!

Legend has it that one of the dear assisting sisters, against
the remonstrances of the often-bereaved parents, deliberately
kept this newborn infant in the trade wind from an open
window. Legend says also that after unavailing objections
Lowell sat beside Abigail's bed saying:

. . . If this child is taken it will be not by the will of God but
by the will of Sister So-and-so.

To Mrs. Gideon Tenney

Honolulu, Sand. Isles.
Aug. 23, 1847.

My Beloved Mother,

Walking in the Furnace

My heart is oppressed with sadness as I . . . think how very
long a time has passed away without your receiving a line from
me. I fear you have had the heart ache too from the same cause.
I was not *able* to write a letter during all the past year. The
principal one I *did* write was to yourself dear Mother—and was
written a year ago. . . . I was six weeks about it and it was
well filled with *family items*—just what I knew you would wish
to hear about—and when I forwarded it, I felt much pleasure in
reflecting that all my dear friends would hear from me through
that. Well, I know you have never received that letter.—It has
doubtless made its bed among the treasures of the deep. *I would*
it were the most valuable part of that vessel's freight—but alas!
many precious lives must have perished also. . . . The vessel
never arrived in China and has never been heard from. . . . I

must leave her there and her passengers, some of them who were
our warm friends, in the hands of a righteous God—and hasten
on with my present communication. As I shall not be able to
recapitulate, you must lose about a year of *items*. Well I was
sick . . . miserably so almost all last year. . . . At the time of
my confinement I was mere *skin* and *bones*. I had not been able
for nine months to make one tolerable meal . . . and was confined to my couch almost all the time. How wonderful that
everything should turn out well at last. . . . I cannot express
my surprise and gratitude to find our *little youngest daughter
dear*, a healthy vigorous child, although it must be confessed
there was little on her bones, save *skin*. . . . The little darling
is now five months old, . . . has never had a sick day.

Our hearts were full of gratitude when we found ourselves
the parents of two living healthy children—and myself more
comfortable than usual. Still we remembered the *past*. . . . I
could adopt the language of Job and say "I was not at *ease*,
yet trouble came." Husband had been a good deal worn down
for some months, and greatly needed relaxation . . . impossible
to obtain. . . . About the time of my confinement an abdominal
disease broke out among our people—so that husband had his
hands and heart full by day and by night. He soon began to feel
ill himself, but still omitted none of his multifarious labors. One
morning he administered to twenty five sick persons before
breakfast, besides the care of myself and children—but nature
could endure no more. He was prostrated himself that day with
the prevailing epidemic. A dreadful fever—agonizing pain, . . .
violent cough. . . . He was immediately taken from my sight—
to our *spare room*, . . . a *separate little* house across the yard.
. . . For ten or twelve days it was extremely doubtful whether
he would ever leave that room alive. He required the most careful nursing—*but there are no nurses in these parts. I* was in bed
with a newborn infant. The mission families and others took
turns, in staying with him, so that his nurses were changed
twice every twenty four hours. Oh! the agony! . . . I would
think of *so many things* that ought to be done, and wonder if
those who took care of him would think of them too. . . . It
rained and *blew* all the time. . . . The Lord *frowned*, and hid his
face, but I know he was behind the cloud. . . . I went and laid

myself and helpless family down at his feet, and then nerved myself to meet what might be sent. O how precious to feel at such a time a *child-like trust* in the blessed Savior. It was . . . my only support during a fortnight of the greatest trial I have yet been called to pass through. Husband had never been sick before—and would never allow me to make any preparation for such an event. Therefore while lying on my couch I had to superintend and aid in the cutting and making of six long bed shirts—five flannel wrappers and a double gown. Then the danger lest his clothes should be put on damp. . . . I would have every article of clothing carried to the kitchen and thoroughly aired and warmed then brought to my bed for inspection —and finally wrapped . . . and sent out through the rain, with a prayer—that He who tempers the wind to the shorn lamb, would ward off the storm, and aid our poor efforts for his restoration. At the end of a week I felt that I could endure the separation no longer and he expressed an earnest wish to see me. It was very early in the morning—the watchers had gone—and no friend had come in for the day—it *rained* as usual—but I was wrapped up in a cloak—and our man servant carried me out in his arms. *Never* if I live a *century*—shall I lose the impression of that dreadful morning! *What a change* disease had wrought in that loved form! But . . . I had presence of mind to prevent any exhibition of the . . . tumult . . . tearing my heart piecemeal. As I held his fluttering pulse in my hand, . . . I spoke cheerfully . . . of his recovery, and I received the directions he gave me concerning some of his papers—accounts etc. in a very matter-of-course way—although I *felt* as if I was receiving his *last will and testament*. But I was unused to practice such duplicity—and pleading my fear of fatiguing him, and a promise to be brought again . . . I was carried back to my little helpless charge. . . . I looked upon my children as fatherless! But I will not dwell upon the agony. . . . My husband began slowly to amend from that day. . . . Kindness and sympathy abounded on every hand. . . . In three weeks . . . we became once more a *united family*. Oh! what a gratitude filled our hearts. It was three months before he was able to commence preaching again, and he has not yet regained his former vigor. He is now absent . . . for the benefit of his health . . . on the

Island Molokai—the place where we commenced our missionary work. . . . He has been absent three weeks and writes me that he feels much better. . . .

August 28th. . . . The first homeward-bound whale ship for the season sails today—and I am very desirous of getting this on board so I shall *hasten* its close. . . . My dear husband has returned home, and is considerably improved in health. . . . There is good prospect that he may be again strong and active in the work of the Lord here—But he has already labored fifteen years—and of course we must not expect the vigor of youth to return,—and it is very sweet to hope that when our work here is quite finished, we shall be permitted to put immortal vigor on—and serve in Heaven. I hesitated about giving you any account of his illness beyond some general allusions I so dread your grieving on our account. But finally I thought a record of it should be had by my friends. Those of them who love God will recognize in it a *father's* dealings. It is through *much* tribulation we are to enter into the kingdom. . . . It was very grateful . . . to witness the . . . sympathy and interest manifested . . . *by all classes of foreign residents*. . . . I never before fully realized how much *he was respected* even by those who dislike missionaries in general. . . .

The disease from which he suffered has made great ravages among this poor people. I have time for no particulars. The children are importuning me. Husband is engaged in the removal of a sick friend—and is not at home.

In Lowell's Station Letter to the board in May, 1848, he tells of his serious illness the year before and of his recuperation on Molokai where, he said he was

healed by pleasant associations, riding fleet horses, daily bathing in cold water, running up and down some of the palis and bountiful, sumptuous living.

His revival of health and good spirits were immediately taxed on his return by the nursing of the brother missionary Richards, his death in Lowell's house, and the subsequent care of the bereaved family and arrangements for their departure to America.

Perhaps we who turn the pages of this volume are minded

to pass over much of this abbreviated letter as still too doleful if we are enjoying the fulness of life. Or if we think life is drab for us, we may wish instead something diverting and enlivening, but if we would know Lowell and Abigail we must go with them into their darkness as into their sunshine. Two months later Abigail could touch a lighter tone on life's harp. Naturally, her letters to her dearest must describe her life at home. This one says:

"Joy Cometh in the Morning"

October 21st, 1847. My hands are now very full—my strength never great. The two daughters dear are always by. They have nobody but their parents with whom they can be left with safety. I never leave them alone with my native domestics—although many of these poor people have obtained as we trust the grace by which their souls may be saved—they have as yet learned but few of the proprieties of life. Conversation that would shock a refined ear is common with them, and their perceptions of right on many subjects are very dim. . . . We have a pleasant yard with shrubbery and flowers—where Emma can run and play to her heart's content, and little Ellen is drawn about it in her little wagon. They are always delighted when other children come to play with them.

Little Emma

Inclosed in this, was a letter which Abigail wrote as from the three-year-old Emma.

My dear cousin Charlie,

You don't know how delighted I am to know that I have so many relatives in America. It is a good many months now since Mamma began to tell me about them, and teach me their names. At first I was quite puzzled to know what the terms "Grandpapa, Grandmama, Uncle, Aunt and Cousin" meant. However, I soon comprehended them. I was the longest learning "Aunt" and I asked Mamma if my "Aunts" in America were like the "Ants in our kitchen and store room—which bite us so sadly." I was very happy to learn that they were quite different. Now I understand you all pretty well—and know your names. I want to see you very much. I often ask Papa and Mamma to take me to America. Now here comes a long stick of sugar cane for me. If you were here we would have a good time. You see it is six or eight feet long—of a red and green color—striped. It is

rather larger round than a man's wrist and jointed every four
or five inches. We will have several of these joints cut off, the
bark stripped off, and then cut into pieces the size of a man's
fingers. Here is a plate full. We will sit down and eat it. You see
it is very juicy and sweet. Swallow the juice only and throw
the refuse into this basket. Be careful and not clutter it over the
matting on the floor as Mamma is very particular and we should
have it all to pick up again. . . . You are younger than I and
have hardly begun to learn little hymns and passages of scripture yet. I have learned a few and can read Boy—Pig—Egg
and a few other words. I hope we shall both learn a great many
good things and grow up to be very useful in the world. Please
write me very soon. . . . You see the "*salutation is in my own
hand*" just as the Apostle Paul's used to be. I suppose you can
decipher my "hieroglyphics" as well as any one else. So good-
bye—dear Charlie.

Thus did Abigail play with Joy when that coveted spirit *Playing*
came to be her companion, and with what maternal pride must *with Joy*
she have folded away the following lines, which evidently accompanied a gift:

With many thanks for your kindness in permitting me to secure a feeble shadow of a true emblem of—innocence, truth, and
loveliness—I would present this to little Emma, and it will ever
be a source of gratification to me, though I may dwell far away
in a foreign clime.

> Still may thou shield her trusting breast
> From each approach of care
> And calmly lull each grief to rest
> Should e'er such enter there

May her life ever be as peaceful and sweet as it is now.

With respect
P. GOODFELLOW

Now, what may it have been, a water-color sketch, a lost
daguerreotype?

In these happy days Abigail delighted in fine needlework,
the only adornment she could afford, on the garments of her
children. She begged from the Mission Depository a few

yards of pink or blue calico, if it was to be had, rather than the apportioned amount, family by family (whether girls or boys) of brown calico by the bolt. In after years, dainty as was her handiwork for her grandchildren, she mourned the failing eyesight that forbade invisible hemming or fagoting of spider-web texture.

Alas, that her song of happy motherhood accompanying her needle so soon flowed into the minor key! Upon little Ellen's death, Abigail exclaimed:

Looking
Upward

   . . . My five precious babes have all died again in my sweet Ellen! . . . I should have sunk but . . . have deeply felt my responsibility as a *suffering Christian* as well as a *bereaved mother.* . . . Looking unto Jesus will just express to you what I have done. *I daily, hourly, constantly look upward.* . . . My sweet children are not dead.

After months of weary struggle to live up to her ideals and finding gradual improvement in her well-nigh shattered health, Abigail writes to the niece, who though much younger was to be one of her dearest friends throughout her life:

   Emma is now six and a half years old. . . . She has regular studies daily and makes good progress. We take the "Youth's Companion" and "Well Spring" for her.

Children's
Reading

   You and S. J. have doubtless made great progress in your studies since we last heard from you. I think you are about thirteen and S. J. eighteen or nineteen. . . . Tell me particularly what studies you have become familiar with—and a good many of the books you have read. S. J. has probably read a good deal of biography, and considerable history and some philosophical and scientific works. I want you should both give much attention to the Natural Sciences and learn to draw skillfully and tastefully. Are you going to be teachers? Tell me all about yourselves. You cannot be too minute. I feel a lively interest in all my young nieces and nephews.

To an older student she wrote:

   How I should enjoy these readings, lectures, etc. That one on "Ancient Egypt" and the one on "Michael Angelo," they are

ABIGAIL AND EMMA

1850

both favorite subjects. How these rich privileges must expand your mind, by giving it a wider range of thought and filling it with useful information.

Again:

Did you ever witness a total eclipse of the Sun? We had one here on the eighth of August last. The scene was sublime. The Sun was entirely obscured for six minutes. We had taken great pains to prepare the natives for this phenomenon, as they have always supposed it to be a forerunner of some dire calamity. Should any great calamity befall the nation within a year—I doubt not that great numbers of the people would believe the eclipse to be the cause of it. *Science vs. Superstition*

This mention of the eclipse has an echo in little Emma's journal.

August 8th, 1850. Yesterday was a wonderful day. There was a total eclipse of the sun. It was more than two hours from the commencement to the close of it and for six minutes we did not see the sun at all. It was very grand. We saw Venus and Jupiter and Mars besides several stars. There were some rockets fired which we saw very plainly. It was quite dark in the house and we lighted a lamp. The fouls seemed very much surprised and some of them went to bed and some stood still until the sun appeared. *Little Emma's Echo*

This quotation and Abigail's letter preceding it were written at Nuuanu Cottage whither our story has now arrived.

2. NUUANU COTTAGE

Early in 1843 with the aid of their church people Lowell and Abigail had

. . . built a comfortable little cottage in the refreshing valley of Nuuanu for residence during the hot summer months. It is a beautiful location, commanding a delightful prospect of the mountains of Honolulu and the shipping, and is also within the bounds of the parish. *Nuuanu Valley*

They had tasted the benefits of brief sojourns during the hottest part of the year at a mission retreat no more than a mile and a half distant from Kaumakapili, yet having a position that received more freely the draft of the trade wind.

This life-giving wind, *Makani mau*, cool, moist, constant, beloved wind, bringing the great cumulus clouds across the Pacific, moors them as treasure ships on the Koolau Range. Thence by innumerable waterfalls the precious cargo is flung, a largess to the woodland gods, a libation for Nuuanu's loving-cup valley.

In Nuuanu, today, trolley, automobile, and subdivisions of land make a greater valley accessible and eagerly sought. The rolling greenswards of the spacious Country Club, the sightly dwellings, well-planned roads, and the quickly grown gardens with trees from many lands, chosen and planted with taste and judgment, denote great gain in the appreciation of beauty among our islanders. But, developed or undeveloped by the hand of man, the lure of Nuuanu is of old; and it will last through the life of the senses. If no one dared whisper to the missionary songs of gods and goddesses frequenting the mountains, to whom many a vine, flower, and fern are sacred, if stories of the faithful and clever *menehune* (legendary dwarfs) and lyrics of forty thousand godlings were denied their ears and imaginations, still, to Lowell and Abigail, the winds sang, violet mountains, delighting their eyes, were changed to mauve, blue, green, or were snatched from sight by the rain; and, as they watched, waterfalls leaped—some of them never to reach the earth but, touched by the wind's wand, to fly upward to the clouds.

Nuuanu Cottage The original Nuuanu Cottage consisted of two rooms of adobe, the steep, brooding roof suggesting the line of the aboriginal huts and wearing, first, thatch and, later, shingles put on by the missionary owner, who must now and again be his own carpenter. The accompanying print from a photograph taken by the first grandson is more eloquent than words in reproducing the cottage, but the additions in wood at the back or sides, made one at a time through the years, are to be imagined rather than seen. The five-foot veranda running around the parlor and sitting-room did not seem

narrow to the grandchildren, and the narrower border of
flowers beyond the white veranda rail still holds in memory
coral and pink begonia, lady-slipper, scarlet plumbago,
lemon verbena, and amaryllis that the New England mistress
loved to call crocus.

One detached room gave Lowell a study redolent of pain-
killer and molasses, and grandchildren's eyes in time were to
know perfectly the geography of the long shelves and just
where stood the glass jar holding the coveted gum arabic,
that pale amber so good to chew and letting you make believe
you were grown up and had real fillings in your teeth! Out
of the great pine desk Grandpa had made himself would come
paper and pencil so that now you could cease from troubling
and "run away to see Mamma."

Near it stood the spareroom, later a schoolroom. Three
bedrooms had gradually joined themselves to the original
structure and a long lean-to pantry, painted blue lead color
inside, never coveted ice, even after its days of island manufacture made it purse-possible, for the Nuuanu draft
through the slatted window blew over the milk pans and
butter bowl and the porous Mexican "monkey" that held
drinking water. Across a "lobby" of bricks was the cookhouse with a dining-room one side, and the other, a storeroom of odds and ends, among them the andirons used in the
kitchen before the day of stoves. Still beyond was the bath-
house, the tub being a small homemade cistern of cement sunk
in the ground. How cold that water was! From the dining-
room steep stairs climbed to more chambers that looked out to
the blue mountains and the Pali, or over the tiny harbor and
the offing once crowded for months at a time with wintering
whale ships.

It was, of course, on account of the great number of sailors   *Bethel*
in this port for considerable portions of each year that the
Seamen's Bethel came into being. This was in 1833, the year
Lowell and Abigail arrived at the Islands—one of their fellow passengers, Rev. John Diell, being the first Seamen's
Chaplain. Under "Father Damon"—the Rev. S. C. Damon,
whose wife was a relative of that Samuel Mills of missionary
fame, referred to in earlier pages—the Bethel Church was

organized in which, listening to preaching in the English
language, many residents came into pleasant relations with
visiting sailors. After the whaling population disappeared
the Bethel Church remained. In 1887, this, the first foreign
church erected this side the American continent, united with
the younger Fort Street Church to form the well-known
Central Union Church.

Emma's
Journal

One idea after another has led us wandering down the hill
and away in time from Nuuanu Cottage! Before Lowell and
Abigail built the additions described that came gradually
with the years, or the mango and tamarind trees that stand in
the garden—long outliving the old cottage—begin to attain
their mature growth, or Emma, at sixteen, climbs her good-
bye-to-childhood-climb in the old koa tree, let us look into
two slim copy books that have survived the years to some
purpose.

One of them has a blue paper cover decorated with a
spread eagle holding the American flag, which boasts but
twenty-four stars; the other, a gold-spangled cover of yellow
paper. On the flyleaf of the first is inscribed, in a hand that
suggests the father's holding the child's, "Emma's Journal
Book, June 4th 1850." Turning a page we find inscribed in
her own writing, with no overhand:

This is my birthday—I am six years old. . . . June 5: I have
just finished arranging Mamma's button drawer.

The little author has intrigued us. Perhaps we shall finish
the notebooks at a sitting.

June 16, Sweet Sabbath day, lovely morning. This is the day
that Jesus Arose from the dead. Look to Jesus.

June 29, We Brought a Stream of water in our yard today.
And I took off my shoes and paddled in the water which
Pleased me much we were much delighted to see it run. Then
papa built up the wall but left a little Place to let the water run
through. I have learned my Sabbath school lessons today.

Going to
Church

July 20: Sweet Sabbath Holy day. I think mamma will let
me go to Church today with Papa but I dont know. Perhaps she
will not let me go today. 3 P.M. I did go to church Mamma did

let me go. I thought she would not let me go. But she did let me go to church.

We can picture the small and very dignified maiden, put on her honor to sit still, opening the gate of the family pew and sitting demurely, the sole occupant, while Papa in the high pulpit stands behind the big Bible and "holds his hearers for an hour or so." Perhaps she is admiring her handmade pantalettes with Mamma's exquisite stitches or patting her skirts out to make them as wide as Mamma's and wondering how long she must wait to have them touch the floor. Perhaps she counts the congregation by way of pastime. Probably she makes sure to remember the text to tell Mamma so that she may be trusted again to play-lady alone in the high-backed inclosure—so like a playhouse!

August 1, I had a holiday yesterday. I had a nice school today. There was a soiree at the palace last evening. But I did not attend.

Although she acknowledges playing "in the mud which was very wrong," there is no evidence that such a lapse from propriety was the cause of the six-year-old's absence from the ball! Nor were other joys lacking for:

August 12, Mamma is making a pair of red shoes for my dolly today.

August 16, yesterday Gussie came and spent the day with me. We had a nice school and a nice play. In the afternoon Mary Ellen came down and Played with us.

> We were as happy as qweens
> In magnificent bowers
> As we skipped o'er the fields
> And gathered bright flowers.

August 21, A few days since I received a very nice letter from Mr Hawley and a present of a beautiful little Accordeon. I have learned to play One little tune on it and mamma plays me to sleep every night.

August 25, Mamma and I are going to make a little flower garden and Gussy Judd has promised us some seeds and roots.

August 27, I have learned to play another tune on my accordeon. yesterday I wrote a little letter to Libbie Judd about our dahlias and she sent me a reply today. To sprinkle some salt on the roots which will protect them from the ants.

September 13. We made a short call at Mrs. Halls, and I helped Kitty fly her kite.

September 17. This morning Mrs. Montague's Canary escaped from its cage and lighted on a tree close by our house where it sang very sweetly. It was a long time before they could persuade it to enter the cage again.

September 18. My mamma is making guava jelly today. It is a very warm day indeed.

September 20. Yesterday afternoon we went into town and after making a call on Mrs. Paty we went to Mrs. John Ladd's and drank tea and passed the evening. We enjoyed it very much. Eddy and I had a grand play. Mrs. Patterson and Doctor Hoffman played beautifully on the piano. We rode home in the moonlight and I fell asleep in Mr. Fuller's arms.

Little Emma might have been surprised if told that evening that one day when grown up and married she would be a near neighbor of Dr. Hoffman and would delight in playing duets with that musician.

The Stars   November 6. My lessons are very interesting these days. I find that Jupiter is twelve hundred times larger than the earth and the largest of all the planets. Herschel is 84 years in going round the sun. Saturn has seven moons and a broad ring. Mercury is the smallest planet and nearest the sun. Mars is very red and fiery. Venus is very bright and beautiful. I often see her in the evening.

November 12. Tomorrow Sammy Damon is coming up with his parents and Aunty and little brother. I love them all very much. I mean to teach Sammy some little sums in Addition.

November 18. I am learning to draw a little but have not done much yet. Fanny Paty can draw very nicely. I wish I could do as well. I have a very interesting Sabbath School book this week. Our horse has eaten down two beautiful morning glories.

December 3. . . . Mamma is sick to day I am taking care of

her besides learning my lessons. I have also been up to Mrs. Andrews on an errand.

December 4. Yesterday I spent the afternoon with Gussy. Her sisters can swim. I saw them. . . . This is Mammas birth day. It is a bright and lovely morning. One of our rose bushes has given us four roses.

January 1, 1851. Today is New Years and I have had a good many presents. One was a little bag and one was a Journal book and one was a fortuneteller and another were some coral beads. . . .

January 2, We had a beautiful sunset last evening and a lovely dawn this morning. . . . The gardens and fields look green and fresh. Our cook has been sick but is better now. I am nearly through my school for today. Then I am going up to call on Fanny and Sissy. I have had a whole week of holidays and commenced my school today.

January 9. . . . A few days ago we planted some grass cuttings and they are putting forth leaves.

January 13. Yesterday the Gentoo a large merchant vessel arrived from Boston around Cape Horn. She brought several passengers. . . . Papa has gone down to see if there are any letters for us.

January 24. This morning I took a pleasant ride with papa. We went into town and brought up Mr Calkin to spend a day or two with us. He has the asthma quite badly. I have finished my philosophy for the third time.

January 25. Mr. Calkin is better this morning. We have got a nice duck. I put it in a barrel of water and let it swim about. It enjoyed it much.

February 18. . . . There is an American Ship of war and also a Frenchman in our harbor. We have heard that there has been a great eruption of the volcano lately.

February 20. Jump for joy. I am so happy. A man has given me a pretty pair of doves and our servant has made me a nice house for them. It is set on a post under my favorite tree and it is made quite convenient with a door and two windows and a little terrace in front. I shall take good care of my pets and give them food every day and water also. Now my puss—my darling Daisy—you must not harm my doves. You must content your-

"Jump for Joy"

self with catching mice and I will give you many a nice bit from the table.

February 28. Yesterday was the saddest day I saw the ship go out with my dear friends on board and it made me feel so lonely. But I do hope we shall live to meet again. . . . We have had a very severe storm of wind. Several houses were blown down. It is very pleasant and cold now.

March 6. Mary Ladd called to see me this morning and brought me a beautiful little present—a real china coffee sect consisting of a coffee pot, cream pot, two cups and saucers and a bread plate. All very tiny indeed, holding only a few drops at most a teaspoonfool. I am delighted with them. Mary is going to California with her parents. I must make her a parting present.

March 9. A psalm of David.

They that trust in the Lord shall be as mount Zion which cannot be removed but abibeth forever. . . .

March 19. Joy—Joy—another letter from Mr. Hawley. I clap my hands at a great parcel of candy red white and pink. Some in long sticks, some in braids and some fine rock candy. I shall give some to my friends. But what *shall* I send to Mr. Hawley. Mamma must help me contrive something pretty.

March 20. . . . I am making a crib quilt for Buddy Whitney's birthday present. He will be a year old in six day's mour. I must be diligent to finish the quilt. I don't like to sew patchwork very well.

April 1. I have had a very pleasant school today. In my recess I went out and built some little stone walls around our water melons that have just come up to protect them from the wind.

April 24. . . . We have also been sick. Now I have returned to my studies until the Missionaries arrive for General Meeting and then I shall have a vacation for some weeks.

April 25. . . . This is a warm day. Papa is varnishing the furniture.

April 28. Last Friday one of our cows got into a taro patch and was drowned. Her little calf is living. Yesterday we had such a delightful packet of letters from America I had a very long beautiful letter from my dear Uncle Lionel.

April 30. I forgot to mention that our cook house took fire some days ago and we had a great fright. The natives were very kind however, and with papas help soon put it out. We were very thankful that our house was not destroyed.

May 2. Sweet May has come again. The little children in America are abroad gathering wild flowers. We have now in bloom in our little garden the Monthly rose and the hiliotrope and the nasturtion and the verbena and the red lily and the Lady slipper and the trumpet flower and the Marigold—Many seeds have just been planted. *The Garden*

May 7. Yesterday papa took me to the opening of the legislature. The king and queen were richly dressed the officers were in grand uniform there were many finely dressed ladies and soldiers and music. Just at 12 o'clock a salute was fired from fort hill and then the king arose and made his speech. It was all very grand. I wish the Legislature w'uld open every day. *A State Ceremony*

May 9. Yesterday I went with papa to Punahou to attend the examination of the childrens school. There were a great many persons present. I did not stay in the school room much but went with many other little girls and had a fine play on the grass.

June 4. This is my birth day. I am seven years old. God has been very good to me in preserving my life and health. I am now a year older and I ought to be better than ever before. I hope I shall be more useful to mamma and very obedient; and always very kind to all my little friends. Some of them are coming to visit me this afternoon.

June 17. Two or three weeks ago we received dear Granmammas degwerreotype. We were greatly delighted with it. Mamma said it looked quite natural altho she had not seen her for eighteen years. She is eighty years old.

June 20. My dear little bird is dead I am so grieved. Yesterday before commencing my school I carried the cage out in the bright sunshine and placed it on the tamarind enclosure In a little while mamma looked out. and found that the wind had blown it to the ground. We went for it at once but the red ants were biting its little body sadly We bathed it and tried to soothe its pain but could not It died in a few hours. *The Canary*

July 7. Last week I did not have my lessons for two days because our servant was sick and I had to do his work as far as I could. Today I have had my school and hope I shall not be interrupted again. . . .

July 30. Yesterday morning we paid a visit to the new deguerreotype artist and sat for our types. Mamma and I are taken together. They are thought to be correct especially mine. We shall send them to America.

August 2. This is my holiday I have hemmed a towel and played a good deal. Papa is building me a new little bedroom. . . .

August 5. Our cook is sick and Mamma and I have much to do.

August 6. This morning Gussie came up to see me in the midst of my studies of my school. I finished my lessons however and we went out and played together.

August 15. Day before yesterday I went with papa to the exhibition of the Agricultural Society. We saw horses and cattle and wheat and oats and corn and potatoes and fruits and flowers and many other things. Those who had the best things received a premium. It was quite interesting.

Her Little Room

September 9. All my things have been removed into my little room. Besides my little bed I have a wardrobe for my cloths and a small bureau, my desk where I keep my writing materials, a tea poy for any little ornaments a stand on which stands my work box and dressing case a trunk for my toys my dollys bedstead my two little chairs and one other one and a few other things. my books are arranged on the top of my bureau.

Monday, September 15. These are the rules which mamma has made to be observed daily for me in my room. Rise early and pray to my heavenly Father then dress wash and brush then take the clothes from my bed and leave it to air than read my chapter in the Bible and commit my verse to memory then walk out or play in the yard until breakfast time. After breakfast and family worship I finish my bed put my room in order then amuse myself in any way until 9 o'clock when my school commences.

American Fruits

Referring to one of her best friends whose sailing away made her so lonely, little Emma writes:

BETSEY TENNEY
1850

September 17. I suppose Sammy Damon is eating apples with all his might and pears also. He has also eaten peaches and cherries and plums and strawberries and currants and I know not how many other delicious American fruits. I hope he will remember his promise to bring some fresh on the branches for me.

September 18. Yesterday afternoon I went down to see Gussy and staide an hour. They have got a new swing and it is a very nice one. It is in their cellar. We had a very nice time swinging in it.

September 22. Yesterday I attended church with papa and enjoyed it much. Papa cannot attend the English meeting very often because he getting so much fatigued in his native meeting.

October 20. It is a long time since I have written in my journal. The reason is because I have written so many letters to my friends. I am reading Gallandets Youths Natural Theology It is very useful. I read it to mamma. My little namesake Emma Paty is very sick. Yesterday they thought it would not live we were greatly afflicted. Today she is a little better. Sweet precious baby.

October 21.

> Now I have finished my last page
> Come dear mamma and look
> And may I go and ask Papa.
> Please buy me a new book?

Probably the new book was bought by the faithful papa, but either it was neglected after the fashion of journals, young or old, or else it had an apotheosis in the eventual burning of the town house. Emma's only journal extant since this one is her teen-age book, too private, as a teen-age book should be, for the general eye!

Very likely the child journal was abandoned by the little girl who must now be sister-mother to a baby brother. We shall follow her as she goes blithely to her tasks and pleasures, and as, throughout the story, the rooftree of Nuuanu Cottage shall offer grateful shade, so Emma shall accompany us, the light of her parents' eyes.

3. SCHOOLING

Teachers   Shall only one chapter be called schooling when school in
Taught   its large sense is the theme of all the chapters, the woof of all
the warp, weaving, now light threads, now heavy, now bright
colors, now somber? Yes, before "the book may close over and
all the lessons are said" we repeatedly enter terms of schooling with our Lowell and Abigail, but this chapter alone shall
bear the name of the refrain occurring and recurring in the
dear lives that from youth to age taught and were taught.

Emma's baby brother, born five weeks after the close of
her "Journal Book," was Augustus Lowell. He was to grow
from an exceedingly delicate childhood to a frail span of
forty years and to pass out a few months after his marriage
and closely following the death of his father. In a letter dated
November 27, 1852, Abigail refers to him thus:

The Baby   Our precious baby is now cutting his teeth and I wish to take
Brother   great care of him. Then there are Emma's lessons to be attended to, for I do not yet send her to school, and all my housekeeping besides. So I do little in the way of letter writing.

Longing to have her best friends know each other, Abigail
writes to her husband's niece:

. . . As you generally spend your summers in the country I
want to have you go next summer to West Cummington and
pass the warm season with my dear friends. You have only to
tell them *who you are*—and they will take you to their hearts.
The place is in the "hill country" about like Heath I "guess,"
(for I was never there). My excellent brother-in-law is wearing
out a precious life to lead a little flock of Christ's followers
Betsey   along the path of holiness. You would love him and my dear
Tenney   eldest sister very much—and Mother—why she is one of the
Again   loveliest old ladies that ever lived, precisely such a grandmamma
as you like. My brothers who idolize her write me that she is one
of the *handsomest ladies in the country*. She already numbers
fourscore years—you must go.

For news, she writes:

. . . The number of whale ships in port is unusually large. I do not remember the exact number, but at least 200. Altho' there were some 4, or 5,000 sailors in the place—our city continued very quiet (notwithstanding the grog shops) until one of the constables killed a sailor who was confined in the fort for drunkenness and disorderly conduct in the streets. I suppose he did not intend to kill him, but he was most culpably careless—to say the least. He was at once arrested and placed in close confinement, to await the new sitting of the Superior Court. But "Jack" was not satisfied, and a large posse of them came on shore and attempted the establishment of "lynch law." For one night the mob ruled the place. The Governor could very easily have subdued it by turning out the native soldiers—but it was thought best to try mild measures at first—but after the mob had burned three houses and threatened vengeance on all the Government Officers—their captains trying in vain to get them on board ship—the natives were permitted to go forth into the streets where the mob were "*promenading*" and seize every one his man—and in this way some 50 seamen were speedily placed in custody—and quiet and order once more restored to our good town—and resumed their peaceful sway. . . .

You must excuse this poor little letter. If postage was high I would not send it. (Probably 7¢) in that case you would get nothing until I could write more and better. . . .

In December, 1853, Abigail wrote to two nieces:

When your letters reached us we were passing through a scene of suffering and woe with our poor people—unparalleled in our experience. The smallpox was here and was literally slaying its thousands. This is the first time this terrible scourge ever visited these islands, but the missionaries have for many years labored to protect the entire population by general vaccination. Thousands have been thus protected—but vast numbers could not easily be persuaded to take sanitary precautions against a disease they had never experienced, so multitudes were found entirely unprotected, and fell a speedy prey to this awful pestilence. As it raged dreadfully—and in fact—commenced in our part of the town—we had our full share of exposure—and of labors among the sick and dying. For three or four months the

greater part of our time was employed in attending to the sick
—preparing food—carrying it to them—and in some instances
putting it into their mouths. I did not go myself from house to
house because we could not both go without taking the children
and besides the constant call of the friends of the sick, and of
those having the early symptoms of the disease rendered it
necessary for one of us to be at home. But no tongue can describe the sufferings of those months—whole families would be
prostrated at a time, with, perhaps, no one to attend upon them
but your uncle. We prepared gallons of food daily and sent and
carried it around—and so did many others—but there was a
great amount of unrelieved suffering after all. Between three
and four hundred of the members of our church fell victims to
this awful scourge and we mourn for the multitude of familiar
faces we behold no more. It was appalling to think that we
might take this loathsome disease but we early lost all dread of
it in our deep sympathy for our smitten flock. Both your uncle
and myself have suffered very much in health by long and continued contact with the disease—and he is still quite poorly in
health although improving now. I have been greatly concerned
about him.

This "concern" of Abigail's for her husband had been of
long duration, for in 1847, after two years of considering the
wisdom of a furlough, she had written an account of his excessive and unremitting toil for twelve years, adding:

. . . I doubt not it would prolong his life many years could
he now revisit our native land and recruit for a year. Were it
not that public opinion in the church is so strongly opposed to
missionaries returning home for a little season, I think he would
do so soon. I have offered to remain here and help along the
work during his absence if he might but go.

Tired   . . . He needs a change of scene and air very much. Not less
than five thousand have died on this one island during the past
summer. The disease was slow in passing to the other islands of
the group, thus mercifully giving the people time to protect
themselves by vaccination. As so many of the laboring class
have died, the price of labor has risen so high that *we* cannot
afford to keep needful "help" so we are performing domestic

drudgery now which no foreigners can do with any comfort in a tropical climate. We are very *tired* all the time, but we hope and pray for brighter days. Our dear children have been preserved in health through all this season of trial, for which we cannot be sufficiently thankful.

Nine-year-old Emma remembered all her life helping keep the fires going and ladling soup through the window.

Emma is going forward with her studies, and with music and drawing. Her little brother is two years old and has just attained to the dignity of pantalets, for which he feels very grand and thinks he is about as big as papa. He is a very darling little boy, having . . . soft delicate complexion, clear blue eyes, golden hair and little cunning aquiline nose which belong to your Grandpapa's family. . . .

Emma

Could you conveniently send for Emma a few pieces of well chosen pianoforte music—suitable for a learner. She has a good talent for music—we wish to cultivate it, not for a showy accomplishment, but that it may increase her usefulness and aid her in obtaining her livelihood if need be hereafter.

Later years of need proved the wisdom of Emma's mother.

Abigail's next letter is addressed to Betsey Learned, who with her husband and his parents had made themselves as own kin to Lowell and his bride while they awaited in New London the sailing of the *Mentor*. Besides picturing missionary life under new difficulties, it throws light upon that much-discussed subject, the "Missionary and the land in Hawaii." We quote the letter at length.

NUUANU COTTAGE, Feb. 1, 1854.

MY VERY DEAR SISTER:

Your letter so full of hope, of sympathy and of substantial aid was received about a month ago. I shall never be able to tell you how like a *heavenly messenger* it was to our desponding hearts. It came to us in *our darkest days* and lifted a weight of anxiety and care from our hearts which was truly crushing us. When I wrote to dear Mama [Learned] we were in the *furnace* along with our beloved people and there we continued until we laid four hundred of our church in the grave—all save twenty-

After Effects

After the
Scourge

five died of the smallpox. Through the great mercy of our God we and our children escaped the disease—but not entirely the consequences of our long continued exposure to the virulent influence. Husband, after a slow fever of three or four weeks continuance, had next what he called four crops of boils. They were doubtless beneficial—though very annoying and painful, as well as debilitating. As these passed away he was seized and completely prostrated with an attack of cholera morbus, which I feared would destroy him, but our heavenly Father was merciful and he arose from his bed, though greatly emaciated and exhausted. Previous to this I had been two weeks in bed in dreadful suffering. Well, we arose once more—and now the disease had left Honolulu. . . . We were called to action.

Reduced
to Lowest
Terms

We found ourselves destitute of domestic help . . . and also of the means of employing any. It was also plain that for the present the energies of our people were exhausted so that for the remaining three months of the year—to say nothing of the future—we must live as we could—We should have fainted had we not trusted to see again the goodness of the Lord in the land of the living. We at once assumed (notwithstanding our en-feebled state) an amount of labor greater than we had ever sustained in our lives before, and also reduced our style of living as low as we thought we could subsist upon. After the labors of the day were ended, my poor husband generally remained in his study until midnight, preparing articles for the paper, reading proof sheets etc. [He edited the native newspaper.] You may ask if we could not have applied for aid from the A. B. C. F. M. as we still continue their missionaries. We could have done so, but we did not wish to, if it could possibly be avoided. We had sympathized in their plans for relieving themselves of our sup-port as fast as might be—and we were willing to endure great inconveniences during the transition state of our mission.

The missionaries were now trying to be dependent for their support on the local churches alone.

The
Missionary
and the
Land

We had looked for embarrassments for a time, but no one could foretell the dreadful plague that was destined to over-whelm us. Well, we wrought on patiently for three months, and as the year drew to a close, we paused to *take our bearings*. We

LOWELL AND EMMA

1855

were forced to admit though reluctantly that we could not labor so hard much longer. I had almost lost the use of my right arm from long continued over exertion, and my poor husband, reduced almost to a shadow, confessed that he must "live better" or he could not sustain his labors and then there was our *Land*. What was to be done? As yet no light arose on our dark horizon. We both felt that we were sustaining a heavy burden. I had spent hours of thought during the past few months in devising ways and means for bettering our condition but they seemed to fail. I suffered intensely. At length I could bear it no longer and I went and laid the great black burden at the Savior's feet. I poured out my soul into his ear which was never closed to the cry of his children. I felt in my heart that we had no other motive in dwelling here than the advancement of his cause—poor and insufficient as our services had been. We had never sought our own—excepting as our interests had been identified with those of his Kingdom. What of this world's goods we possessed had come to us almost as if direct from above. The purchase of this land was the first direct effort we had made to increase our possessions, and we should not have done this, had it not seemed very necessary in the new arrangements for our support. If we had taken too much thought by so going—if it pleased our Heavenly Father that we should live more by faith and trust him to provide ways and means—or if we had felt too independent and anxious to take of ourselves—I now gave it all up. I felt only anxious that the path of duty should be made plain *Prayer* and I was ready to walk in it. I besought our heavenly Father to direct all our affairs after his own good pleasure. Oh it was so sweet to commune with Him, to leave all my cares with Him, with the lively assurance that He cared for us! It was a day long to be remembered—I gave up all, and I arose from my knees with a calm, trusting cheerful feeling I had not known for many months.

Betsey, *the next day your letter came* with all its words of *Answer* love and tender sympathy, and that one hundred dollar order! It seemed to dissolve my very heart. O, thought I, could these precious friends but know the *comfort* they have brought, their generous souls would feel a sweet reward. How my poor husband's countenance lightened, and my arm did not ache for twenty-four hours at least although the pain in it had by no means been imaginary. Well, this was the beginning of brighter days. Our dear people began to rally from the stupor in which the plague had left them. Meetings began to be well attended, and when they were called upon to tell what they would try to do for our support during the new year, with their numbers so sadly diminished, they the surviors arose and cheerfully pledged themselves to attempt quite as much and a little more than they promised at the commencement of last year when they numbered one third full more than they now do. At our first communion in the Year, three weeks since, they made their first quarterly payment, and it was more than they ever gave in one quarter before! So that with that and your generous gift we have been able to make another payment towards the land, and also to employ some domestic help, which had become indispensable. Has not our Heavenly Father cared for us? and shall we not always trust Him in all our future days? You said, my dear sister, that you and your dear husband sent fifty dollars—so I supose that dear precious Papa Learned added the other fifty dollars. May God's best blessing rest upon you all forever more, and may you never *want any good thing*.

Land Again   I mentioned in my letter to Mamma Learned that there had never been any land connected with our station while all the other stations had more or less. No one is to blame for this state of things. In Honolulu it has always been more difficult to secure land than at other places, though no doubt we could have obtained it here years ago—but we never thought of making provision for the future, also it would no doubt have excited the jealousy of foreigners who would have made use of it to injure our influence among the people. But now things are different and the changes in our manner of support as well as the progress of things in the nation generally—gave the thing a different aspect even to the minds of the enemies of the missions. Land here costs a great deal—but it will never probably cost less than now and perhaps our Heavenly Father designs this to be a comfort to us and our dear children in future years and so has brought us into circumstances to oblige us to provide what we should never voluntarily have done.

We shall have to live very close until this debt is cleared off, but we now feel a sweet trusting spirit that we shall be carried through. We naturally desire to live in a comfortable and respectable way—so that our strength may be sustained—so that we may be able to take the lead of our dear people in the various objects of benevolence in which we and they are interested—so that we may be able to use hospitality without grudging—so that we may make a decent appearance in the foreign community with whom we mingle, and lastly so that we may give our dear children, if they are spared, *a thorough education*. This last is the only *personal* luxury I crave.

Education a Personal Luxury

I wish to say that our people seem to love us better than ever, and we fully reciprocate the feeling. We have passed through great trials together: . . . We never loved our work better than now, and we are full of labors. . . . We have always been very happy missionaries, though as a family we have had many sorrows and trials.

Happy Missionaries

As far back as 1851, before this awful scourge of disease, Lowell had written the Board that his church a plebeian, a poor church compared with the congregation of the chiefs' church, and was unable to contribute for all causes more than four hundred dollars during the year, with monthly concerts, i.e., missionary gifts, of one hundred dollars more a year.

In June, 1854, Lowell had called the attention of the Board (oh, how far away was Boston!) to the fact that his was the only station in the Islands where more or less land had not been given to aid the missionary family. We recall the precious one-half acre given for the Kaumakapili Station by the High Chief Paki and his wife Konia.

Financial Straits

Lowell quotes domestic help since the epidemic as costing forty dollars a month, and as difficult to obtain at any price. Native produce, also, at this time was more expensive and great economy was needed to get through the year on a salary of one thousand dollars.

The better to get an understanding by his far-away employers Lowell sets forth his "present expenses for the Year," thus:

Domestic service	$480.
Five cords of wood	80.
House keeping	52.
Milk and butter	104.
Beef and pork	52.
Potatoes and taro	52.
Three barrels of flour	45.
Clothing for self and family	100.
Tea, sugar, molasses, and coffee	25.
Soap, rice, pia, etc., etc.	25.
Newspapers, stationery, postage, etc.	25.
Repairs	50.
Sundries for wear and tear	50.
Total	$1140.

He then expresses a hope of receiving six hundred dollars from his church as support of their pastor and asks the Board for four hundred dollars for the current year hoping to ask for not more than two hundred in 1855. Apparently the matter needed more consideration, for in a few days he penned a request for a loan from the "Prudential Committee" of five hundred dollars, to be refunded to said agents in the course of five years without interest.

Abigail to the namesake niece wrote:

Business Economy

May 14, '54:—My very dear Abby, your welcome letter of March 12, accompanied by another from Alfred—together with the "invoices" of our goods—was received three days ago. I know your uncle will write your papa and Alfred about the business—still I cannot help expressing my gratitude to them for the promptness with which they have attended to our wishes—and especially for their gratuitous services. I cannot call it anything else—for the trifle they allowed themselves is not to be considered at all like remuneration. *May God reward them.* You would know how to appreciate the favor had you been obliged to pay twenty, thirty, fifty, or one hundred per cent for everything you ordered from home through the agent here. I know we shall like *everything* they have purchased. I feel entire confidence in their judgment and good taste. The flour seems particularly providential as it was put down last on the list, we thought it doubtful if the funds held out to procure any. And after hearing of the war and the failure of the crops in Europe we had come to be some what anxious about our *bread,* and to wish that we had ordered it more definitely. Their forwarding us three bls. we regard not only as providential, but also as evidence of their good judgment and forethought. Bread stuffs will be very high I have no doubt for some time to come—but if nothing untoward happens, our flour will arrive by the time we need it.

Let a familiar story interrupt. It is current among us of island birth that in the days when a voyage around Cape Horn sometimes rendered the cargo of flour wet, moldy, and so caked that it took a mallet to break it before it could be laboriously sifted and resifted, the missionary mothers of large families would cannily say, "Now, children, the one who eats the most taro shall have the most bread." And thus the capacity for starchy food was largely satisfied by the home-grown article!

Abigail's letter continues:

I rejoice greatly, my dear Abba in the evidence your letters impart of your rapid advance in intellectual and moral culture.

We are in usual health—excepting that your uncle has a turn of his asthma and I a turn of my neuralgia. Neither of these are very agreeable companions.

Our annual meeting of the mission is about to commence and we are daily expecting a family to stop with us, besides much other company. So we are very busy just now.

Now it is Lowell's turn to carry on the story of their life. On November 27, 1856, two and a half years after the last record, he writes to Lionel Tenney and his wife Mary, at the Marietta Seminary in Ohio:

DEAR BR. AND SISTER,

. . . My apology for not writing you frequently is first a never ending amount of missionary work on my hands and 2d my dear Abba holds the pen of a ready writer and communicates to her friends like a book. . . .

Holiday   I will announce at the outset that this 27th of Nov. is my birthday 54 years old. It has become quite fashionable here for parents to give their children a holiday when their birthday comes around. Having labored and toiled more than 20 years for the benefit of this poor people perhaps it will not be amiss for me to have a holiday, unbend a little and commune with those I love. My first wish is O that I could invite our Marietta friends to come and spend the day with us, and talk of the past, the present and the probable future. This being impracticable, O that we could commune on the electrical wires. But no. So thirdly I must resort to pen and paper. So you see, I am de-

1856   termined to have a holiday with my friends in Marietta, communicate some ideas, cast them upon the waters, with a well-grounded hope that after not many days your full souls will reply with "good measure, pressed down, shaken together and running over."

54 years old! Some people are in the prime of life at this age. But not so with me. I have some unmistakeable symptoms of decay and a premonition that I never shall be able to endure, physically or mentally as I have done in years past. Still my prayer is that I may live to hear many times yet from the dear native missionaries whom we have sent out to Micronesia and to the Marquesas and of the blessing of God upon their labors; may I hope to live to see other missionaries go forth from this 2d Honolulu church under my pastoral care to the Islands of the Pacific.

You are aware, I presume that I am subject to Asthmatic turns the cause I know not unless it be hereditary. Both of my Grandfathers were afflicted with asthma in their old age. I never had symptoms of asthma till after I was 40 years old. . . . During the present year have used Davis painkiller, putting a teaspoonful into a small tumbler of water, well sweetened with molasses, and sipping it, by little and little, till the stomach was well warmed and the spasm would yield. The relief is very sud-

Anxieties   den. . . . I have prescribed this remedy to natives and have become quite celebrated among them as an asthmatical doctor. . . . We are usually favored here at Honolulu and Nuuanu Valley with one of the best climates in the world. . . . When I left the U. States that cold bracing climate of N.E. I did not

ABIGAIL'S BROTHER LIONEL

ABIGAIL'S BROTHER AUGUSTUS

presume that I should live more than ten years in this tropical climate. But I have become so thoroughly acclimated here now, that I fear I could not endure the N.E. winter, should I ever see my way clear to return thither again.

Your sister Abba was an invalid all the fore part of our missionary life. Had she been favored with health and strength, there is no telling what amount of missionary work she might not have accomplished ere this. Her illness, together with our oft repeated bereavements well nigh crushed her spirits for many years. Sometimes she tho't we ought to return to the States on her account. But our physician and Missionary Brethren and Sisters have never thought it best for us to return inasmuch as, for the most part, I have been able to go forward with my work. *Fears of Invalidism*

With all her infirmities she has made me a comfortable home; and on her couch, she has talked to and done much for the women. For the last few years she has been gaining strength, till she has resumed her favorite work, that of teaching school. While I am now writing, she is in her school room surrounded by 60 native children and youth, boys and girls, teaching them the English language. She has been thus engaged for the last two years. Two classes have already graduated and gone to the Royal (English) School. Tomorrow is the last day of the present term. Rev. Mr. Armstrong, Pres. of the Board of Education, has been into the school this a. m. and says he wants another class of ten to go to the Royal School. Several other schools have been commenced in the vicinity, but both parents and children refuse to patronize them, because they wish to go to Abba's school, where everything is explained, and where the scholars go ahead. One year ago the pressure was so hard, that I went into the business myself, and taught four hours a day five days in the week. We then had over a hundred scholars daily and everything went on swimmingly but it was too much for me to keep school and do all my other missionary work. I held on till I was called to go and visit our mission at Fatuhiva. Since then I have not kept school. *Teachers Again*

My dear Abba can now endure more than I can in mental labor and for aught I know she will soon have an academy here as flourishing and celebrated as that which has long been under the tuition of her dear brother and sister in Marietta, O., U.S.A.

Before Lowell begins his next paragraph, and since we know from him that Abigail is in the schoolroom next door to his study, let us slip away for a few minutes to the contemplation of her work. Not that we shall interrupt the devoted schoolmistress, but that we have in hand a document or two that may help us. We must remember that the missionaries *Hawaiian* in coming to the islands seemed not to conceive that this *Language* people might be divorced from their language. And just as they were careful in every way to be obedient to the wishes of the sovereign and to help and uphold Hawaiian law, so they set themselves, as we have seen, the task of learning the Hawaiian language, translating the Bible and other books into it, and teaching that language alone in the schools. But the desire for foreign things was inevitable and in her later life Abigail wrote of the teaching of English in Hawaii in which work it seems she was pioneer. She described it thus:

Teaching Rather early in our missionary life, some of the more ambi-
English tious among the native boys besought me to teach them the English language. I was so pleased with every evidence of interest and progress among them that I gladly complied and it so came to pass that I had a large evening school in the English language composed chiefly of young men, and another during the day for children, in successful operation before the Government had established the system of English schools. When that system was fairly inaugurated I became a teacher under the direction of the "Board of Education" with a large school of boys and a few bright girls. Then followed years of very delightful and successful work.

Abigail's friend and fellow teacher Mrs. Amos Cooke wrote of this venture as

. . . the first English common school taught on these islands, June 1854 to 1860 . . . a popular flourishing school of eighty or more pupils.

Abigail's daughter tells of it thus:

It was her school of eighty well trained Hawaiian boys and
girls who gave several yearly exhibitions in the English language in the old Kaumakapili Church that inspired King
Alexander and Queen Emma to resolve that the nation should
have the same opportunity in education with these few. When
the necessary laws had been passed and arrangements were completed they took my Mother's school for the nucleus of the new
department and moved it to the Royal School on Emma St.,
inviting her to be its first principal. Being unable to accept the
position she gladly passed on this fruit of her labors to the
larger future awaiting it and continued teaching in her own
home.

The later pupils were children of her foreign friends and
neighbors. But while she was still in the midst of the early
school she has mentioned, there came to Abigail the following
letter of encouragement. Written by a neighbor at beautiful
Rosebank, that spacious home site on Nuuanu Avenue distinguished by the dark grove of mango trees and the long-
curving drive bordered by royal palms, it bears a cherished
signature, that of the Hon. R. C. Wyllie, who was one of the
early bulwarks of constitutional government in these islands.
The letter runs:

MY DEAR MRS. SMITH:— *Mr.*
It does me good to meet your little native scholars, boys and *Wyllie's*
girls, on the Nuuanu Road. They afford me a pleasing remi- *Letter*
niscence of the crowd of Boys and Girls, all good humored and
laughing Imps, who welcomed me when I first landed in Honolulu from my yacht, the "Daule," on the 10th of May 1824,
who went with me wherever I went, and who only disputed with
each other for the privilege of carrying before me, (looking
back and chattering all the while), what little purchases I made,
and even my Umbrella!
Your scholars prove that they, the young Hawaiians of 1857,
are as mirthful and as kind as were their Predecessors of 1824.
I have to shake hands with them on the road as I walk up every
day. Being all *alike* favorites, I wish you in my name, to make
them, each, holders of one share in the "Morning Star," taking
care to fill in all their names, and send me an exact list, the *boys*

in one column, and the *little ladies in another.* I will pay the
amount for them all, to Bishop Dick, alias Richard Armstrong
alias Limaikaika, &C. &C.

Admiral Thomas, with whom you were always a very great
Favourite, and who writes to me by almost every mail, never
fails to particularize your name and your Revd. Husband's, for
his special regards. I wish you could spare time to write to the
old Hero, now upwards of 80, but taking his long morning walks
as usual; and, I believe, praying for the Hawaiian King and
people every evening before he goes to bed. If you write to him,
send your letter to me, and I will forward it. I enclose herewith
20 Blank Certificates of shares. If your little pupils exceed that
number, let me know, and I will send you as many as may be
wanted. With compliments to Mr. Smith and "aloha" to each
of your scholars, I am, My dear Mrs. Smith

Yours most respectful
R. C. WYLLIE.

We shall have much more of the *Morning Star* anon, but
now let us return to Lowell's study and see how he is coming
on with his long letter. We left him writing of his Abba and
it is of her he is writing now. He is joking mildly again over
the thousands of miles as nothing between friends.

Abba's birthday comes just one week after mine. . . . It will
then be vacation with her and I presume she will have a holiday
with our Marietta friends, unless the "Ladies Strangers' Friend
Society" should have a meeting on that day, and even in that
case she would be very happy to introduce you to that interesting circle.

Strangers'
Friend
Society

Oahu
College

Our missionary school at Punahou has just been converted
into a college called the Oahu College. At present however it is
more of an Academy than a college, for they have only a small
Freshman class. Young gentlemen and ladies now attend as in
an academy, but this feature will of course be modified, as the
number of collegians shall increase. This like every other institution must have its beginning.

Emma has joined the institution and rides to and fro daily
with two of Dr. Judd's children. She is especially pleased with

the school. President Beckwith is a superior teacher and all his pupils are wide awake and progressing finely in their studies. The distance from here to Punahou is about three and a half miles. Emma has been to the Royal school several terms. She is in advance of most of the children of her age, and for this you must give credit to her mother who has taken much pains with her when out of school. She has been taking lessons on a piano for a year or two; is passionately fond of music, and plays very well for one of her age. We have recently received an excellent piano for her from Boston. She also plays church music on a melodeon, and we feel or ought to feel under very many obligations to God for sparing this daughter to us, for giving us the means and opportunities of educating her here, at our Island home. She was twelve years old last June. . . .

Emma at Punahou

Oh, there comes another package of letters from our missionaries at Micronesia, from Ascension. But on opening them I find they were written last February. They have been off cruising after whales all summer. Our last intelligence from that mission was . . . three months later than these letters. Report says that letters have come into town from Fatuhiva. All these things give variety to my holiday. I must be excused a few moments to go to the post office and see how Zion prospers at Fatuhiva.

While Lowell is gone to the post office (and it will take more than a few minutes for him to harness his horse and jog down the then steep Judd Hill to the wharf, and then let the horse climb back again) let us consider the freshness of this man's spirit, as pleased with his little "holiday" as Browning's Pippa, as interested in the human beings that pass before his mind's eye, young and old, familiar and strange, in the sunshine of Honolulu, amid the wintry storms of Ohio, under the burning sky of Micronesia's atolls, white or brown people, throbbing hearts, immortal souls! Like the little girl Pippa, with a rare holiday, Lowell could turn his eyes sad from disappointment, from fatigue, from longing for that which he did not see, and in spirit exclaim with a trusting heart, "God's in his heaven!" but Pippa could say, "All's right with the world!" Not so easily, Lowell. There are heavy burdens on his heart of what *he* must do that *others* may be saved.

Here in his study is a rough sketch of Honolulu in 1856 we may be sure he would share with us.

Our harbor is now visited by some sixty or seventy whale ships and the city is full of sailors who go about seeking whom they may pollute and destroy.

Honolulu in Shadow and Sunshine

Honolulu like all other civilized parts abounds with Beer Shops and grog shops—bowling alleys, theatres and a circus. And no pains is spared by ungodly men to rid this community of what little virtue they have. I trust, however, that we have some Christians in our native churches who will stand the test, whether those who come from our American churches do or not. There is a great rage among the pleasure loving citizens at this time for public balls. The Chinese merchants in this city recently gave a ball in honor of the King and Queen, which cost them about $4000. And last Friday evening their majesties gave one in return and some of the English men of war in the place kept it up till 6 o'clock in the morning and then took breakfast with the Queen. You are aware that some professing Christians are great advocates for the innocent amusement of the Ball room; when they sup at midnight and dance on innocently till 2 or 3 in the morning, but who think with their liberal minded neighbours that it is outlandish to hold a prayer meeting over an hour or an hour and a half and the best of sermons must not last over 30 minutes. Where a man's treasure is, there his heart and affections are!

But beside this picture—gay-colored, doubtless, to the participants, grievously dark to Lowell—lies another, tear-stained it may be, but in happy as well as artistic contrast. It is by the same hand.

Sarah Iki

At 7 o'clock this morning I went to the funeral of Sarah Iki.

Of her Abigail spoke as "that nice native girl that I 'brought up.' " Barring this parenthesis, Lowell continues:

She was some 23 or 24 years old. She lived as a domestic in our family for several years, was received into the church at the time of our great awakening and has lived a very exemplary Christian life. Unwearied efforts have been put forth to draw her into the snares of the Devil. Libertines have often boasted that they could buy any Hawaiian girl for a dollar. But thanks to the God of Missions Sarah has withstood all their temptations and has gone to her grave in peace. Her parents have stood firm. Several years ago a libertine knocked at their door late at night. The father stepped to the door and was presented with two bags of dollars $100 in each, one for the father and one for the mother. "Take them" said he "and give me your daughter." The good old man slammed the door to and told the scamp to be off with himself. A beautiful young merchant sent her his gold watch with a note stating that if she would call at his store, she might have as many nice things as she wished, if she would but fall down and worship him. . . . But she spurned his offers with contempt. I apprehended that very few girls ever withstood such temptations as this dear girl did. Last March I married her to a graduate from Lahainaluna Seminary, with the hope that in a year or two they would be ready to go out as missionaries to Micronesia. But she went into a decline soon after they were married, and she died yesterday morning at nine o'clock. . . . We are obliged to bury very soon here in this tropical climate. . . . To feel that we have been instrumental in saving one soul is enough to reward us for all our self denial, toil and labor in a heathen land for 20 years. But we hold that tens and even hundreds have gone from this second Honolulu church to that which is prepared for the people of God. . . .

Lowell is returned from the post office with news from the South Seas of friendly chiefs and people welcoming and desiring missionaries—American and Hawaiian—to teach them the gospel of Christ.

Our souls are fired with zeal on receiving such communications from those who have buckled on their armor and are in the field, watching every favorable opportunity to communicate the glad tidings of salvation to the perishing heathen.

"Our Souls Are Fired"

He begs his relatives in New England to interest themselves personally in that romantic boat, *Morning Star*, being built in Boston, saying:

The more who are personally interested in this work the better. Some may give pence, some shillings, some dollars and

Oh that some may give themselves a living sacrifice to the cause of Christ among the heathen.

Lowell's holiday is drawing to a close, but he must attack one more subject.

I suppose, it is known ere this through the U. States who is to be your next President. I do not allow myself to become very much excited on the subject of political elections; though I am aware that very important consequences will follow. The kings of the S. Islands are hereditary and whatever may be their characters or qualifications, they must be honored, accepted and endured even until death. Our present king is a youth—a young man of considerable talents, has a pretty good knowledge of the English language, but he has certain advisers and counsellors about him who in all probability will involve him in ruin, both temporal and eternal. When a king rejects the counsel of long and well tried friends and regards himself wiser than seven men who can render a reason, and when he selects infidels and scoffers of religion for his most intimate companions, we can not confidently expect the providence of God will long smile upon him.

Lowell on Politics Again

It is our prayer that the U. States may be blessed with a President who will fear God and who will seek the highest welfare of the nation. Slavery and intemperance are probably two of the greatest evils in our country and it is exceedingly desirable that Presidents and Governors should have correct moral principles on these subjects. But it is difficult to tell what a man will prove to be in the course of 4 years if entrusted with the affairs of State. We hope he will be *square* and *upright* but from the past we must not be disappointed if he shall prove to be a pentagon or an octagon, and lean over at an angle of 45 degrees from the Bible standard of truth and righteousness. "When the wicked bear rule, the people mourn." The halls of legislation at Washington have become very corrupt; and it makes my blood boil with indignation to hear of the war and bloodshed at Kansas. Verily I wish the good people of Kansas could arise like the citizens of San Francisco and drive their infernal neighbors back to their own homes, where they can

HONOLULU SHOWING DIAMOND HEAD, 1857

OLD WATER FRONT, HONOLULU, 1857

OLD FORT FROM WHICH FORT STREET WAS NAMED, 1857

wallow in slavery to their own eternal shame. But I must stop. The Lord grant to send deliverance to the people of Kansas.

The *Morning Star* has been referred to by Lowell and the Hon. Mr. Wyllie, but it is for Abigail to picture the vessel's arrival at Honolulu and departure for the South Seas. In a letter to Mrs. Martin, a generous friend in New York state, we read, 1857:

The "Morning Star" has at length dawned upon our longing sight and we c'ld say—How blessed are our eyes which see this heavenly sight—which other missionaries have longed and prayed for—but died without. Our anticipations were more than realized. I will send you a paper containing a full account of the manner in which we have prepared to receive her.

All the foreign residents (it seemed) and thousands of the natives assembled on the wharf to witness the presentation of a Banner we had prepared for her. As soon as the Captain received it, it was instantly run up to the "mast head" and as its graceful folds of white unfolded to the breeze—displaying the "Star and Dove" such a shout as went up from those assembled thousands as has been rarely heard on these shores. It did seem as if the Kingdom of Christ was gaining the victory over the Prince of darkness to hear men of the world "hurraing" for the missionary vessel. My mind reverted to the scene presented on this very spot only one generation ago when the first missionaries landed on these shores. The veriest sceptic must have been convinced of the utility and efficacy of christian missions in reclaiming a lost world. The dear children of Honolulu—who were stock holders in the "Morning Star," enjoyed the great privilege of visiting her beautiful arrangements to their hearts' content. So also the natives, hundreds of whom were owners in the concern. The Capt. was very kind and accommodating. We liked him very much, and think him well fitted for his position. The vessel was detained here but a very few days and then sailed away for the Marquesas Islands—richly freighted with supplies—letters—love tokens, and two precious missionaries besides several other passengers—all of whom were connected in one way and another with the blessed enterprize.

In the fitting out of this vessel and all the increased interest

awakened thereby in thousands of hearts for the advancement
of the Redeemer's kingdom—I realize the answers to many mil-
lions of prayers that have ascended from pious souls, many of
whom have exchanged prayer for praise in the upper sanctuary.
I regard the building and sending forth of this vessel as a great
step onward in the conversion of the world. What an increase of
interest will the dear little owners feel in the good work. Many
more I doubt not will give themselves to it personally than w'ld
otherwise have done so. It cheers and quickens our churches and
sabbath schools here wonderfully and it is so much needed
among the thousand Isles yet unvisited by one ray of gospel
light. Eternity alone will reveal all the blessings it is destined
to shed over these benighted regions. Remember it constantly in
your prayers. . . .

Books

By the "Morning Star" we received two packages of books
from the Messrs. Carters. Tongue and pen alike fail to express
what I feel in my heart in view of this inestimable gift. . . . I
have so longed for books. Here are helps for my husband, helps
for myself, and helps for my dear children. O what a treasure!
I have not recovered from the first excitement of opening these
packages. It was so unexpected. There was no . . . word of any
kind. . . . I suppose my dear Friend, it is through your influence we have been the recipients of this rich gift. Blessings on
you and blessings on the Messrs. Carters. . . . I hope we shall
be made better and more useful by the perusal of these choice
volumes. . . . The little book of "Sunday pictures" for my dear
little boy—how I have wanted something like it for years—and
the little family, house and all, from your dear daughter quite
overcame Emma I had often heard her express a wish for such a
doll—but they are quite expensive here. She does not really play
with them much, altho' she has been so bereaved of sisters and
brothers, I have encouraged more play with dolls than I otherwise might. . . .

A Twelve-
Year-Old
School-
mistress

. . . Emma has written a brief note. . . . As we are just
closing our school term—in which Emma has been my assistant
—and the families are convening for the Annual Meeting, we
are in such a bustle of labor and interruptions that neither of
us can write much. . . .

In a letter of even date to Hattie, the young lady daughter of Brother and Sister Coan, who was pursuing her studies in "the east," Abigail writes:

Emma has had a little school since Punahou School closed. I have put an end to this for the discipline is of too stern a nature for a little girl who has not yet entered her "teens." She likes it very much however. She is going forward with her music and drawing and will now resume some studies at home. Her mind and character are developing well. She still looks forward to teaching as the way in which she is to fulfill her part in life's labors. Still she sometimes wavers in her mind—for instance— the other day I allowed her to do some nice work on a silk dress I was repairing. She succeeded so well that she almost decided on the spot to be a dressmaker! To interfere with this idea, she was invited over to Waialua to pass a few weeks. She quite startled me by the announcement that she had a great desire to learn to milk cows. I replied that it w'ld be of little use, as our pasture was at so great a distance! "I know that, Mamma, but I may be a farmer's wife and would like to be prepared for emergencies!" She can put a horse in to a carriage—better than the Irishman did—wash dishes, darn stockings, play the piano and some other things about equally well.

Many thanks, my dear for your full account of your travels, visits, impressions, etc. I entered into them all with much relish and delight, especially that little scene at Niagara where you responded to the whistle of the little "Maid of the Mist." That was a sweet romantic occurrence to be long remembered. My heart warms to all such little things, just as it did when I was at your age. Are you not glad to know that you may preserve that same heart of yours warm and fresh—e'en to old age?

Lowell's and Abigail's Youthfulness

Lowell, too, in his own way kept his youthful heart and when away from his heavy duties at home could joke in his letters to his family. On a little tour on Hawaii in October, 1857, he wrote his Abba:

I broke away from the tender chords, the affectionate liga- ments, and the brotherly Bonds at 10 o'clock this a. m. and rode over here (Waimea) in a little more than five hours. From Kohala. Have an excellent horse, a kind sociable and compan-

ionable guide and the very best of Hawaiian weather for travelling and am enjoying my visits and journey thus far "first
rate." . . . This family are all surrounded with shrubbery—
their garden is a rank wilderness and the children I think need
some more open sunshine cultivation and also those at Kohala.
All growing up rapidly like the flowers in the garden with an
obvious lack of something. They are so afraid of our public
schools that they must be kept at home.

*With the
"Lions"*   . . . Have been with Brother Lyons to visit his new house of
worship—even to the top of the Bellfry. A very nice convenient
little house. . . . But I see no good reason why I should tear
down ours. Br. Lyons is having a school for a few days, with the
school teachers in his field—here at the station. I have just held
a meeting with them of half an hour—talked to them on the
subject—nature, self denial, &c. of pioneer missionaries. They
appeared much interested. I hope they will be better school
masters here—if none of them ever go to heathen lands.

Br. Lyons *ma* sympathize with me in improving this good
weather for my overland journey, and though both the old and
the young *lions* would like to hold on to their prey for several
days—they will probably let me off unmolested about 12 o'clock.

*Parents
and
Children*   In August, 1858, writing to Emma of pleasant voyaging
to San Francisco for his health on the bark *Fanny Major*,
Lowell glories in the comforts of a

. . . nice state room six feet square with bowl, pitcher, looking
glass, towels, two berths, hook, and a round window on the side
of the ship as large as the mouth of a large cannon. If we do not
live well and grow fat, the fault must be our own.

I suppose that you are going to school again at Punahou.
You must keep on good terms with Star—have no falling out,
not falling off by the way—treat him kindly, and I presume, if
you give him enough to eat and drink, he will serve you faithfully. Remember the 10th commandment and do not covet your
neighbor's house nor anything that is his.

From brief and hurried notes from Abigail to her daughter
on one of Emma's vacation trips (always on horseback) over
the other side of the *pali*, we glean items of the busy life, the
interest in the growing son and his friends, the difficulty of

finding a suitable schoolhouse when the large school was turned over to the Government and Abigail was starting her small school for the children of foreigners, the tax of studying Latin at her age (fifty plus), her delight in meeting cultivated strangers. Returning home one evening,

. . . soon after tea as papa could not go was glad I did come home as I found Mr. Edwards here and he might have been disappointed to see no lady. He made a long evening—was very pleasant—knows every lady of note at home. Is a great grandson of Rev. Jonathan Edwards, of N.Eng. celebrity—grandson *A Caller* of Pierpont Edwards once chief justice of the United States *of Historic* courts—and son of Judge Edwards of N.Y. His father is an *Connec-* intimate friend of Gen. Scott. He showed me autograph letters *tions* from Gen. Scott. I told him he ought to preserve them with great care—as in a generation or two hence—they w'ld be of historic interest. He said that reminded him—that at the time the traitor Arnold's property was confiscated, all his papers came into the possession of his grandfather then chief justice of the United States; that he himself some years ago overhauled them and made a valuable selection for the historical society of N.Y. His father who of course was cousin to Aaron Burr took care of that poor man during his last days—when this gentleman was a boy—I was astonished to hear him talk, but I happened to be at home on most subjects! I wonder how it happens that he is not acquainted with people here. He only knows the Damons.

November, 1863, gives us a letter from Abigail to Mrs. Hiram Bingham, Jr., missionary in Apaiang, Micronesia:

The Morning Star sails today and with her goes our warmest *Strong's* aloha to you and all our dear patient self denying missionaries *Island* in Micronesia. There also returns in the Star a native youth *Boy* from Strong's Island. He came up a year ago and has been in our family all during that time. He is such a good boy. Our hearts are very sad at parting with him, but we hope and pray that he may be very useful among his people, and a great comfort to missionaries. He has been a great comfort to us. . . . Our little son has devoted himself to him very closely and has assisted and taught him many things and now he feels like part-

ing with a brother. Paitok told Gussie the other day that he had
never cried after his old home since he had been with us but that
he should cry a great deal when he left us. If he is a fair specimen of your converts from heathenism you have the greatest
reason to thank God and take courage. We like the appearance
of the new missionaries . . . [bound for Micronesia]. They all
dined with us a few days ago. I hope the box of oranges will
reach you in a state fit to eat. Emma made you a little jar of
jelly which you will find in the box. I only wish we c'ld do all
that is in our hearts for all the dear missionaries.

In spite of acknowledged illness all the winter of 1860–61
and the spring of 1863, Abigail was still teaching—Emma
with her now, for

. . . Emma graduated last June (from Punahou) with much
credit to herself and much comfort to her parents. . . . She
bids fair to become a successful teacher. Is very fond of the
School business. Our school is down the valley near Mr. Hall's. We are
down the absent from home six hours daily.
Valley
Besides this we have two lady boarders. One of them is about
18, a protege of Mr. Wyllie. We have the care of her and the
Boarders superintendence of her education. She is Irish of *highish* birth,
but the family are "decayed" as to fortune. The other lady is
Miss Brown—a member of the Mission. She is in her 84th year
and quite infirm. Our time is very fully occupied, and we feel the
need of more strength and more grace. . . .

Emma teaches drawing and music among other things. . . .
She is anxious to earn money enough to go to the States and
spend a year, and we are desirous she should do so. She recently
received an invitation from California to a situation of music
teacher in a young ladies' seminary—but we did not feel as if
we c'ld part with her to go so far away at present. She may go
in the spring if all goes well, it w'ld be an advantage in some
respects.

The only references any letters we have make to the war
are a premonition of Abigail's in the spring of 1861:

Civil War The world is in a state of revolution—strifes and tumults
agitate the nation—our own dear native land is being drawn

THE SEAMAN'S BETHEL
1857

PUNAHOU SCHOOL
1860

into the vortex—but above all reigns our covenant-keeping God —and he will bring order out of confusion.

The other reference is to two nephews—one in camp life near New Orleans; the other brought home with a fractured leg by his young wife, who traveled over eight hundred miles to reach him.

He will live and his leg will be saved—perhaps to lose it and life itself in some future battle. How long, O Lord, how long shall this terrible strife be suffered to continue?

Doubtless Abigail had much to say on that subject so deeply stirring the hearts of true Americans even so far from news as the Sandwich Islands, for, after all, few of the many letters she wrote were sent back to her daughter.

That daughter in her "teen-age" journal wrote in 1861 of boys playing with miniature homemade forts and cannon, and of her own preparation to celebrate the Fourth of July by wearing "Union colors" made into decorations for hat, breast, and belt. She also relates that on passing a neighbor's house she saw a Secession flag waving over the door, plainly indicating what their political feelings were.

The visit, in 1863, of Dr. Anderson, Secretary of the American Board, is mentioned more than once by Abigail as an occasion of great joy and satisfaction. Little did she dream of a sequel a few years later that was to bring great sorrow to the little family in Nuuanu Cottage.

Visit from Secretary of A.B.C. F.M.

In July, 1864, almost thirty-two years since he and Abigail had bade farewell to their friends in New England, Lowell wrote the officers of the A.B.C.F.M., suggesting a visit home and supposing their "friends would cheerfully contribute more or less to the expense." He wrote that an old friend and classmate had invited him to "come home and attend a class meeting at Williams College at the commencement in August 1864." He had, however, replied to the kind invitation that duty required a postponement. But if the furlough is taken later Lowell hopes that the Board will contribute to the return passage, and supposes that his salary will be available. This "salary" we understand to be paid by the Kaumakapili Church. As we have seen, for some years he

A Visit Home

had tried to relieve the Board of the burden of his support. In May, 1861, he had written that his wife was again an invalid and obliged to have a female servant, and, reminding the Board that his congregation was made up of poor people, had appealed for $400; but in November of that year he requested that only $200 be sent him for 1862. His zeal in self-denial was not only for his own missionary work, but also for the mission in the Marquesan group, to which some of his flock had gone as laborers. In November, 1864, finding his "attacks of asthma more frequent and prostrative," Lowell asked the Board that the date of his (first and only) furlough be set for the spring of 1865.

For twenty years Lowell and Abigail had felt the need of respite from toil. Was their long prayer now about to be answered?

4. FURLOUGH

The joys of anticipation! When the children and grandchildren of Lowell and Abigail step, with little preparation, upon one of the big liners that leave the deepened and widened harbor of Honolulu, one of many in a week—going on waters smoothed by the bulk of the vessels, equipped with clean, luxurious cabins, excellent meals, commodious decks, guidance of a gyroscope compass, conveniences of room telephones, safety of wireless connection with the world, travel so swift, so comfortable, so frequent for business or pleasure as to seem but a ferry-boat excursion of sometimes only four days to "the coast"—does any one of them bethink him of the tiny *Mentor* that rolled his forbears around Cape Horn for half a year, or the *Comet* that took them to California thirty-two years later in seventeen days? In our everyday aspect of travel have we not lost some power of thrill? Perhaps the airplane still holds it for us. What will take the charm when that pales?

Preparation for Travel

Emma's dream of "going to the states" was coming true, and her children have a little tangible proof of her preparation for that great event. Her earnest work in pencil and crayon drawing, for which she felt she had no special gift but great determination to improve, was followed by an attempt at painting. Her friend Hattie Baldwin, later Mrs. Samuel M. Damon, loved for a lifetime, recalled visiting Emma at Nuuanu Cottage for a fortnight sometime previous to the "trip east," and in an album are extant an india-ink Diamond Head and two paintings of roses, results of lessons during that visit. How much was done by the young teacher and how much by her comrade pupil no one can say, but one marvels at the delicate strokes of pen and brush, the stipple then in vogue, the iridescence of the dewdrop on the fragile petals and the finely veined rose leaves. This volume was to contain later a colored drawing of the bark *Comet* that bore a happy company of Islanders on the first lap of the expedition to New York *via* the Isthmus of Panama. It holds also pages bearing imitation calling cards, drawn in pencil as if scattered on the page, with the names of the passengers, and, farther on, the autographs of relatives visited in the homeland.

The young Augustus reports voyaging on the *Comet* thus, in a letter to his "dear teacher," Professor Alexander:

We went along to Diamond Head very well. . . . Next morning . . . we were in sight of land, Maui, Lanai, Molokai and Oahu. We had to lay off and on, first we would be near the back side of Oahu, it looked near, then we would be a good ways from it. We saw four or five whales that day . . . humbacks I believe they were. I did not feel very well for about a week. . . . Forty eight passengers in all. We played a good many games, Consequences, Authors, Shuffle Board or Skittles was a game played by gentlemen on deck . . . like that. . . . I cannot make it look very good with ink. We played other games such as Magic Wand, Copenhagen, etc. We made a very good passage of 17 days. We had two calms we only went 60 miles one day 31 the other. . . . A pilot came on board. He said he had bad news for us that our beloved President Lincoln was killed by the hand of an assasin. It was terrible news for us. The papers were all dressed in mourning. We saw the new vessel D. C. Murray which was taking the news to Honolulu. The people all felt like crying. Some of them did I think. The city of San Francisco is all draped in mourning. . . . They will kill Wilkes Booth

Augustus on Voyaging

when they catch him, that is if they do catch him. . . . They
have a great many things here which they do not have in Honolulu, such as horse and steam cars, gas lights which are equal to
five common lamps. There is a good deal of noise and bustle in
the city, a great many things to see. . . . Their stores are large
and there are a great many of them.

Anticipa-
tions
Realized

Letters and journals testify that the realization fully
equaled the rosy anticipations. The tropic son and daughter
had their first experience of train travel, jumping into snow
banks, sending and receiving telegrams, tasting the sweets of
going "home for thanksgiving," which Emma celebrated in a
commemorative poem to the delight of admiring kin. Mourning the deaths of the fathers and sisters of both families,
there were, still to be revered and treasured, the mothers
with their terse and spicy remarks, joking uncles, hospitable
aunts, admiring, teasing cousins, who seemed brothers and
sisters to Emma with her lifelong hunger for such intimacy
and congeniality.

Cold
Comfort

Separated from their parents, who must make many journeys telling about the mission work, visiting friends, and
gathering up new vigor for their remaining years in their
far-off island home, the young son had the stimulus of New
England schooling in a rigorous climate, while Emma wor-
ried her mother almost sick by her rapt attention to the
study of piano and harmony while living in such desperate
cold as a hall bedroom in Boston could offer. But those island
children showed no enervation of physical endurance or
mental acumen, once opportunities were theirs.

Emma's
Music

Emma's hard and persistent work in music was enriched
by her intense enjoyment of "Philharmonic Rehearsals at
the Academy of Music" and by her first hearing of opera.
She clutched eagerly at every such treat and at lectures and
sermons by noted men, feasting on them as she feasted on the
companionship of her congenial kin—preparing for a long
famine in years to come.

That Little
Item,
Expense

As Abigail wrote, "that little item of expense will peep
out," and so it was easy to make excuses why she should not
accompany her husband as far as Chicago, where she was determined he should go for the annual meeting of the Board

and it was a delicate matter going to places where friends could offer necessary hospitality. In her letters to Emma discussing the business of shopping at the great Stuart's [sic] in New York and elsewhere, Abigail's taste and love of things beautiful and intrinsically good were ever in evidence and her advice and judgment were ever for the true economy. All this was well understood by the daughter, who during her teens had kept her hair ribbons fresh and enduring by "ironing" them around the bedposts at night and putting everything away clean and smooth.

Among Abigail's experiences in New York are these:

Mr. and Mrs. Prime were *very* kind. On the day we left she . . . took me to a number of grand places where she visits—to Delmonico's to lunch and to Stuart's [sic]. She is known to all the clerks to whom she introduces me as a friend of hers who has been absent from the country more than thirty years, and who wished to see all the improvements of the times. So they were very polite and showed us everything, especially the $3000 shawls. I c'ld not appreciate those but suppose they are very grand. She ended by purchasing a present for me in the shape of a handsome French Broche shawl—cost $30 or so. You may believe I was astonished—but she insisted upon it, said she came to the city on purpose to do it, etc. Mr. P. also put a new hat on papa's head and said he sh'ld send the old one to Barnum's! She also gave you a handsome parasol and one or two little articles—and a number of books for us. O they were *so kind*. . . . Went to Henry Ward Beecher's church to attend the sewing society where the ladies send off to the freedmen a hundred suits of clothes every week. It did my heart good. Promised . . . to spend a Sabbath with them before we leave and hear H.W.B. preach. . . . Wrote a long letter to Grandma Judd [Dr. Judd's mother] thinking it w'ld make her happy to hear about her good brother and his excellent wife (Mr. and Mrs. Thomas Hastings). While there I was visited by Teddy and Tom Gulick, Nat. Emerson, James Daly, Nevins Armstrong, Munson Coan and Willie Rowell just arrived. Had a splendid time with them all. Mrs. Hastings said it did her good to see them cluster around me just as if I was their Mother. I was disappointed at not seeing Sam and Willie Andrews. Papa saw them both, and they would have come to see me, only I was out of the city the evenings they c'ld have come. Anna Paris is at Vassar College.

*Broadening
Sympathies* Although the "English Church," as established in Honolulu, had not found the greatest favor among the missionaries of the A.B.C.F.M., Abigail gives a sympathetic description of the communion service she attended in the Episcopal church in Westchester, New York, the home of her beloved niece Abby. And despite the fact that *puhi paka* (tobacco smoking) had been made a subject of church discipline by Lowell and his brother missionaries for years, Abigail in recalling her visit in one home could write back in genial remembrance of

Your dear husband and Mr. E. . . . taking an occasional little smoke together and talking quietly.

In March, Lowell, in Greenfield, Massachusetts, where his aged mother was making her home with the youngest son, wrote to Abigail:

*Sugaring
Off* New Sugar! Sail ho! What, sugaring off today! Only a little for Mother. She has been longing for some new sugar, but alas! she loathes the sight of it. Well, I took the saucer and found a market for it at once. They will keep the molasses till you all come and then we shall have a good time. . . . About two barrels of sap this year. . . . The Sugar Season about over. . . . The frost is coming out of the ground; and soon they will commence plowing, sowing and planting. The singing of birds has come. Oh, what a winter!

*Homeward
Bound* The last visits paid and the heartbreaking farewells over, our little family embarked on the steamer *Costa Rica* for a safe but rough passage to Aspinwall. The train ride across the Isthmus was enjoyable and the country seemed vividly green to eyes that had looked on snow in New York but ten days earlier. The *Constitution* was waiting to take the passengers to San Francisco, and in all this voyaging Emma seems to have been the belle of the boat. The travel-weary Abigail writes of a providential delay in San Francisco for

LOWELL

THE SMITH FARM AT GREENFIELD, MASS.,
TO WHICH LOWELL'S PARENTS MOVED
SOON AFTER HIS DEPARTURE FOR
THE SANDWICH ISLANDS

A sketch by Emma

a period of four weeks, during which she recruited her forces and Lowell took the opportunity to go

. . . on a mission up into the country on behalf of our Hawaiian Board, visiting *Kanakas* at Don Pedro's Bar and at Grape Vine Gulch.

Hawaiians in California

Spending a Sabbath in each place with a group of Hawaiians, fifteen in the first and twenty-five in the second, Lowell then went on eighteen miles to see the Big Trees. He found the Hawaiians in these raw mining towns

. . . very glad to see me, and they presented me with $16.50 when I left them. They are well supplied with Bibles, testaments, and hymn books; but they are unstable as water in their locations; for they are washing over dirt which has been worked before and they stay but a few months in any one place. Their habitations must be much like those of the soldiers in the army; mere temporary huts.

Oh, how the mining towns do look, verily everything has been turned up side down—the soil has been all washed off into the streams and the otherwise beautiful fields are barren rocks—deserted shanties—with very few inhabitants. The surface mining is nearly exhausted in this region; only quartz mining is now profitable—and none but men of wealth can work them; they require a fresh outlay of machinery; they employ day laborers to dig and work their mines. . . .

On my return from Big Trees to Murphy's received a telegram from Columbia requesting me to attend the funeral of a child in that town. I did so, and the people wished me to spend the Sabbath with them so I went and held my meetings with the natives during the week days and came and addressed the people of Murphy's three times on the Sabbath; for which they footed my bill at the hotel and gave me $5.00 besides. Next day came 70 miles in stage and 100 miles in a boat and joined my family on Tuesday morning.

My journey, visiting, exhorting, preaching, . . . travelling over hills and through gulches, camping out with the natives etc. etc. for almost two weeks, has done me good. I grew stronger daily and feel much better prepared for the remaining voyage than before this mountain jaunt. . . .

We hoped to arrive in Honolulu by the first of June so as to be with our missionary brethren in their annual meeting. But for some unknown good reason, we are detained and shall not be there. . . .

San Francisco Preachers

Called on Dr. Stone yesterday. He is a great and powerful preacher and draws a large congregation. Dr. Scudder is another very powerful preacher and there is Dr. Wadsworth and others, but I expect the people will learn bye and bye that Christ has said "Without me, ye can do nothing." All the great preachers and wealthy churches must learn this great truth and humble themselves before the Lord, as well as poor missionaries and humble preachers every where. All will be like sounding brass and tinkling cymbals unless the Holy Spirit come down to convince men of sin, of righteousness and of a judgment to come.

Abigail wrote of Lowell's visit and of

California as yet Partially Explored

. . . the Great Tree Father of the Forest which has been ruthlessly cut down. . . . There is much that is very beautiful and also much that is very wonderful in the scenery of California, and it has as yet been but partially explored. Being our nearest neighbor we of course feel a lively interest in all things pertaining to its development. Have you seen "Across the Continent" by Bolles of Springfield? He was one of the Colfax party. The book is worth reading.

We who read simple comments in letters must, to make a picture of "the coast" at that time, fill in commonplaces to them that, to some of us, are startling. Little Honolulu was three decades older than San Francisco and in the fifties received children from California and Oregon as pupils in the Punahou School. Honolulu also exported to the continental frontier wheat and potatoes raised on Maui. The furnishing of the first printing press in Oregon to the mission there by the mission here is one of the monuments of early civilization in these islands and is already passing into glamorous legend.

A joyous welcome home crowned the happy furlough. Abigail wrote of it to her niece:

. . . Just at the right time our vessel was ready for sea. It was the "Comet" the same one that carried us over last year. We had a safe and pleasant passage of fourteen days and I gained a great deal of strength so that when we arrived I felt much better than when I left New York. It was a glad day when our mountains loomed up to view—towering majestically above the clouds. Your cousin Emma was the first to cry "Land ho" much to the discomfiture of the Mate who was on the lookout and who expected to be the first to announce the glad tidings. The sun was setting in golden splendor the same evening, tingeing with glory the masses of fleecy clouds which crowned the different Islands in sight, just as *"Coco Head"* the nearest promontory of our own beloved Island (Oahu) burst into view, and early the next morning were just off the harbor waiting for the steam tug and pilot to take us in. Oh, what a homecoming was ours. . . . Some came off in boats to meet us . . . and as soon as the vessel's bows touched the wharf there was a grand rush on board. Such warm greetings from friends white and brown. . . . Our fellow passengers . . . mostly strangers . . . were exceedingly interested in witnessing the joy of the natives at the return of their missionary. Four carriages were waiting . . . to convey us to as many different homes. We accepted gratefully the one which took us nearest to our own cottage. The distance from the landing was a mile and a half, and we met warm greetings all the way. After breakfast we went directly to Punahou where the examination of our College School was then in progress and where we were welcomed by the missionaries, their children and many friends.

Emma's Land Ho!

In that day of oral examinations, whatever the discomfiture of the pupils, their parents and friends made a gala event of the affair—a whole day session—with lunch in the low adobe dining-room as an interlude. This custom was still extant through the seventies. Abigail continues:

One gentleman remarked that there had not been an arrival for a long time which caused so much excitement! So we had a merry time over it. . . . It was a time . . . of fervent gratitude in view of all God's wonderful mercies to us during the past fourteen months.

5. AFTERMATH

Thanks-
giving

Abigail and Lowell have their one furlough behind them. The longed-for experience has been theirs; the dream is become memory; the cup of realization has brimmed, the joy being pressed down, shaken together, and, for the rest of their lives, running over with thanksgiving.

Welcome

Table entertainment was offered by the good neighbors who had been tenants in Nuuanu Cottage during the family's absence.

"We thankfully accepted their kindness for nearly *two weeks*—abominable, wasn't it!" exclaimed Abigail; but Kukui, the old servant who had held things together during Abigail's strenuous years of school teaching had died while they were away. Moreover, warm weather, constant interruptions of callers, and general settling, made a delay in "housekeeping and entertaining company after a fashion as of yore," comfortable if not necessary.

Shock

Kukui's death was not the only shock they suffered. The old lady who had boarded with them had lost her life, being burned to death, and the old home at Kaumakapili had vanished also in flames. With the loss of that home, which, with no insurance, was total and irreparable for $3,000, came also the loss of needed income from its rental, $30 per month.

But Abigail can smother sorrow and take delight in her children. Emma is now settled in the "spare room" at Nuuanu Cottage where

Emma

. . . a young, fresh tamarind tree shades one of the windows, and the yellow blossoms of the Acacia [probably *Kolomona*] look smilingly in at the other two. A pretty set of cottage furniture—fresh and new [and bought with money Emma had earned] and all her little fixings, pictures, etc., with delicate white muslin curtains looped back from the windows, all combine to give a chaste air to the room, quite in keeping with the little mistress.

During the long vacation the boy, Augustus

. . . is reading Caesar with his sister for teacher and trying to get ready for Algebra with the same gentle helper. Emma has

two music pupils and she has also received the appointment of
teacher in music and drawing in our College School. . . . All
the patrons of the school are pleased with the appointment.

In early December, 1866, Abigail writes in glad remembrance of the year:

At Home. . . . It is winter again and the little snow birds *Memory*
have gathered amid the shorn branches of the vine which creeps
up the pillars and under the windows of that sacred room where
I spent those two blissful weeks. God bless the dear occupants
of that room and provide for all their future as he provides for
my little snow birds. . . .

You inquired about postage. This is the regulation for this
country. Ten cents is the charge on every single letter from us
to you or from you to us. We must prepay the whole on those
we send away and seven cents on each one we receive, so if you
really wish to pay for your letter you can do so by enclosing a *Postage*
two and a five cent stamp. It would be useless to put it on the
outside. Our postage bill is of course large but it is joyfully
paid for it is all we have left for intercourse with our loved
absent ones.

The goods we sent via Cape Horn have arrived in safety and *Webster's*
among them is my splendid copy of Webster's Unabridged. It is *Unabridged*
a treasure. I am making pies of the apples I dried in Albion.
How precious are all the associations connected with our visit *Apple Pies*
home. O the good you did us! I sometimes fear that we shall
need recruiting again before a tithe of the next 30 years have
passed away.

At present the influenza is raging fearfully among our poor
people and our hearts and hands are very full of care and labor.
During the month of November there have been about 300 *Influenza*
deaths within a circuit of five miles—nearly all from the effects
of the influenza. . . . A few of these have been foreigners—but
they are mostly natives. It was scarcely worse than this when
the small pox was raging here.

About the same date Abigail says in a letter to her brother
Lionel's wife in Northampton, to whose care she had taken
her mother from Ohio:

I am deeply grateful to you for all your cares and labors for our precious mother. How glad I should be to relieve you of them I can never tell, but God has ordered my path in another direction and so the blessing is for you. May you find the same kind and tender care in your declining days which you now bestow upon her.

I have had no efficient help since I came home, and as I have entertained a good deal of company, I have had to labor very hard, I believe not less than one hundred persons have eaten at our table since our return. One young lady spent four weeks with Emma and we now have a dear friend from San Francisco come to pass the winter with us for the benefit of her health. I love to extend hospitality and to see people happy. It seems to me that we never had so much to do as now, but I suppose we have. The reasons why it so seems are that we have had a year's vacation from labor, and also that my old servant is no longer living. I have now a young boy and a little girl. I teach them both every day if possible from books and they help me all they can. But of course I have to be on hand to attend to everything.

Hospitality

Meteoric
Shower

By the way, did you see the meteoric shower the other night? There were more that 300 counted here—a few of them *were* quite brilliant.

Lowell writes:

We remember our visit home among our relatives and friends with deep interest. The blood courses more freely in our veins; we have seen you all at your homes, and firesides; the distance between us seems almost annihilated; the great Cable is laid and we get news from England in 14 days. They are pushing on the Great Western Rail road, and if you and we live long enough we shall see some of you here in Honolulu; fresh from North-ampton, only fourteen days travel. The mail steamers from San Francisco to China are to touch at Honolulu going and return-ing. Six days by rail and eight by steamer! Only think of it. Don't it make you feel young and resolved to come to the Sand-wich Islands!

Atlantic
Cable and
Western
Railroad

Church
Givers

Since our return we have re-shingled the large roof of our House of Worship, at a cost of $1100.00. Native carpenters and others belonging to my church performed the work gratui-

AUGUSTUS
LOWELL'S BROTHER

LUCRETIA
LOWELL'S MOTHER

tously. Carpenters would have charged $250. for the job. The work is done well and you will be glad to hear that the debt on our hands is about twenty dollars.

Our Sunday School is quite flourishing; never more so. Some 200 including the teachers. Abba has a large class of native boys and Emma of girls and young women. Her class averages from 15 to 19. Joseph Cooke had a large class of young men, Mrs. Hayden, Miss Helen Judd, Sarah and Julia Dimond, Henry Waterhouse and Robert Andrews all have classes in our school, which gives it character; and the little folks are quite ambitious to learn their lessons and be on hand to join in singing, both at the commencement and close of the School. Your correspondent has a good smart native man to assist in superintending the School. At three o'clock p.m. we have six district Sabbath Schools each averaging from 20 to 25. The teachers above named except my own family (Emma has a class in the Bethel between 12 and 1 p.m.) go out and conduct them, two and two. We do with our might what we can on the Sabbath for the children; the government are so anti-sectarian that they allow no religious instruction during the week!

Sunday School

District meetings conducted by deacons and leading church members were organized for the aged and infirm.

During his stay in New York, Lowell had purchased an "American Organ" for his church. Since its arrival

Lowell's Organ

. . . our choir of singers have made great improvement. A native by the name of Stephens taught by the son of a missionary, is our organist and choirmaster. He plays very well and has already taught about a dozen so that they perform well on the organ. Please give us a call some Sabbath morning and hear their voluntary, and other tunes as sung by "Natives who are ten times worse than they were before the American missionaries came among them."

This letter goes on in hopeful strains and is joyous over a new revival of religion, especially among foreigners, apparently the continuation of revivals in various parts of America, and says:

My dear wife was never more active and useful among the natives than since our return home.

At the close of this epistle Lowell presents a theme which must, under cover all the while, have been harrowing his soul.

I now purpose to fill out this sheet by copying a letter recently received from the Missionary Rooms, Boston. It was dictated by Dr. Anderson [the Secretary of the A.B.C.F.M. whose visit to the islands already mentioned had set their hearts aglow!] but written by his successor, Dr. N. G. Clark. After pondering for some time upon this letter, it occurs to me that these two Doctors have been taking lessons of the men of this world; Christ, you know, says that "the men of this world are wiser in their generation than the children of light."

During the recent American war, lots of commissioned officers were dismissed, and others appointed to take their places; some perhaps on account of old age; General Scott, for instance, to retire, under full pay—etc. I have said enough to give you a clue to what is coming—

MISSIONARY HOUSE, BOSTON
Nov. 24, 1866

HONORED AND DEAR BROTHER,

The Sword   I have recently had a conversation with Dr. Anderson, in re-
Falls   gard to your work, of which I feel that I ought to give you the
results. He is very strongly of the opinion, in which from your age and infirmity and the immense flock you have to look after, I fully share, that it is best for you, much as you love your work, and highly esteemed as we know you are by your people, to divide your field into several parishes, each under a native pastor; or to relinquish it as a whole to one active well esteemed native pastor. We can not but feel that it must be just impossible for you to look properly after so large a people. They ought to have a great deal of care to keep everything snug, to keep alive a true, wide awake christian spirit, to develop a spirit of christian benevolence, and a healthy piety, able to withstand the peculiar trials of the time.

You can afford to retire from your labours. You have done a good work, a man's work, and can afford to rest on your honors, and rejoice in the fruits of your toil, in a good happy old age. Your example and words may be to young men for counsel, to bid them go forward with renewed energy to meet the issues and responsibilities devolving on them.

You know I wondered at the idea of such large parishes as some of you have on the Islands. They would do in other days, but I am sure a change is necessary. It would not meet the wants of the case to have assistants. It is better to put the full care and responsibility on well trained and faithful native pastors, of whom the Lord has given you many, and more are to be raised up in the future.

With kind regards, etc.,

N. G. CLARK
Foreign Sec. A.B.C.F.M.

P.S. To be on the retired list of course would not affect your salary. Your people could well support a pastor of their own. C.

After copying this letter for his brother-in-law's eyes, Lowell adds:

This you see is turning over a new leaf and introducing me into a *"state of rest"* such as I have never desired or anticipated. My wish has always been to be at my post, watching and serving, when my Lord should call me home! My missionary *"titles," honors and "rest"* all come unsought, unasked for, and undesired, by me. An old classmate secured "D.D." for me. May the God of Missions give us wisdom that we may honor him and his cause in this proposed change.

It is a sweet and chastened spirit that closes this letter with the words:

A great deal of love to Mother Tenney from us all—and also to you, all your families, and to all enquiring friends. Yours in Christian fellowship.

LOWELL.

This was a hurt that, in Emma's words, "almost killed my father." At this time his church people decided the matter as the following letter from Abigail to her brother Lionel shows.

September 20, 1867. . . . Well, here we are hard at work as usual. Our people would not consent to give us up for a younger pair of laborers and so we may continue on until God calls us to rest from our labors. Our school enterprise is very popular —we hope much from its civilizing influences. It has increased in numbers from twenty-eight to one hundred and fifty. Our two young teachers are indefatigable. Our Sabbath school is under a good organization and is doing well. We have over 200 connected with it. Our people are in a wakeful, hopeful, state and we are cheered in our work. Husband is remarkably well. I have *Teaching* been obliged to resume teaching in order to eke out our salary *Again* which never covers our necessities. I teach from three to four hours a day and enjoy it much. Still, as we approach nearer the millennium the churches and mission boards will grow so enlightened as to know that it is best to give their missionaries a comfortable support so that they can give themselves entirely to their legitimate work. It will not be in my day, but I do not complain. . . .

The Emma has returned from her summer ramble and is at home *Daughter* at present. Her year of teaching was so severe upon her that I was afraid to have her go on without a longer rest. She has been very busy making shirts, coats, and pants for her brother, getting him ready for a new school year. Her being at home makes a golden period in our life's calendar. She lightens so many burdens and smooths away so many rough places and keeps perpetual sunshine about us.

Tell our precious mother . . . I am more and more happy to think we went home and had such a precious time with her.

Dear Abigail! her interests were many. The same letter, fraught with unspoken feelings, could turn gaily to a description of an idol of which she had sent home a photograph. It reads:

The Idol The old Idol is at least eight feet high and looks exactly like the photograph, being principally mouth and teeth with very little in the way of body or legs. Did it frighten Mrs. Parson's little children? I was afraid it would. It was "cast down" at the time when idolatry was abolished here. It fell into a Kalo patch and sank down through the water into the soft mud where their food, the Kalo, or Taro, grows. There it has lain for almost fifty years until the generation who assisted in its overthrow had passed away, and the present occupant of the land knew nothing of it. One day, about a year ago, the land holder in working over his mud, and feeling something hard under his naked feet, fished it out, and lo an old idol rose to view, in a state of almost perfect preservation! Its exhumation created a great sensation among the natives as well as among our children. They never saw one before until they saw them in the museum in Pemberton Square. There were one or two ancient natives found who retained so much regard for the old times that they predicted dire consequences to the poor man who had so unwittingly set up an idol. It was found at a place about thirty miles from here, was brought to this place and presented to the museum of our college. So far as I know it is the only genuine specimen of the ancient objects of worship remaining on the Islands, although the natives have an *honest* habit of carving out innocent specimens of idolatry and selling them to strangers as genuine, much in the same way as the papists sell the fifth leg of the ass which carried "the young child and his mother into Egypt."

Letters to a Child

Writing to her grandnieces she always had some bond of interest in pets to write about—her delight in all pigeons until she saw fantails, when they filled her imagination; joy in mating ducks, sorrow in their tragic death and honorable burial to satisfy the child owner of the pretty pair; multiple cats until nine to put out of the house at night were too many for even a tireless grandmother—all these interests gave zest to her letters to children. On one occasion she wrote a little girl:

I just want to ask you if you ever study out loud, because your cousin Gus does—not in school you know, but when he is getting his lessons at home. . . . As I pass to and fro I often get hold of a nice passage in some Latin or Greek translation, or a little treat in astronomy. Since I have been writing here at his study table he has been saying over and over a description

of the dozen stars which form the head of Medusa, which is part
of the constellation Perseus. So you see I have had an opportunity to refresh my memory with a little bit of astronomy
while writing to you. I must say, however, am glad he has gone
off to the parlor to practise his music.

Emma's
Marriage

The year 1869 brought Emma's marriage to Benjamin
Franklin Dillingham, a good man and true who was to prove
an affectionate, generous, and loyal son-in-law as well as
husband.

Here it were easy to follow a tempting path and to trace
the odyssey of this young man from his birth in West Brewster, Cape Cod, through his childhood on a farm in Westboro, Massachusetts, through seven years of youth on the
high seas from the fo'c'sle of his uncle's ship to his accidental
settling in Honolulu, and, from that point, to forecast the
drama of his business career in Hawaii. But the life of B. F.
Dillingham, as he is remembered today, deserves a tale of its
own, and, refusing an excursion into his story here, we continue with our Lowell and Abigail.

This same year, 1869, brought to Abigail and Lowell the
outcome of long doubts and fears regarding their missionary
work. In April, the month of his daughter's wedding, Lowell
wrote to Abigail's eldest brother, John Tenney:

Another letter came about Dec. 17 assuring me that I must
comply with the wishes of the A. Board—otherwise I must look
entirely to my church and people for a support, but if I would
resign and consider my work as done, they would continue my
salary as long as I live.

In a letter to her namesake, Abigail said:

God over
All

Your dear uncle and myself were deeply touched by your true
sympathy in the loss of our church and people. There can be no
doubt that a great mistake was made—but God is over all. We
have lost none of our self respect, or true position as christian
missionaries and we have received much sympathy from friends
and neighbors many. We shall, I trust, always remain true to
ourselves and to the blessed Master in whose name we came here
to live and labor for our dying fellow men. We are not opposed

to the march of improvement in church or state. Everything
must advance and we have always had "Onward" for our watch-
word. It was thought by the youngish members of the mission
that thirty years was long enough for a man to be in active
service, and so we must give place to our young brother—while
the work was prospering in our hands. Perhaps this is the way,
and yet, if our master had thought so, would he not have weakened our strength in the race, or given us some indication of
inability to perform our duties? Your uncle now goes out every
Sabbath 4 or five miles and holds service in two churches. He
also spends much time with the sick. He visits the hospitals,
sometimes daily, and has lately taken to carrying pure spring *The Cup*
water to the inmates of one of them, because it is better than *of Cold*
they get elsewhere. He does not think anything of these humble *Water*
duties, he is so used to doing for others, but they remind me of
the "cup of cold water" of which our Savior speaks.

Months rolled by, and in latter January, 1871, Abigail
wrote to Dr. N. G. Clark, Secretary of the A.B.C.F.M. as
follows:

NUUANU COTTAGE

. . . So what with a flourishing medical practice (under a
government license) and his editorial labors, this old missionary *Abigail to*
of 68 years is fully occupied all day and all the evening and is *Secretary*
happier than he has been for four years! He is in excellent *A.B.C.*
health and bright in spirits once more. *F.M.*

As for myself, I am always teaching and my hands and heart
are full of work all the time. As I am obliged to teach in order
to eke out our daily bread and a sufficiency for a modest support, I can not be too thankful that I love the work and have
strength to do it and that I desire to do it for the Master.

To a friend she wrote:

I have known all about a teacher's life in my own family.
First my father, and then my brother were noted teachers in
their day, for more than 40 years each. My father, however, did
not teach constantly, but my brother taught continuously a
large school from 20 to near his 60th year, and from that time
until his death six years later, he was seldom without a few boys

in his family in whom he delighted, and whose education he was superintending.

Undoubtedly it was partly to unite forces economically as well as to cheer the hard-working parents that a year after her marriage Emma, her enterprising young husband, and their baby daughter took up their abode at Nuuanu Cottage. Here, while her young brother was away, first working in a store in Hilo and later at business college in Pennsylvania, Emma helped her mother and shared her children with their fond grandparents. It was a happy period in all their lives. Sorrow was theirs, too, for in 1874 came the death of the second child, a bright and robust little boy with radiant blue eyes. The grandmother's heart was crucified afresh. "To bear, to nurse, to rear, to love and then to lose!" Sorrows are not always lightened by sharing; sometimes they are increased as one's own pain is reflected, doubled, trebled in the sufferings of those best loved. Therefore daughter Emma must rise to the occasion of bearing a mother's loss bravely lest the grandmother's stricken heart break. With quiet resolution Emma became once more assistant teacher in her mother's school, for, since the brief furlough, school is again the major theme, as it has always been the most recurring rhythm, in Abigail's life.

To Love and To Lose is noted in the left margin alongside the preceding paragraph.

This school was made up of about twenty-eight Anglo-Saxon children, from four to thirteen years in age. Alert and vigorous in manner in spite of variable strength, she held a steady course as teacher until almost seventy-two years old.

Abigail's youngest pupil in this her last school was the grandson she called (unbeknown to him, with his wholesome awe of her authority) the apple of her eye, Walter Francis Dillingham. Fifty years after the schoolroom door at Nuuanu Cottage was closed finally, this grandson invited all available pupils, and there were twenty-three, to a celebration of "The Smithsonian Institute" as Lowell named Abigail's "academy." Much anticipation was indulged in by the grayheads bound for a holiday in their happy past.

Nuuanu Cottage had been accidentally burned after Lowell's death and the land sold. But thirty miles from Honolulu, at Mokuleia, near the mission station of Waialua

Lowell and Abigail had so often visited, the grandson had built as a small ranch house a charming replica of Nuuanu Cottage. First, a private railway car decorated with coconut leaves, Hawaiian flags, and school banners made for the occasion; then, at the terminus, automobiles carried these "old children" to a little green yard surrounded by white palings and cherishing both flowers of the long ago garden and also a singing *auwai*.

Replica of Nuuanu Cottage

If there were tears they were happy tears as one and another called "The dear old roof—so perfect!" "Oh, the same narrow veranda!" "The high railing!" "There's 'Father's study'!" "And there's the schoolroom!" Happy exclamations, all. Chinese orangeade, a childhood beverage, refreshed the visitors who finally gathered at a long table where old-time foods were served. Who were there? Father, grandfather, old bachelor, business man, banker, capitalist, ex-governor, rich man, poor man, doctor, lawyer—one almost adds Indian chief! The girls? Mother, grandmother, spinster, ex-teacher, ex-librarian, traveler, social worker, organizer, counselor, friend. How they talked, how they laughed, how they loved it all!

To start off the reminiscences already bubbling in the table talk, the following extract was read from an address written by Abigail for her Golden Wedding in 1882.

Mokuleia Reminiscenses

Of her early Hawaiian school she had written:

My scholars made rapid advancement in civilized and christian education. With scarcely an exception they gained a clear and distinct enunciation of our English tongue. As the years went by, they advanced to higher grades of educational progress and were transferred, many of them, to the Royal School, and some attained to honorable place at Oahu College. As they reached maturity almost all of them turned out well. Several of them became excellent teachers of English. A few died young after giving bright promise of usefulness. Some of the girls married native ministers and teachers. Then there are now living stalwart farmers, mechanics of various kinds, printers. And some time ago a bluff hearty sailor called upon me and, giving his name, I recognized one of my own bright pupils. There was in my school a merry, wide awake, but law-abiding boy who bore a name that has been celebrated in song and story from the olden time. He is now known as Captain William Tell, the efficient leader of the Police force in Honolulu. Then there was a very handsome boy, who was also a very close student. I destined him for the noblest career in his country's service. He has since occupied some of the highest positions of trust in the nation, and at present fills the position of Postmaster General in Honolulu.

Of the dear children of my foreign neighbors and friends, who in later years came under my teaching and training care, I could give many pleasing reminiscences. I must only take the time to say that they made me feel that the wide earth never furnished a happier teacher. Many of these have already arrived to mature years and have taken their places as representative men and women in this and in other lands. From some of these I have received congratulatory letters for this anniversary. God help them all, and may each one ever prove a pure and shining light and a controlling influence for good in the world.

There is a large group of little ones who have but recently passed from under my watch and care. Their tender feet have but just entered upon the untried path of life. My heart yearns over them. May the good Shepherd have them in his loving keeping and may the covering shield of God's protecting care be their defense through all their lives, that none fall by the way.

May God grant that when I meet my pupils at the last great day in the presence of our Divine Master I may be permitted to present them all and to say with exceeding joy "Behold Lord here am I, and the children whom thou hast given me."

A few furtive tears were brushed away by one and another and lo, the teacher of half a century ago and her little schoolroom, with its girls wearing long braids of hair down calico backs, and its barefooted boys in short trousers, had replaced the scene and the company. And that was no surprise. Did we not know as we closed wee Emma's Journal Book that the gentle shadow of Nuuanu Cottage must ever and again fall across the path of our life story?

Grayheads nodded sympathetic memories and no glasses were needed for far-away pictures. Nor was any stimulant other than happiness required to loosen tongues.

Here are some of the reminiscences given at the Mokuleia luncheon:

Julie recalled that soon after the burning of the first Hall's Store, Oscar in some school prank climbed into his desk (the desks were of all shapes and sizes, being furnished by the parents of the pupils), whereupon his sister Lucy cried out that he must not break his desk for his Grandfather Hall would have to pay damages and he needed all his money to rebuild his store!

Oscar remembered that when he and another boy had by persistent quarreling in recess, exhausted the patience of the teacher, she arranged that they should take recess separately, one after the other. Finally, her philosophy rose to the dictum that, as every dog had to have his fleas, so her school, she supposed, must endure the annoyance of Oscar as its flea. His own recollection of himself as a trouble maker was borne out by others present who had found him a baneful tease. He declared that in his career at Punahou, the influence of this former teacher was "all that saved me!"

Margaret presented for the host's memorabilia a little glass hat which she had received as a school prize fifty-seven years ago.

The subject of prizes reminded the granddaughter that she had always supposed her grandmother was "very rich," because she was so free in giving prizes and presents.

Margaret did not recall, but others did, the consternation felt at school when she inadvertently thrust a steel crochet needle into her arm. Mercurochrome was not known, was iodine used then? But as far as we children knew there were no germs, so perhaps that helped recovery.

Julie remembered her sister Haunani's stand in saying that she would kick the teacher for punishing Julie. The threat was carried out only to discover the rebound of a hidden hoop skirt which saved the recipient of the blow and surprised the offender. Sister Pauahi thought this, then, must have been the occasion when her two sisters, Julie and

Haunani, also her cousins Laura and Emma occupied simultaneously the four corners of the schoolroom.

Such pictures raised the question as to "the size of that schoolroom, anyway," with desks enough for the children, recitation bench, teacher's table. Three walls had each a window, and an open door led to the yard for play or across the veranda to the room where teacher's daughter, between nursings of her children, taught higher mathematics, music, and penmanship. In front of the bench stood the pupils in spelling lessons, when one "went to the head" or "went to the foot." Reference to spelling reminded Belle that the word "skunk" was always omitted from the list. Was this on the idea that "nasty" is a "nasty word"? Abigail's granddaughter retains a similar connotation with the Hawaiian translation of the last word, *pilau*. Being forbidden its use in childhood, she finds it abhorrent still.

George, referring to the idea of "carrying on" habits of schooldays, remarked that he had been true to that philosophy as regards the matter of spelling, being aware of its snares unto this day.

Johnny and James were referred to by various members of the group. They were two young boys who in succession were boarding pupils in Abigail's home. Johnny was mentioned by George as one whose tongue made it easy to escape punishment. On one occasion when he and Johnny were guilty of "hitting Laura," Johnny returned from being sent to look for a stick for retributive punishment with the easy lie of being unable to find one. Whereupon George was sent on the same errand. Unable to "tell a lie" (where have we heard that of some other great man?) he fairly macerated the stick with such efficiency as to remove the teeth from the weapon, so to speak. Fleeing from the wrath to come, George ran away, leaving his hat. Across the meadow of the cemetery playground, through the old homestead of his grandfather, "Sweet Home," down the then steep Judd Hill, George soon found himself hidden under the Nuuanu bridge at its foot, where the cool waters of the Pauoa stream purled that day—at times it threatened or stole the bridge. Refreshed by the shadow of the echoing rafters and the earth walls grown with maidenhair fern, he was all too soon interrupted by breathless Johnny. Once again Johnny's expedient of smooth fib took him back to school, as unable to find George as he had been to find a stick.

All went well with George until time to go to school next morning. To go to school barefooted was usual, but bareheaded—unheard of! One could not endure remark or question. What to do! The despised checked cap of an avoided "Scotch suit" was donned and all questions from his schoolmates as to "Where did you get that hat?" (or rather its earlier equivalent) were answered by a quenching air and the statement that he was wearing his cap because he "liked it so very much"!

George was not the only one of his family to run away from punishment. Cousin Kauka told of the fleetness of Charlie, George's older brother, who, prophetic of the requital for using a "bad word," nimbly crawled under a row of desks and escaped while the bowl of symbolic purity was in preparation. Among questioning smiles and sneers Kauka stoutly maintained that his selection by the teacher as an example in place of the escaped Charlie was purely vicarious; but he cherishes the taste of the Hawaiian-made brown soap and lathering water as an effective warning that has preserved the immaculateness of his diction to this day.

The rotund, slow-footed "missionary horse," Old Whitey, was called *Elelu Keokeo* (White Cockroach) by some of the children and "once," said Oliver, "in an altercation over something with the teacher, Horace and I declared we would shoot Old Whitey."

Abigail at threescore years and ten, despite many remembered scenes of her discipline, must have had much understanding of youth. The price of enrolment in her little school included barefoot walks over dusty hot roads without sidewalks for some, and, as Pauahi recalled, a ride for herself and her brother Bonny of five and a half miles twice a day, sitting double on horseback all the way from Waikiki to Nuuanu Valley. Pauahi added her memory of teacher's Golden Wedding celebration as the grave responsibility of deftly slipping into Abigail's palm a two-and-a-half-dollar gold piece when shaking hands in congratulation. The mention of the Golden Wedding recalled to Carrie how many years she had treasured a gold-printed piece of white ribbon, the "Pupil's Badge." The gold coin reminded Albert of the great impression made on his mind by the plateful of gold coins seen at that party—a vivid contrast to the contribution boxes in church. He said he and Walter were the school babies. To be sure they were—being only six years old when "dear teacher" sent her last class to Punahou. Albert said that, since seats had given out, he literally sat on a little hassock at Abigail's feet! With other children he remembered "the peach trees that Gus planted," protected by a high-for-children whitewashed inclosure, and quoted Walter as saying, "Uncle Gus is more fond of those peach trees than he is of getting married." So much for observations on a bachelor yet a decade from his wedding.

Many in the little company remembered vividly the same things—the tamarind trees, their delicious but forbidden half-ripe fruit; the needle tree, a Monterey Pine, with long, flexible needles that looped into delicate links for neck and arm chains, or offered "knotted" thread and needles for sewing leaves and flower petals into dainty costumes for dolls, also made from Nature's offering to children's seeing eyes. Coveted half-ripe mangoes, also forbidden and delicious, and mangoes hidden under the leaves of a trash fire in neighbor Campbell's yard for an appetizing roast, were retasted in memory, as was the cool water from the water-monkey standing in a draft in the pantry, when ice was an unwonted luxury. Stronger in associative power than taste were the remembered "smells" from Father's study, redolent with Jaynes' Pain-killer, Carminative Balsam, and many another aromatic remedy for human ills. Others besides the granddaughter had witnessed the bleeding of a patient's arm. Laura thought she remembered "helping" by holding the necessary cup!

A letter from Nellie mentioned neighbor Campbell's monkey,

a terrible beast if I remember correctly, and tales of "what it might do" if released filled our hearts with a fear that has

lasted all these years. The little low-browed missionary cottage
has a frame of rosellia in my mind. Surely long sprays were
never more flower-laden than those around the old pump.

Listening, some of us could taste again the honey sucked
from their tiny stems, and hear the pop of the wee "fire-
cracker" buds snapped between our finger tips, and remember finding in old books little circlets of the flowers slipped
one within another without thread and pressed for sentiment's sake. Nellie's

first memory of the little school room is of Henry Green measuring his spool work twice across the length of the room and the
big girls watching him to see if he was cheating. That little
school room has tender memories—I could linger long with
them for they fostered foundations on which many of Honolulu's best citizens built character. The multiplication tables
were drilled into us all so perfectly that multiplication has
never had any vexation, and beautifully penned mottos taught
precept and penmanship from Aunt Emma's guiding hand.
. . . The framed signals on the front "stoop" where Gus could
watch the tower on Whitney's store for duplicate signals of
ships coming into port (long before the days of the lookout at
Diamond Head). . . . The cool parlor,—and there one morning I was permitted to come in to morning prayers. Willie
Damon had died and there would be no school; we were all
dismissed but "Nellie could stay and play with May after
prayers." In the grandfather's sonorous voice now I can hear
those words, "In my Father's house are many mansions; if it
were not so I would have told you" and the children's hearts
were quieted and death had no sting. . . . At last came a great
day. We had mastered "long division" and the principal of
Punahou School was to come to see if we could pass the examination. At the moment he drove into the garden I was a very
active pig for Horace to drive to market; but we "grew up"
that very day. . . . Punahou was to be our next stepping stone
to learning.

Nellie's letter had also referred to "the low stile" over the
stone wall from our school lane into the cemetery as "such a

joy." So did the others remember it, for the great grassy
meadow, awaiting graves of another generation, was the
playground, the campus of our little school. George referred
to it with great reverence and affection. We had as little fear
of death or ghosts as Wordsworth's "simple child that lightly
draws its breath." Her "two of us in the churchyard lie"
were matched by little graves of our own. In season, we
gathered as little earning chores the great green army worms
from the long grass standing about our knees. Nellie, recalling them, wrote:

. . . The short cut home through the graveyard was always
more exciting when it was caterpillar time—bless the mynah
birds, do the children of today know why they were imported?

George had been "among those present" when graves were
moved for the new entrance, and with other children had been
interested in the finding of little exhumed bones. But every
day the sun shone while the showers fell; we wore to smooth-
ness little hills of grass for sliding; the wee red tassels
bloomed nowhere else; the linnets sang over our heads. We
were children, happy, happy children!
An absent former pupil paid tribute to

. . . thirty two years of teaching given to us island children.
. . . Every quarrel on the playground, every lesson and song,
was made to teach in some form the old, old story. Only God
can measure the abundance of the harvest, as children's children
shall scatter broadcast the seed of her sowing.

We follow the grayheads with eyes shining through tears
as they leave the table at Mokuleia and in their several automobiles glibly feed the miles with further reminiscences all
the way home. But now they are gone and we return to the
pages of sixty years ago.

*Captains
and Kings*
"The Captains and the Kings depart." The seventies were
beyond the day of the whalers. The Kamehamehas, under the
rule of three of whom Lowell and Abigail had lived, were
gathered to their fathers. The young and charming Lunalilo
had reigned his few months and gone to the great democracy
of death. Bernice Pauahi (Mrs. C. R. Bishop), daughter of

the High Chief Paki, had more than once declined the crown of the Kamehamehas and now in 1873 Kalakaua had come to the island throne. Abigail writes of political matters to her son, in business in Hilo, Hawaii:

We finally have a king settled over us, *chosen by the people* (altho he *was* the rightful heir) who insisted upon their legislators electing him, in spite of opposing candidates and some show of resistance. It was a time of anxious solicitude among us all while the political agitation continued and much prayer went up to the throne that the right thing might be done, and we think it *was* done. The new king is very popular with all classes, affable and friendly and sympathising with his subjects, but it is a time of great depression in every department of business, and our business men are longing very ardently to bring about a reciprocity treaty between the Government and that of the United States. The king, I believe, desires this. Of course, the U. S. can get on without this little dot, mid-ocean, but the dot cannot so well get along without aid from that great power.

A little more than two years later, Abigail's pen rejoices in the following news:

April 8th, 1875, Thursday eve. Joy for us and for the Islands in general. The "City of Melbourne" came in this morning bringing the unexpected news of the passage of our treaty. The town was jubilant. There is a torchlight procession this evening and at this moment they are holding high carnival before Henry Carter's house. [Henry Carter was the able Minister from Hawaii to Washington.]

The Treaty

Rockets, cheering, speeches, etc. and he deserves a better ovation than we can give him, for his *pertinacity* has triumphed as nothing short of it would have done. There is *talk* on the street that the opposers of the Treaty mean to spend two hundred thousand dollars in buying up the representatives so as to defeat the treaty in the end, but as they have given it publicity I guess the Republicans will have a little too much regard to their reputation to be bought. It is said that the Democratic members have put this treaty through. *I like them for it.* They are opposed to monopoly. *I like them for that.*

Showing   That is a fine concession, Abigail, for so staunch a Repub-
One's   lican. For in 1882 we are to see your political color in these
Colors   poignant words:

> So we are to have democratic rule for the next four years. It
> was a great shock, but God knows best. We need chastisement.
> May it be sanctified to our whole nation, especially to the
> church of Christ.

Abigail is always delightfully open-minded and often
plain-spoken. So her friends sometimes thought. But Abigail would be willing for them to think and to say so, for she
would declare:

> I allow my friends to differ from me in views and sentiment.
> Let us still be friends.

The following extract shows her vigorous thought, practical judgment, understanding of child needs, praise, condemnation, each in its place. It is from a letter to her son.

Wrecked   The "Syren" arrived here from Boston just a week ago.
Babies   Somewhere near the Falkland Islands she picked up a boat
containing the captain, his wife, with two babies, one a year and
the other three years old, together with the boat's crew who
had been obliged to abandon their sinking ship 18 days before,
off Cape Horn, and had been drifting about that frozen region
ever since, frozen and famished and yet alive. The good captain
of the "Syren" gave the lady all of his shirts, the only things on
board she could use for herself and babies. Those babies had not
been dry for 18 days. Judge of the condition of that year old
baby! only the mother love kept it alive, and the men say they
should have died in despair long before help came but for the
courage and fortitude of that woman! None of the company
could stand when taken on board the Syren, and when they arrived here the lady could not come on shore until clothing was
taken off for her use. You know just what a commotion such an
event caused among us here! It was not many hours before their
wants were met and they were all comfortably located in the
Sailors' Home. The wrecked people were English. I had of
course been down to carry some things and to see just what was

most needed after the first necessities had been met. . . . I
thought the little girl ought to have a doll. . . . You'll see the
notice of this rescue in the papers and also another disaster
wherein the crew of an English ship in a sinking condition were
refused succor by an American ship, and would have perished
had not an Italian vessel appeared and rescued them after there
were four feet of water in the hold! I declare I dont know what
punishment is severe enough for that hard hearted captain. He
was going to San Francisco and I hope will get his deserts. This
wrecked family think Honolulu a perfect paradise and want to
live here always, and you know, it *is* a good place for people in
trouble of any kind.

Turning over the memories of the seventies and eighties,
some of them written in letters, others, only on the tablets of
the mind, we realize that Abigail was always much more than
a teacher. Her first three grandchildren with their parents *Adjust-*
were a part of her household until the return in 1876 of her *ability*
son, Augustus, from an eastern business school, and the arrival of her son-in-law's relatives, made it necessary for two
separate establishments. During the transition the schoolmistress was housekeeper for a family of eight under what
we should today call such primitive conditions!

In the following three years, illness and care in the junior
family brought not only the tax of anxiety but sometimes the
superintendence of two households. If the daughter and her
husband must be absent on business or recuperation of health
there was no trained or even practical nurse to be requisi-
tioned for service. "Mother" might even move her then small
school to the dining-room of the daughter's home, returning
now and then to Nuuanu Cottage to see that her men folk
were faring as well as could be expected. On such an occasion
she would say:

With my school and the little ones and two fresh importa-
tions from the "Flowery Kingdom" who can speak only Chinese,
I shall be much occupied. . . . Ah Fat (the name sounds appropriate) is leaning on the broom handle in the front yard. As
it is the third day since he commenced, I hope he will be able to
finish sweeping it today.

Once the almost-wreck of an interisland steamer brought terror to the home-keeping grandmother lest the young parents be lost at sea.

Lowell had long been anxious to have her lessen her toils, but knew she was persisting for the education of their son. Now her son may

chafe at the thought of my teaching, but he can not yet assume the extra care and expense, and I am so thankful to be able to work.

And in preparation for the homecoming of that only son, what extra work hadn't she done!

For years Abigail had known within herself that she would be "old and worn out" did she not "live by faith." As it was, *Second* she could be gay, laughing and saying to a contemporary on *Wind* the celebration of her birthday:

I am astonished that you are allowed to be so old. My son will not let me get much beyond fifty!

Or she would gleefully meet her grandson's heart's desire with a noisy drum "as big as an old fashioned band box" and tell her daughter that she must endure "grandma's folly" while the slipping years allowed. How she enjoyed the grandson's Christmas greeting, "Merry candy!" and she was not afraid to say she loved "to have children pull things about as they want to."

Ready to help in any emergency, just before the return of her son from college she let her tired daughter go to San Francisco to meet her husband, and assumed the care of the little ones although there remained five days of her school year.

It was a very hard five days and nights, but I got through, examination and all, and then had four days left in which to clean house, whitewash, do outside painting and various other matters in the tidying up line that are more difficult in an old rough house than in a nice one.

Her glad sympathy put by fatigue, including that of a restless, teething child at night—harder to bear than when

BENJAMIN FRANKLIN DILLINGHAM
1876

EMMA LOUISE DILLINGHAM
1876

she was younger—because of her joy in the rest for her daughter. The welcome-home motto and green wreath for the returning son were scant expression of the thrill to the waiting souls from the moment Lowell's eye at the spyglass saw the pole in town signal, "Steamer coming past Coco Head!"

"Shall I ever forget God's goodness to me in that hour, that perfect homecoming!" cried Abigail. At the end of December, 1877, Abigail wrote:

A little more than two months ago our precious children and grandchildren had a narrow escape from a fire with which some fiend attempted to destroy their house. . . . Of course we brought them all home where they remained for six weeks, when they entered a new house. . . . The past fifteen months has been a long period of suffering on the part of our poor Frank and consequently with us all. The three months of Husband's illness during the summer was another great strain, besides the daily care of family and school, so that when this last shock of the fire came I fairly succumbed. My nervous system is much shaken . . . and I suffer . . . from a kind of apprehension of I know not what. The feelings are all new. I never had a headache in my life as most people do and know not what to make of these new sensations. I continue to teach as the doctor says it keeps my mind occupied and teaching is my "normal condition." *Under Fire*

In the following spring Abigail wrote her namesake:

I am planning to give up teaching. I know it is too much for me and the domestic cares are all I ought to attend to. I have never been in the habit of taking any recreation to speak of and this is wrong for anyone, old or young, and I want you to bear it in mind. If possible do not take holiday time for receiving boarders or doing more work than comes in term time. I know why this has been done and I have overtaxed myself so often and for so long that I cannot bear that others should do it. God give you wisdom in this matter. We do talk a little of going to San Francisco in the summer. It is all uncertain as yet. *Holidays?*

The school teaching was not abandoned for another three years, but June saw Abigail, her daughter, and grandchildren off for a holiday in California. There is ample testimony of the anxious watchfulness of Abigail and her daughter for each other during this visit, but Lowell's letters bring them refreshing philosophy during their absence.

Lowell the Home-Keeper

Kahele comes with the clothes every Saturday, makes our beds, sweeps the bedrooms, takes her pay all right thus far. Ah Ling eats his allowance, looks after the horse, washes and oils the carriage, feeds the hens, gathers the eggs, 1½ dozen of which I have sold. The hens are now all having a vacation, but I think their egg factory will be in operation again ere long. Ah Ling has been up several times cutting weeds and burning them in the pasture. I have school with him five evenings in a week and have given him writing lessons by day. But I think he is off more or less evenings.

. . . You say "I feel as if it is not quite right for me to be here doing nothing but spend money." Indeed, are you doing nothing else? Are you not eating and drinking and enjoying yourself, receiving calls from old friends and acquaintances, and making many new ones? Having taught school for forty years, is it wrong for you to have a season of rest from toil? Most teachers have their annual vacations and recuperations. Please do not spoil this vacation because of a little expense lest you become penny wise and pound foolish. . . . It is moved and seconded that you make haste slowly about returning. Now then, as I call for the motion, Mrs. Chairman, let me say I wish this vacation to be one of uncommon magnitude. I wish you to recuperate and rejuvenate, to see and be seen; to attend the female prayer meetings and the meetings of the Woman's Board, to get good and to do good as you have opportunity, and not hide your talent under a napkin. You need not be afraid or ashamed to tell the good people there what the Lord has done for the poor Hawaiians through your instrumentality. . . . I am not in the habit of making long speeches—especially on subjects which are perfectly obvious. Motion? Those in favor of your holding on to return . . . October will say "*ae*." . . . Carried unanimously. Now then we shall not expect you to return until October, unless you can give some good reason for so doing.

Upon the return in October, Abigail wrote her niece:

Our dear ones here were very indulgent in sparing us so long, and our homecoming was a very gladsome one. Home duties were never more attractive, or home comforts more prized. We had much to do, but have both found our health much improved. I am not wholly recovered from the nervous derangement from which I suffered so much a year ago, tho my nerves are stronger, and much more equable. For days together I feel quite well in all respects, and sometimes for weeks. I am never irritable, but a little inclined to depression, tho no one knows it. When my "nerves" keep me wakeful at night, I suffer most. But my dear, I have just had my 69th birthday and what can you expect. My hand rests in my Savior's and all my times are in His hands. I am up early in the morning, seeing after Gussie's early breakfast and keeping all things bright for him and your dear uncle.

Treasure Trove

Emma brought from San Francisco by sailing vessel a large tin box of marshmallows (unobtainable then in Honolulu)—and how long the supply lasted, two or three delicate morsels apiece being the after-lunch-on-Sunday treat! A greater treasure from California was the first carnation plant in the Islands. The first flower, so spicy and dark red, crowning the tiny plant made a day of rejoicing in the household.

But soon nursing more serious than that for flowers was required. In 1878 a fever swept through the town, taking many victims, and in our junior household father, mother, and daughter were laid low. Wrote Abigail:

The Presence Chamber

We came very close to our God during those trying days in prayer and deep humiliation. . . . A few days before Emma's fever reached its crisis I was prostrated . . . and for six of her worst days I was unable to go to her. They strove to keep her great peril from me, but there was no mistaking your uncle's prayers! I knew we were walking on the confines of a great calamity and I entered into the very presence chamber of my God and communed with him as a dear friend! . . . Our God was most merciful and the uplifted rod was stayed.

A joyous convalescence for all the sick ones brought plans for better living conditions. The boyhood days preceding his seven years at sea were remembered by the young hus-

Daisy   band and father. Daisy, a Jersey cow, the first of the then unthought-of Woodlawn dairy herd was bought and became a pet in the tiny rented back yard. How ridiculous it seemed to Frank Dillingham that his children, used to the blue milk of the Portuguese dairymen, would not touch Daisy's cream!

The Honolulu of today has almost forgotten the dusty waste that once lay between the shore and the foothills, a harsh stretch where practically only *kikania*, thorny member of the deadly nightshade family, and *kalu* (*Acacia far-*

"The   *nisiana*) thrived between gullies made by the occasional and
Plains"   torrential rains. The brave algaroba, sprung from seed sown inadvertently by pasturing horses, or hopefully by human foresightedness, struggled into life in the seventies. The eighties brought a government water-piped system, neces-sary precursor of the buildings for homes, schools, and other purposes that now crowd from the fast-disappearing salt swamps to the hilltops back of "The Plains."

Despite these conditions in the region just described, Frank Dillingham looked beyond them in space and time and, as his first step into his dream-farm, purchased fourteen acres of land adjoining the "Punahou Lower Pasture" and bounded otherwise by Punahou, Beretania, and Alexander Streets, although the last was nonexistent then. Removal to that spot, two miles from town, seemed almost a Daniel Boone adventure to the two children, for, as we have indi-cated, no homes or trees intervened between it and the site of the present electric pumping station, at that time a quarry of volcanic sand. Two irregular tracks, now Beretania and King Streets, with frail wooden bridges over the deep gullies the annual freshets made, crawled across the waste of sun-cracked ground. But through thorny *kikania* and *kalu* one might drive at will, just as horses (their tails stiff with burrs), turned loose by their owners, wandered over the wilderness.

"Wood-   September, 1879, saw the young family of four Dilling-
lawn"   hams moving their walnut "sets," latest style of the seventies,

together with cheaper pine accessories and an iron stove that would burn the green algaroba wood thornily hedging the premises, into a simple one-story cottage. The house had encircling verandas, many doors, windows that worked with ropes and pulleys instead of the customary notches and stops, green wooden blinds, and floors covered with Chinese matting, tacked down save for annual housecleaning. To the minds of the older generation Frank was risking the family health in establishing bath and toilet in the main house instead of an out-house. But 1879 was twenty years too early for Honolulu's first sewerage system.

By 1881 our forward-looking city had established a Bell telephone and Abigail could easily arrange dates when she would drive Old Whitey at a slow jog trot, with frequent rests or interspersed walks, the prerogative of a "missionary horse," away across the plains to spend the day. She was sure, if it were Saturday, to bring a friend to play with the exiled granddaughter May. *Bell Telephone*

Frank drove daily to his hardware store in an open express wagon (and his was never a missionary horse!), so May could ride at least part way to Grandma's school at Nuuanu Cottage and often stayed with her several days. At six years of age Walter was riding his pony, Flyaway.

Dodd's bus, *hapa ha* (twenty-five cents) the round trip to town, with wheels that sometimes came off in the deep dust-or-mud-filled ruts, was a later convenience, antedating by some years the English tram-car's service with its galloping mules that, as often as might be, ran away when being transferred from one end of the car to the other at the terminal. *Dodd's Bus*

Emma was so busy with her new babies (three in three and a half years), her chickens, ducks, weeding, tree planting, etc., that the monkey-pod sapling found in her wilderness which "must be cut down because a dirty tree—too hard to sweep up leaves!" lives on to this day and is now the glory of the "Church in the Garden." Strangely enough grass has been found that thrives under its great shade, nobody is troubled by the falling leaves, and, with its many noble qualities, it is replacing throughout our city the beautiful but shallow-rooted and uncertain-lived algaroba. *The Monkey-pod*

Artesian wells were the pride of the seventies, Frank's well, one of the first. Walter and his playmates must fall in line and dig wells, too, long and laboriously. One of the miniature derricks Frank had made to protect young trees from the cattle that pastured in the big yard was borrowed to help the boys work the post-hole digger, on its rope, sawing back and forth in serious play, as if their whole vocation were endless imitation!

Emma could philosophically spare one of these derricks. Had not bull, time after time, put his shoulder to the whole army of them and made her lawn, next morning, look like a dismantled chess board! How did her trees ever survive repeated destruction? She had planted great clumps of ginger, saying "That will be too hot for the cows to eat," and then a young colt had been "tickled" to kick them to pieces!

Troubles Little and Great

Old Egypt had its plagues and young Woodlawn was not without its plagues. At one time grasshoppers sat in unbroken ranks on the rail fence surrounding the farm, ready to devastate the premises, and were interfered with only to the extent that the children could make themselves into a beheading army. The brand-new wall paper was sadly defaced by a scourge of millers that swept in from no one knew where to fill the air with the dust of their wings. Roasting pans of burning oil bound to rakes and carried like torches of destruction through the house were the combating, and finally triumphant, force. It was a time of power against power. If the house must be painted, the patient vines were ruthlessly laid low and a mother must still be sweet when the children's pet goat butted through the rare English ivy on the front doorpost. All this, plus drunken milkmen and departing cooks, was as nothing when "the reaper whose name is death" plucked the "morning glory baby" whose short half year on earth is still a bright memory. Abigail's "seven times wounded heart" once more brought forth renewed trust as the fruit of bereavement.

Water in a Thirsty Land

The eighties, through the enterprise of Mr. S. G. Wilder, Minister of the Interior, brought a piped water system which soon made "The Plains" a rival residential section of the dear old "Valley." The developments of Manoa, Kalihi and

THE GRANDCHILDREN—MAY, WALTER,
HAROLD AND MARION, WITH "FRITZ"
1885

Palolo valleys, the tract at Kaimuki, the Makiki, Pacific, and
Alewa heights, and more new sections were undreamed of as
Abigail drove Old Whitey across "The Plains."

In other ways Honolulu was expressive of growing pains. *Growing*
With a somewhat childish vanity Royalty returned from a *Pains*
trip around the world with a planned innovation for the
miniature kingdom—a real palace of concrete to replace the
hip-roofed, wooden *Hale* of former kings, and a coronation
with real crowns, even if seven years after his accession to the
throne. Abigail, promising her brother a pamphlet descriptive of the event and a sight of her "royal invitation,"
commented:

It has not been a popular thing on the part of the king. Such
a needless expense. A small country is great only as it walks
modestly. Any attempt to ape the grandeur of powerful nations
is, to say the least, ridiculous.

Eighteen eighty-one brought Honolulu a second visitation *Smallpox*
of smallpox, with attendant fears and arrest of business. But *Again*
Abigail said:

Losses in business are not to be thought of when compared
with the sufferings of the afflicted ones.

Distress called forth energetic expressions of help from
all.

. . . Our poor people . . . not previously protected are
falling before it. . . . We still hope . . . with fresh vaccina-
tions and the care of the Bd. of H. that the disease will ere long
be stamped out.

This year was marked also by "The Flow of Eighty-One,"
the great river of once molten lava being one of the sights on *Lava*
today's tourist trail on "the Big Island." Abigail briefly *Flow*
describes it thus:

The great eruption that started it occurred three or four
months ago on Mauna Loa, and the molten stream started down
towards the plain, through the forests on its way to the sea.
We have had several great flows since we came to the islands,

but they have either reached the sea at some isolated part of the island or else ceased to flow just before reaching the inhabited parts of the island, i.e. with one exception. But this flow is steadily advancing towards the pretty town and lovely bay of Hilo. It is now but seven miles distant, the molten stream is a mile wide, and the light and smoke and unearthly sounds are plainly seen and heard by the people in Hilo. It moves slowly so that the people can flee for their lives if necessary, though they would have to leave their homes behind them. We still hope that the flow will be checked at its source, as was the case some years ago when it approached within two miles of Hilo. The bay of Hilo is almost as beautiful as that of Naples which it a good deal resembles. We hope it is not to be filled with this dreadful lava.

The flow continued; space and time for hope grew short and tense. The Princess Ruth, remarkable for her prodigious size, daughter of the great line of the Kamehamehas who had repudiated the ancient religion, reverted (or had she always been faithful?) to the old gods and in this great exigency came from Oahu to Hawaii. With her train of retainers she approached the unwieldy mass of death and destruction. She made the stipulated sacrifice, red fish, white chicken, black pig. The flow stopped one-half mile from the seemingly doomed town, Hilo, the crescent city. Christian and pagan rejoiced together. God was over all.

6. ABIGAIL

The Closed Schoolroom

Abigail had closed forever the door of her little schoolroom in June of this year, 1881, but there were always chances to help the grandchildren in their studies, and two new babies were born into her grandmotherly care before her childward activities ceased. Staying at the little farm during a necessary absence of her daughter she could tell of incidents like this:

I have just been in to help Walter dress and heard his spelling lesson and Roman numerals at the same time. Leaving him

to draw on his stockings, I took his shoes out to be blacked.
Finding the man at the churn, I took the crank and gave him
the shoes. I "brought" the butter by the time the shoes were
ready—felt quite proud.

Abigail confided to her distant brother:

I had a great desire and curiosity to be seventy years old. I *Threescore*
thought there would be some sudden change of feeling in body *Years*
and mind to mark the event. But there was none and the strong- *and Ten*
est feeling I had on that day was gratitude to God that there
was something left for me to do in the world, and that I had so
much strength for the service that remained.

How much indeed, dear Abigail, of all manner of things!
As late as in 1883 she was equal to this, once again superintending two households in Emma's absence. As mother to
daughter:

Yesterday morning early arrived the "Coptic" with 1100
Chinese for this port, also four mission ladies en route for the
eastern states, health seeking. We hurried round and impro- *An*
vised a meeting of the Woman's Board. A large attendance, *Improvised*
including Mr. Damon and Frank, Dr. Hyde, Mr. Forbes, Chan- *Meeting*
cellor Judd and other masculines. I presided of course but invited Dr. D. to pray and the rest to aid in making the meeting
a grand success—and it was. The strangers made addresses,
answered questions, etc. It was an inspiring time. When it was
over I felt that we had had a good large piece of an annual
meeting of Woman's Board in Boston, such as we read of in
"Life and Light." . . . After the meeting I hurried up to the
house [her own in Nuuanu] made beds, etc. Everything looked
well. I hurried back, it being late, drove Dolly [not a "missionary horse"], liked her very much. . . . More to say, but
no time.

Although the longed-for and long-expected brother did
not come on October 2, 1882, Lowell and Abigail celebrated
their golden wedding—but not as anticipated. The son and *The*
daughter had planned an elaborate reception in their spa- *Golden*
cious grounds but—Abigail may tell the story. *Wedding*

Six days before the day and just after the four hundred cards of invitation had been issued came that fearful crash in the fatal accident to Frank's only brother Charlie.

"So swift trod sorrow on the heels of joy." I must hasten over the agonies of the next few days, as my head already begins to ache at this brief review. Of course all thoughts of a celebration were given up, but in three or four days friends gathered about us and insisted that we "receive" in our own cottage home, and we consented. Two hundred came (our place is small). The little pamphlet will tell you the story for I cannot as yet write much about it. It was an ovation, most unexpected and surprising. We knew nothing of the arrangements that had been made, of the gifts prepared, of those precious home letters of the outgushing hearts that were coming to us and hands freighted with loving gifts. It was all a great surprise, and you see, my dear, that two great extremes met us on that occasion joy and sorrow, as they seldom meet. Well—it proved too much for my naturally sensitive nerves and I have been obliged to take a long rest from all mental effort . . . and such a blessed quantity of letters I longed to answer! I am very much better now and if I can only manage to do just enough and no more I get along very well, but as yet I can write and read very little at a time—can go out and exercise in various ways, keep up little Walter's lessons, etc.

The little pamphlet Abigail mentions contained a poem by her daughter full of joy and thankfulness for the day, addresses in reminiscent vein by Lowell and Abigail, quotations from which appeared elsewhere in these pages, and precious testimonials from others both present and absent.

Who Is Known? Admiring friends thought they knew Abigail well, but how much are people really known to friends or to others? Did anybody know that Abigail had once hidden and fed a deserter from the navy? If anybody had known, how would she have been judged? Why did she do it? Probably she, the frail boy a world away from home, and God were all that knew. Did people think it odd that the body of a woman found in a neighboring woodshed forty-eight hours after suicide was given a beautiful casket covered with flowers and

a funeral in Nuuanu Cottage? She had been a "most esti-
mable lady," said Abigail.

Was she ever weary in well-doing when girl after girl
whom she was teaching and training in her own home fled out
through the window into the tempting darkness of night,
leaving her clothing rolled up in her bed to deceive the kind
mistress passing the open door?

Who could guess pains of rheumatism, or neuralgia, or
utter weariness in Abigail's light step, out-stretched hand,
welcoming voice, smiling eyes that invited confidence and
promised interest to everyone who approached her?

What were the thoughts that occupied Abigail's mind as
she waited each Sunday morning for Lowell to call, "Time
to start for church"? As far back as she could remember, the
granddaughter, playing on the floor of Abigail's bedroom,
had watched her dress herself in dainty clothing—the black
grenadine with the narrow green silk stripe, the satin shoes
with elastic up the ankle sides, the real-thread-lace jabot
fastened at the throat with the gold-nugget pin sent by the
Hawaiian friend in the California mines, or perhaps the
brooch containing "Little Lowell's hair," the chaste fan, the
delicately perfumed silk gloves! Bonnet strings tied, Abigail
would recline on her green-baize-covered lounge by the window, her Bible in her lap, her eyes closed in meditation or
prayer.

Sunday Morning Medita- tions

Perhaps she was thinking of missions, on this wise:

A good man in New London has died and left half a million
of dollars to the A.B.C.F.M. Wonderful are the ways of God.
He has some great designs to be accomplished right speedily.
. . . . I am more deeply than ever interested in the missionary
work in Africa since dear Beulah's nephew went to the dark
continent, and when the Herald comes I look first of all for
news from "Bilunda." So many precious lives have been surrendered in that trying climate. Things look very hopeful in
Bilunda, and in some other places. I see that the young lady
who went out in Mr. Fay's party has married one of the
brethren. I should think this an economical arrangement considering their limited accommodations in house room.

Missions

Is she laughing softly?

I do wish I was rich, and could put a million of money into the hands of the A.B.C.F.M. How they do long to occupy waiting fields and also better support those already being worked. O, that more wealthy men might be converted to Christ! what a privilege it must be to be entrusted with much wealth—to be a steward of God's bounty, and what a mistake people make in thinking the treasures committed to them are their own. God will surely ask an account of their stewardship.

Religion is so much of her life, we can almost see Abigail's lips move in a meditation like this as she pictures far-away loved ones:

Everlasting Love

How dreadful it is when we lose sight of the tenderness of God. We may not always be able to feel it but we know it is there. . . . Leaning on the arm of everlasting love, no such precious trust shall be lost. In God's own good time and way he will reward it. Never falter . . . never faint. "They that trust in the Lord shall be as Mount Zion, which cannot be removed, but abideth forever." How precious are the promises of God.

Immor-tality

Turning in her mind to one gone before she murmurs:

He is not dead—he lives forever more, and continues to bless me in my precious remembrance of him.

Marriage

Perhaps marriage crosses her mind. She reasons with herself:

When a man is courting he makes himself as agreeable as possible to the lady he wishes to wed. He shows her many and constant little pleasing attentions. He is watchful for her comfort and pleasure and tender and gentle in all his manner towards her. . . . He does all he can to win her heart. . . . The same means must be employed to preserve the love of that heart after it is won, else love will die out or burn with a feeble flame in spite of promises and vows. . . . Although we know that God loves us, yet we do not rest satisfied without desiring and asking and yearning for daily fresh manifestations of that love in our hearts. What is the meaning of daily communion with God? It means something more than our efforts to build up his cause in the earth. It is a constant renewal of the sympathies that exist between our soul and God. We are so constituted that we crave fresh assurances daily. This by no means implies doubt or distrust of the Divine or the accepted human love.

She ruminates sadly on a young friend:

She seems to get along comfortably in her married life, but I guess there is not much romance about it!

Again she ponders:

I should never choose voluntarily a single life for a woman, but very many of the brightest and best and most useful of our sex have chosen this life, and oh, how infinitely preferable it is to an ill favored marriage.

A smile passes over her face as she pictures an engaged couple of her acquaintance

. . . and all the pleasant little arrangements and consultations in active progress. I always did love to watch young birds build their nest, and this reminds me of it.

How does her mind work on education? We know from her *Education* many written words how vital it was to her conception of life —a large part of her father's religion. And do we not remember her saying that a thorough education for her children was the only personal luxury she craved? Thinking of young kinsmen in the far-away homeland, she muses:

They have had the best home training. . . . Their future is safe with God. They should have some freedom now that there may be symmetry in their development of mind and social bearing. . . . Things may not develop just in your way, or in my way, but if God is entrusted . . . in the best way.

Of manners and character she murmurs:

Fitted to grace the highest circles of society. . . . Perhaps *Manners* such have the most courage and fortitude to meet the privations *and* and vicissitudes of life if called to it, just on the principle that *Character* I have always found it easier and infinitely pleasanter to make a true gentleman or lady comfortable in my modest home than to try to do it for a shoddy upstart.

Naming over her friends as tenderly as one would finger a rosary, Abigail would come to Bernice Pauahi Bishop, daughter of the High Chiefs Paki and Konia, and she would recall how eagerly Bernice used to come to Nuuanu Cottage to spend a day with her. Bernice would ask the pleasure of brushing Abigail's long hair, and would chat merrily and delight in teasing the child Emma. When long ago her betrothal to Charles R. Bishop was rumored, how *kanalua* (uncertain) Lowell had been lest the engaging young American be not the equal of the royal-natured and beloved princess. But how the years had proved the wisdom of her choice. Gratitude filled Abigail's eyes as she recalled the many times she had returned from the Bishop home

. . . strengthened and braced up for more earnest endeavor for the people of our love and care. . . . At last may we find each other in the Golden City of our God where we may renew with joy and gratitude our humble life among the beloved people of these Islands many of whom we believe are being added to the great multitude no man can number who swell the choirs of Heaven. . . . Now she is gone, the last and best of the Kamehamehas, the strongest bulwark of this nation, a christian lady and my precious friend these many years. There is no one to take her place in any degree.

Does she dwell on old age?

Renewed claims, some of more than fifty years have been resurrected since our golden anniversary. . . . There is pleasure and some pain in renewal of intercourse, but much more of the former than the latter. . . . Though I have written at least a hundred letters . . . it will be impossible to keep up with more than three or four of the most precious ones. . . . I have just had my seventy fourth birthday and what are you to expect from such an old fossil! Husband is eighty one, has ridden in his buggy at least 10 miles today and is still active and vigorous, going about among the sick and sorrowing. . . . Vigorous . . . that word needs moderation . . . not the vigor of youth by any means, as when one sets out on a journey in the early day but rather the quickening of the footsteps as the evening draws on and one sees the lights of home in the near distance and is anxious for the rest home coming will bring. So we two old young people who hope to die in the harness go cheerfully on, hoping for the gathering together and the joyful . . . meeting . . . above.

Her thoughts light like a bird upon a young friend in a far-away garden. Her eyes kindle and she whispers: *Bring Back Eden*

Bring back all of Eden you possibly can—and that will be a great deal.

On receiving a letter from a friend in Philadelphia describing his daughter's parties—beginning at bedtime, five hundred guests, and $600 worth of flowers—she muses:

A useful christian man. I guess his children are nice, too, only they have had to contend with some of the disadvantages that wealth and position bring. . . . I am so glad that our lot has not been cast in that line. *Contentment*

No Franciscan courting of Lady Poverty, this, but a humble contentment.

Abigail dear, it is the year 1884. The parting with Bernice seems to be hastening the sands in your own glass. You are aware? Yes; and long ready. Three years ago you wrote to your brother, "We must speak often to each other for the time is short." Hark! Abigail. In forty years Katharine Lee Bates will sing: *Sinking Sands*

> Because the years are few, I must be glad;
> Because the silence is so near, I sing.

Your brother has been writing you oftener of late and what joy it has given you—so long the "hungry-hearted," as you told him. You say:

I have kept my heart young always and so have you, and bye and bye we shall put on immortal youth and vigor. *Much To Do*

How much happiness is being crowded into your days— and how much there is still for you to do! The making of calls had not gone out of fashion. The increasing presence of strangers called for more and more welcoming of the coming and speeding of the parting guest, many of these, too, were missionaries needing heartening for their new tasks or, on return, healing of broken health. For many years Abigail had been president of the Women's Board of Missions of the Pacific Islands. Her heart was in all of its activities. The work of the Strangers' Friend Society was a vital need when the long list of Honolulu's societies was unborn. *Po Elima*, or Friday, was from Abigail's early mission days to this present a day sacred to the "female meeting" of the Hawaiian church. The arrivals and departures of the successive *Morning Stars*, and, after the last wreck, of the schooner successor, *Jennie Walker*, were seasons of activity, hospitality to passengers, and gifts of all sorts, including household goods, farm implements, and domestic animals.

Few of Abigail's pages remain, but probably they are all the letters she wrote in those busy weeks previous to her home-going. What more could we ask her to say? She expressed the greatest satisfaction in her home life, including a fine recognition of her deep friendship with her daughter. A last look at the starry heavens:

Star of Love   We had a lovely view of the great planets in conjunction, and Venus at her perihelion was the finest planetary sight I ever saw, large and clear and bright like a small sun . . . looking, I thought, just like the Star of Bethlehem when it met the rejoicing sight of the wise men as "it came and stood over where the young child was."

Finally, this, to Betsey Learned, her spiritual sister who had sped her on the white wings from New London to Honolulu so long, long ago:

In Remembrance   Yes, dear, our supplementing the wants of the missionaries was in a very small way like the same blessings conferred on us so many years ago. Tears came to my eyes as I thought of the eager faces, the willing hands, and the loving hearts that did so much for us. How often and often they rise before me. Perhaps it is because they are so near me now in spirit. We hope to hear from, or rather to see our little "Jennie Walker" and to hear

from her precious passengers early in December. Did I tell you
that I prayed for the lives of the animals, as well as their own?
It was right—was it not? and can you think how happy it made
me to see my children and grandchildren doing with eager glad-
ness for those dear ones, just what you and your dear ones did
for us? God is kind. I bless Him. Again and again has my
Emma said to me "It makes me so happy to be able to do any
good in the world." That is her highest aim and joy.

At the turn of the year the arrival in Honolulu of an   *The*
Englishwoman to hold many evangelistic meetings for which   *Broken*
Abigail must plan and work, brought her to the final efforts *Pitcher*
of a spent body. The pitcher was broken at the fountain.
The letter to Betsey Learned, just quoted, had closed with
these words:

No, dear, I didn't remember that Job said that. Have I got
to lose my "understanding" as I advance in age? May he take
me away before I have become such a sorrow and care to my
friends.

This, Abigail's last wish, was granted when she "entered
the fair schoolroom of the sky," January 31, 1885.

The memory of Abigail permeates the years as an attar of   *Attar*
roses—roses many, varied in quality, color, texture, sig-   *of Roses*
nificance, sweet, thorny, real, lasting.

IV

"IF WINTER—"

1. LOWELL

Alone

ALONE! Molokai, the Lonely Isle, had not been so lone as this! But had not Abigail said, more than fifty years before,

the Missionary husband and wife are all the world to each other. A separation is felt in all its agony?

What was true for youth must be doubly true for age.

In February, 1886, Lowell wrote to his niece, Abigail's namesake, correspondent, and confidential friend, as follows:

NUUANU COTTAGE
Feb. 18, 1886

MY DEAR MRS. HARRINGTON:

Feeling pretty well this morning for an octogenarian, I propose to write a few lines to you. More than a year has elapsed since your dear Aunt Abba fell asleep in Christ. For several months after her death my health was not good, and I often felt that the sands of my life were disappearing rapidly, and that I too should soon be numbered with the dead, but we have been favored this winter with the good old trade winds and refreshing rains, and my health is much improved. But my house is left unto me desolate, and only those who have been thus bereaved can fully understand the bereavement. But God has been very gracious to me. I have had a good home in Emma's family, all of whom have truly sympathized with me in the loss of their mother and grandmother. I have had enough to eat, and to drink and to wear, and with my own horse and carriage have daily taken Gus to his store in town. There I have met those who wished medical advice and treatment, and then I have passed on up to the Old Homestead in Nuuanu valley, and often find others here wishing the same. Here I spend the day with my dear wife's picture standing on the table and apparently looking upon me, while writing or reading or eating my lunch, or

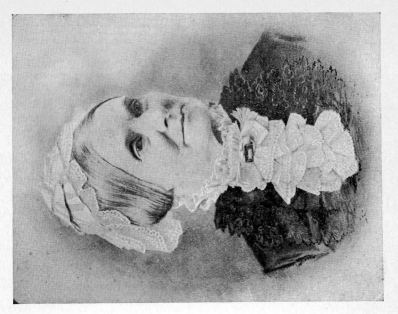

ABIGAIL, 1882

LOWELL, 1882

conversing with callers. Here also I have Dr. S. Irenaeus Prime's picture, a dear friend of ours. He was my room- and class-mate in Williams college and we have always had the New York Observer on our table—an invaluable newspaper. I feel greatly bereaved in the death of this good man. Irenaeus' two books of 100 letters in each lie on my table and I often read some of them.

Often, too, doubtless Lowell had read his friend's beautiful tribute to Abigail, published in his paper, the New York *Observer*. Probably by now Lowell knew the kind words by heart:

. . . A lady of refinement and cultivation, fitted to adorn the best society and able and willing to adapt herself to any company into which duty called her, . . . as a missionary, a teacher, a friend, as wife and mother she exerted the happiest influence. *A Tribute to Abigail*

Her house was the resort of travellers and others who greatly loved to enjoy its hospitality. The corps of Christian laborers at the islands held her in the highest esteem, the heart of her husband safely trusted in her, she did him good and not evil all the days of her life; she opened her mouth with wisdom and in her tongue was the law of kindness. A woman that feareth the Lord shall be praised.

The girl Lowell had found in the schoolroom, had taught him through the years many a lesson of forbearance and love and, very early in their married life, called by him "my dearest earthly companion," had so remained. Were love and marriage ever more discussed than in our immediate day? Divorce, a word practically unknown in Lowell and Abigail's vocabulary, remembered by their granddaughter as a rare expression during her childhood and spoken always under the breath, is now on every printed page and bandied about on the tongues of the multitude. Love and marriage. Does Russia think she has buried their old significance? Many in our own circle have been ready to criticize the matter-of-fact marriages contracted by missionaries of a hundred years ago when going to a foreign field. Boards did not wish to send *Missionary Marriages* single missionaries. A young man looked about for a suitable wife. Someone suggested "just the one." A brief meeting, a publishing of the banns, the making of a trousseau to last through years barren of replenishing, a marriage ceremony, a voyage to the uttermost parts—"how awful!"

Recently a group of gray-haired missionary granddaughters met at luncheon. One cousin turned to another and said: "But Grandpa didn't love Grandma when he asked her to marry him! Wasn't it awful!" Let me not crowd these pages with the names of living descendants of that happy and successful marriage! Such beginnings may have been true of some of the marriages, but not of all. But is there a case known where the common purpose, the deep consecration to a worth-while life, the close companioning under hardships of every description, the rearing of excellent and devoted children, did not build up mutual admiration, patience, trust, and shared interest—did not deepen spiritual understanding and affection of the finest caliber?

After one year of married life Lowell wrote of his delicate wife to her older brother:

Be not over anxious about your sister. I have often heard her say that she never regretted for a moment that she has enlisted in this cause—and also that the last year has been the happiest in her life. Yes, brother, kindred hearts have united for once at least. Our joys and sorrows, hopes and fears are one.

A few years later he confided to his journal:

Abba's birthday—thirty one years old. This has been a very happy day with us both—the contrast from constant excitement and vexation from one [a long-time and trying house guest] . . . to a day of quiet and comfort by ourselves is so great and so happy.

Abigail's words in 1835 recur like a musical refrain, "When such friends part, 'tis the survivor dies!" And from his old age fifty years later comes an echo from Lowell, "Only those who have been thus bereaved can fully understand!"

Lowell has been looking at the catalogue of the names of

the pioneer missionaries and the seven or eight reinforcements from 1820 to 1840 and exclaims:

I am quite surprised to see what a number of necrological stars are affixed to their names. Not less than seventy. How few of us left! You will not be surprised to have me say that I feel lonely—only four or five male members left and we are old, feeble, and can do but little. But I seem to hear my Lord and Master saying "Occupy till I come."

Occupy
Till I
Come

Considering Lowell's strong feeling for necessary aloofness from matters political during the heat and burden of his missionary experience, it is noticeable that in the last years of his life he followed with the eagerness of a chess player the movements of the pawns in this tiny kingdom rocking on its foundations. As keen was his interest as if a physical earthquake were threatening. Far more, indeed, for he grieved, as he always had, at the probability that the autonomy of this land would be lost. Never having been willing to sacrifice his allegiance to his native land, always to his dying day a staunch American, yet, for his long services to this foreign land, he had been granted papers of denizenship which he prized. With all his heart he had echoed throughout the years the dictum Kamehameha III had uttered in Kawaiahao Church at the restoration of the Hawaiian Monarchy by Admiral Thomas of the British Navy: "Ua mau ke ea o ka aina i ka pono (The life of the land is perpetuated in righteousness)."

Lowell the
Observer

Because of the instability of the Hawaiian throne, with weak and wicked advisors buzzing in the ear of a selfish and shortsighted king, Lowell's son-in-law, B. F. Dillingham, and, also, his neighbor, the progressive Samuel G. Wilder, had suffered great delays in business matters important to the welfare and future development of the Islands. These interests lay upon Lowell's heart.

Of the following letters, some show Lowell's alertness of mind in watching developments of history-in-the-making about him. Others show his growing thoughtfulness and interest in the younger generations, the mellowing of character that sweetens and brightens the memory of his last years.

June 30, 1887

Good Morning, Frank:—

Thanks for your good letter of the 4th inst. 24 days from London to Honolulu.

Excitement 100 Degrees

The political excitement in town is about 100 degrees Fahrenheit. Gibson *ma* have become hot enough to return their portfolios to the King and his Majesty says hold on till I can form a new cabinet. The citizens are to have a mass meeting at 2 p. m. today and will probably have something to say about the new cabinet.

I trust the excitement of Queen Victoria's jubilee will have abated when this note reaches you. Your expenses must be great at such a time as this, and I fear little or no progress in accomplishing your business. You will be patient of course if by moderation you are likely to succeed. We will all wait patiently praying for your success, and your safe return home by and by.

Aloha nui olua me Emma [Great love to both you and Emma],

Your father,

L. Smith

July 28 '87

My dear children Frank & Emma way off in London, *Aloha olua.*

By our last letters you will get some idea of the state of political affairs here on the 30th. of June, the mass meeting, the demands of the community upon the King, giving him 24 hours to say yes or no, and how he was advised by American, English and French ministers to comply immediately with the demands of the community. The Gibson cabinet were all dismissed, the

A New Cabinet

Hon. Wm. Green was called to help form a new cabinet, and appointed himself minister of Finance, Godfrey Brown of Foreign Affairs, Lorrin A. Thurston Minister of the Interior and C. W. Ashford, the Attorney General. The new cabinet together with the lawyers at once revised the constitution promulgated by Kamehameha V and made so many alterations that they call it a new constitution. Then called on the King to abrogate the old and adopt and promulgate the new.

The schooners were all detained in the harbor 24 hours waiting for his signature. The new constitution has clipped off the
King's wings, and put him into pretty close quarters. I hope the
London capitalists will now remove the blocks from the wheels
of your colonization scheme, and also from Mr. Wilder's railroad scheme and bid you both God speed. *Clipped Wings*

The Queen Kapiolani and her train arrived, all well, by the
Australia on the 26th. *Home from Abroad*

Portion of a letter to his absent children, August 12,
1887:

I am happy to hear that you had such a splendid visit at the
Hawaiian Club at Mr. Hunnewell's in Charlestown and that the
Queen and her party so behaved that you felt proud of them.
But we are none of us proud of the King's Hawaiian Club in
their scandalous opium bribery transactions, which have just
been fully published by the Hawaiian Gazette. You know we are *Opium Bribery*
commanded to fear God and honor the King, but how can we
honor any man whose private conduct and maladministration
is so abominable and outrageous? I should think that if his conscience is not seared as with a hot iron he would abdicate and
flee if possible to parts unknown.

WOODLAWN, HONOLULU
August 25th, 1887.

MY DEAR CHILDREN, FRANK & EMMA.

Your London mail of July 26th came to hand about noon on
the 23rd, inst., for which we all feel very grateful. Glad to hear
that you are both well, but sorry to hear that our glorious and
bloodless political revolution has so frightened the good mil- *Bloodless Revolution*
lionaires of London. The political and mercantile prospects of
these Islands from my standpoint are brighter now than they
have been for twenty years. I think it is wisely ordered that you,
Emma, are with Frank during this time of suspense, and I trust
it will all come out right by and by.

I have been greatly comforted of late to know that the good
influence of the pioneer missionaries and their descendants is
not dead and that even the Hon. Clovenfooted Gibson has testi-

fied that there is quite a mistake and that the missionaries now in power are among his best friends.

Cargoes of aloha from us all.

YOUR DEAR FATHER

HONOLULU, WOODLAWN
September 23rd, 1887.

TO FRANK AND EMMA.

MY DEAR CHILDREN—

Prodigals to Date

The Old Constitution, which allowed the King and Gibson to act like the "Prodigal Son" has been abrogated and a new one adopted and promulgated and accepted by the people: The Wm. L. Green ministry are doing with all their might to stop up the flood gates of waste and insolvency; have prepared the way for an honest election of nobles and representatives, and on the 12th inst., the "Reform Party" elected twenty-four nobles and twenty-two of the twenty-four representatives for the next legislature. The Opposition or Old Gibson party were very certain they would gain the victory and restore everything back to the Gibsonian party. But you see the great majority were ashamed of the waste of public property and wheeled into line with the Samaritan foreigners, and who ever heard of such a glorious and triumphant victory at the polls, as the Reform Party had here on all the Islands on the 12th, inst.? A *political*

A Political Jubilee

jubilee. Gibson has left the Islands, . . . all ran for representatives and all left out in the cold . . . also, who figured so largely to get the opium bill for the King to disgrace himself with a bribery of seventy-one thousand dollars—he too is left out in the cold. Now if you will hold on till our mails of September 20th, by the "Sydney" and "Mariposa" September 23rd, and "Australia" September 27th, together with a telegram from Bishop & Company and another from Mr. Spencer, come rushing into London, I trust they will sweep away the fog from your eyes, so that you can see political prosperity as far off as the Sandwich Islands.

Portion of a letter of September 23, 1887. Lowell had asked the elder granddaughter

. . . if she could write a journal like that of her dear mother.
"No indeed." "Where did your mother get her education?" "At
Punahou." "Well," said I, "what is the use of your going to
spend four years in Boston? If you are aiming to become the
wife of a lawyer, I think Punahou is quite sufficient. But if you
wish to qualify yourself to become the Principal of a Ladies
Seminary or go on a foreign mission, then you might go
through a female college, study medicine, etc., etc." Marion
called on me this morning and said "This is my birthday." "Oh
Yes" said I, "Four years old! What a nice little girl you are."

In reading these letters in his clear hand we must remember that Lowell was in his eighty-fourth year and very deaf.

On Sabbath morning, Rev. Waiamau being in affliction
wished me to conduct the exercises of public worship. The
Lord's supper was to be administered—six adults were to be
received into the church and six children to be baptized. I told
the deacons that perhaps the ordinances had better be postponed, but they said "No" everything was ready and they
wished me to officiate. So I walked up on the platform, read a
hymn, offered a prayer, read a portion of scripture which re- *The*
ferred to the Lord's supper and explained it to the candidates, *Pulpit*
prayed again repeated from memory the church covenant of *Again*
belief, faith, hope, etc., etc. to which they assented, and the
church arose and accepted them as brothers and sisters in
Christ and promised to cooperate in building up Christ's kingdom wherever their lot in life may be cast. Baptized five of them
and then baptized the children, prayed, read a hymn for the
choir to sing, administered the sacrament, and pronounced the
benediction and dismissed them at 12 noon. I am feeling so well
these days that I am expecting to occupy the desk there again
next Sabbath a. m.

HONOLULU, December 10th, 1887.

MY DEAR NIECE—

Thanks for one or two cards received by our family some
time ago informing us that Emma and her husband had arrived
from London in good health and spirits, and would soon be on
their journey homeward. As Emma holds the pen of a ready

writer, she will of course tell you of their many pleasant but hasty visits on their way home . . . due here on the 25th of November with the big mail. A curious coincidence of anniversaries clustered together about that time. November 24th was American Thanksgiving, November 25th. was Gussie's birthday and the appointed day for the return of our precious friends from London, and yet the steamer may be delayed waiting for the mail. On the Sabbath, November 27th, was my eighty-fifth birthday. On November 28th, was a national holiday "Restoration Day." As a family we wished to have one, but not five thanksgiving dinners and we wished to all sit down together at that joyful feast. Now then we were all agreed to have the family Thanksgiving dinner on Monday, the government holiday. This was "multum in parvo" and we all rejoiced together. Emma said "It is too good to be true. . . . No place like home." As a family and as individuals we have a great many things to be thankful for.

"Multum in Parvo"

In my mishap on the 13th of August I was apparently within a few inches of instant death. My physician said it seemed to him that an angel must have been present to protect me. My left ankle, leg and knee were dreadfully bruised, the hand and arm so crushed it was very doubtful whether . . . I could . . . have their use . . . again. But . . . I am now able to walk, and to dress and undress myself, though my arm and side are very sensitive and I must be very careful in using them. I am able to ride out in a carriage and to go to church in pleasant weather, and to prescribe for poor sick natives, who feel greatly attached to their spiritual father in the Lord. It is a great comfort to me to be able to do something for others, to be "diligent in business, fervent in spirit, serving the Lord" or some of his poor people. At the time of my beloved wife's death I was quite unwell and presumed it was my last sickness, but God ordered it otherwise. Feeling of my pulse they seem to beat as regularly as they did ten years ago. Dr. —— says that I have a remarkably strong constitution and that I rally from ill turns, quite as quick as do the young men. One thing is obvious. I have always been temperate, my system is not saturated with beer, gin, rum, wine, tobacco, or opium or any other narcotics.

A Young Man Still

How different our tropical winter is from what you have in

West Chester and Greenfield. Good refreshing trade winds, a cottage and yard surrounded with a large variety of roses, flowers and shrubs of every kind. Verily, the lines have fallen to us in pleasant places and we have a goodly heritage and we ought to be therewith content.

Your affectionate uncle.

L. SMITH

HONOLULU, June 23rd, 1888.

MY DEAR NIECE—

Many thanks for your early morning call, May 16th. We ask no apology for early morning calls. In this tropical climate our fingers are not cold for want of a fire in the parlor, or elsewhere. Half dressed, we can sit on the verandah to chat for an hour if necessary, without any inconvenience. But if you were really to call here half an hour before breakfast you might have to wait a little for me to return from my morning walk. I now rise with the sun, and take a walk sometimes in one direction and sometimes in another for thirty or forty minutes. This gives me a good appetite for breakfast. After morning devotions and breakfast, I drive a gentle horse in my carriage down town to Gussie's store, where I usually find natives waiting for medicines, or wishing me to go to their houses to see and prescribe for their sick. . . . *Walking and Driving*

July 30th, 1889

. . . *Grand riot in town.* Robert Wilcox, ringleader of one hundred fifty natives, marched from Kapalama this morning and entered the palace yard and took possession with a part of his men and with the rest took possession of the Government House, determined to overturn the present Government and have a new set of Government officers, etc., etc.

The Commercial Advertiser of today . . . will explain the result of one day's work of rebellion and treason and Guss proposes to cut out the article and send it to you in his letter, fearing that the whole paper may be waylaid. There have been many revolutions here during the last fifty-six years, but all without the shedding of blood until *now*. The government party *"Riot and War"*

all escaped, Wilcox surrendered with a white flag and he and all
who had not deserted him were taken prisoners.

My old mission house was a house of refuge last night for a
dozen or more women and children from town. I went in and
read the fourth chapter of James to them and then offered a
prayer, and in the course of an hour Captain —— telephoned
that Wilcox was taken prisoner and locked up in the station
house.

August 1st. The "Morning Star" did not sail yesterday
having lost a day of preparation by the Wilcox riot and war.
But the farewell meeting was held this p.m. from two to three
o'clock, and a very interesting meeting it was. I was requested
to be present and pronounce the benediction. All who took part
stood near to me, and I heard nearly all that was said, or read,
or sung.

Portion of a letter to his daughter:

July and August 1889

Frank tells me that you and he are corresponding about the
propriety of Walter going to a Boston school the coming winter
rather than coming home to enter Oahu College in September.
Dr. —— and several other intelligent gentlemen and some intelligent gentlewomen, advise that he by all means stay there at
least one winter, and I must heartily "kokua" [second the mo-
tion]. And not only that, but I give the same hearty advice to

you, to prolong your visiting in New England and New York
till the spring months of 1890. This blessed recuperating visit
has been postponed some four and a half years on my account.
No, my dear daughter, please make haste slowly about returning to your good home at Woodlawn. I have had a talk with
Frank, and he says "you just write to Emma and tell her how
you feel about her spending the winter there." Can't you have
a central station and be near both children?

Portion of letter, 1889:

Now one paragraph to Harold and Marion. Please tell them
that Grandpa is quite comfortable and happy in his old Nuuanu homestead and that Mr. and Mrs. L—— are expecting

that when they come back to Honolulu with dear papa, they will come up here and live with them till Mama shall return from her visit to her American friends. Grandpa will expect them to tell him a thousand and one things that they have seen and heard on board the steamer "Umatilla" and their ride on the cars in San Francisco and all about the Lions and Tigers and Elephants and Bears and other great curiosities they have seen. . . . Yes, yes, lots of questions.

For the Younger Grandchildren

HONOLULU, July 4th, 1889

Grandpa's aloha. . . . *Aloha nui ea!*

Your mother's letter dated Auburndale, June 12th, and 14th, came to hand on the 28th, ult., and gave us all great pleasure to hear of your safe arrival in Boston, and that May had been received into college. And I trust you will be glad to hear that all your family friends at Woodlawn and at the old homestead in Nuuanu are in their usual health and that your grandpa is rejuvenating and feels much better than usual.

To the Elder Grandchildren

The Fourth of July you know is one of America's great annual holidays. So also here at the Sandwich Islands. According to the program the pleasure portion of this community have a pretty hard day's work before them.

Regata at eight a.m.

Yacht at nine a.m.

Rifle competition nine a.m.

Baloon ascension nine a.m. Melville.

Oration ten a.m. in Opera House

Athletic sports and baseball match at Makiki in the p.m.

Public ball in the evening at the hotel.

Perhaps I will enclose a printed program for you to read at your leisure, or send you a bulletin. Holydays are far more numerous now than when I was a young man. The Fourth of July, Thanksgiving and Christmas are all that I remember that we had in Heath, some seventy-five or eighty years ago. The sports, pasttimes, presents, luxurious dinners and public balls were little or nothing then, compared with what they are now. Now, in the latter part of the nineteenth century, who can count the anniversary parties given by parents for their young children and others grown up to man and womanhood? There are also the wooden, the tin, the silver and the golden wedding anniversaries, next come centennials, inauguration of towns, states, and empires and Presidents, etc.

You of course will think this a strange kind of a letter for a grandpa to write to his grand children way off here in New England. Yes, it is my Fourth of July composition to you, who are in a travelling, visiting, and sight seeing school, and I want you to realize before you graduate that all these wonderful things like the Temple in Jerusalem, are earthly, and will soon pass away; and when you shall be called upon to die, you will want an interest in the Lord Jesus Christ, such as the world cannot give nor take away. I want both of you to often read the third chapter of Proverbs and in all your gettings be sure and get wisdom. Mark and make a note of objects truly good and praiseworthy, but touch not, taste not, handle not that which is evil and tends to evil, for the wages of sin is death.

May God in his wise providence watch over you both for good, and in due time return you in health and strength with full purposes of heart to spend your time and talents and influence in his service, is the prayer of your affectionate

GRANDPA.

NUUANU COTTAGE, October 22, 1889

DEAR DAUGHTER EMMA—

I am very glad you could see some of our surviving friends of the third or fourth generation, as well as the hills and vallies, roads, houses and cemeteries where my grandparents, uncles and aunts and my old acquaintances are resting till the bright morning of the *Resurrection.*

Heath Remembered   But after all the glorious description of Heath and the homestead of my nativity and its surroundings, I think I shall prefer to spend the remnant of my days in this tropical climate and have a resting place for my body in the Nuuanu cemetery, by the side of your dear mother.

The Railroad   October 23rd. We are having splendid weather this month— good refreshing showers at night and cool invigorating winds by day—most excellent weather for out door work, for house

NUUANU COTTAGE

WOODLAWN, 1883

carpenters, and bricklayers, and for the one hundred fifty men who are making a railroad to Pearl Harbor. Frank says the ties and rails are now laid about one-half mile per day and engineers say it is a good substantial road. He seems to be very happy in superintending the work. I am glad he can now partake of some of the first fruits of this business, which has occupied his mind for several years, both day and night.

The October Supreme Court are in session these days and are *hookolokoloing* [investigating] Wilcox and others for their treasonable attempt to overturn the government on the 30th, *Politics* of last July, and roll everything back into the slough of *Gibson ma.* If you receive the weekly Hawaiian Gazette you will have an opportunity to wade through the testimony of witnesses, some of whom were among the conspirators but have turned States evidence and thus save the hemp that might swing them up. It is obvious now that the King himself was the grand *kumu* [origin] of all this trouble; Wilcox was expecting the King to be with and sustain him, and that makes the grand *pilikia* [trouble] in the prosecution and decision of the court. After all the developments that have come to light, one would suppose that the King would be so ashamed that he would absent himself from all public entertainments and gatherings. But no! being infallible and unaccountable to mortal man for his treasonable conduct, he goes to the public circus, the theatre, to dinner parties and balls, both on board the ships in the harbor and respectable families in town, and has a great dinner party and ball this evening at the Palace, and all this too as though he were as "wise as a serpent and as harmless as a dove."

To his daughter:

November 21st, 1889

Regarding the meeting of the A.B.C.F.M. I am exceedingly pleased with the addresses and speeches of Dr. Stores, President of the Board. . . . I am glad you were there and saw and heard to your great satisfaction, and that you had the privilege of addressing the Woman's Board. Dr. Judson Smith and wife were so happy in making your acquaintance that he has written me a letter of congratulation that I should have a daughter so deeply interested in the foreign missionary work in which I have

*Meeting
of A.B.
C.F.M.*
spent my life. He says they would have been glad if I had been
with them; presuming I attended the meeting of the Board when
they met in New York city in 1832. I left that fall for the
Islands, but did not attend their annual meeting. Dr. Anderson
had summoned us to be in New London, Connecticut, on the 9th
of October ready to embark for the Islands on the 15th, on
board the whale ship "Mentor" Captain John Rice. But on
arriving there, the ship was lying on her side being coppered,
and we were detained there more than a month. In those days
there were very few old or *new* missionaries to attend their
annual meetings. But when at home on a visit in 1865, I attended the annual meeting of the Board in Chicago, and had a
seat on the platform with several other returned missionaries,
and we were all called upon to address the great audience. It
would seem that a number of returned missionaries were at
home this year on business and that each one "cried aloud and
spared not" calling upon the man of Israel for help. It was
doubtless good for those who have ears to hear and hearts to
pray "to be there."

Dear Daughter, did you not almost wish that circumstances
would allow you to go in person as a missionary to the heathen?

*A
Mission-
ary's Life*
You are aware that your parents and M.'s grandparents
have spent their lives as missionaries of the cross of Christ and
have never felt that they made a mistake in accepting and obey-
ing the commands "Give me thine heart.—Go and preach the
gospel to the destitute.—and—Lo, I am with you always, even
unto the end of the world." Is it too late for us to pray that
when May completes her education she may conscientiously
consecrate herself to the work of trying to save souls, either as
a home or foreign missionary?

To his niece:

March 1890

Frank had to purchase locomotives, cars, etc., etc., for the
road. Then he wrote to Emma requesting her to make arrangements to meet him at San Francisco on the 21st of December to
spend Christmas and New Year's days there, aid him in select-

ing new furniture for their Woodlawn cottage, and then come home together. . . .

Frank's prospects are now far more promising than they would have been had he succeeded in getting a loan of money in London for his railroad.

Only think of it. In 1865, after I had laboured thirty years without a vacation and felt that my missionary pilgrimage was drawing to a close, consulting our family physician, he told me that I had no chronic disease—what I needed was *rest*, and a *change of climate*. "Get a furlough of the A.B.C.F.M." said he, "go home to the States, ride on the cars, visit your surviving relatives and friends, spend a winter there, be absent a year, and you will return invigorated and have ten years more added to your missionary life." Well, we thanked him for his prescription, swallowed it whole without vomitting, and home we went to the States, visiting high and low, rich and poor, bond and free, and the thermometer went forty below zero the month we stayed in New York with Dr. S. Irenaeus Prime and family. In the summer of 1866 we returned to the Islands, and your Aunt Abba lived till 1885—twenty years—and here I am yet, March 1890—twenty-five years. How many more are to be added the Lord only knows. Some persons do not live out half their days, because they cannot spare the time to take care of themselves.

Regarding Furloughs

P.S. March 6th.

Before closing, I suppose you would like to hear something about your octogenarian uncle. Well, my days and nights are passing rapidly and as happily as I can expect, all things considered. On the 27th of last November I rounded out eighty-seven, and am now in my eighty-eighth year. My general health is better now than it was five years ago, when your Aunt Abba fell asleep in Christ.

During my pilgrimage, I have several times had a "stitch" in the small of my back, which was soon relieved. . . . But the grip must turn the screws two or three times, which assured me that I now have a new customer.

As ever, your affectionate uncle,

LOWELL SMITH

Extract from a letter by Emma, May, 1890:

Lowell's Lunch Party

Yesterday was a very precious day to me—it was the fifty-seventh anniversary of father's arrival here and I surprised him with a *lunch party*. I got *six* of the old missionaries here to lunch with him—four others were too feeble to come. They were so bright and said so many cute, witty things, it was delightful. Reminiscences were very many and they would not allow themselves to be cast down by present prospect of governmental action. They had a season of prayer before separating and when they parted they all wished each other such smiling good-byes, and *"Hoped soon to meet again in the New Jerusalem!"* It was just as sincere and lovely as it could be, but was too much for me. I had to go off and have a good cry. Father was considerably older than any other present—but as young and spry as the youngest. He was intensely gratified at the reunion —and I shall never cease to be thankful for the privilege I enjoyed.

HONOLULU, April 4th, 1891

Lowell's Last Letter

MY DEAR MRS. HARRINGTON,

Many thanks for your good letter of February 27th, . . . received March 4th. It is a long time since I have written to you and several other of my American correspondents. . . . But during the political changes that have taken place by the death of King Kalakaua and the promotion of his sister, Liliuokalani, to the throne as Queen . . . , I have tried to keep my friends posted up in our political affairs, by sending them some of our Honolulu newspapers.

In December and January I was afflicted with sore eyes, sore ears, and a sore throat, and for a season was so deaf that I could hear nothing. A dark cloud hung over me for several weeks, but to the surprise of us all by the wise treatment of Dr. ——, my organs of sight, hearing and speaking have been so far restored that I now feel as if the Lord is giving me a new lease of life. With my gentle horse and carriage I go two miles to town daily, to my son's new store, where I usually find several natives wishing me to prescribe for some one or more sick in their families, and often they wish me to go and visit them at their houses.

I am happy to hear that you had a good birthday visit on the 26th of January with Mrs. Dr. Emmerson in Amherst. I made her acquaintance some seventy years ago when as a school teacher she boarded with my parents in Heath. And it was then and there, in mother's parlor that Dr. Emmerson arranged with her to become his wife. When at home on our visit in 1865 I called on her at her home in Amherst. Please favor me by passing my *"aloha"* (my Hawaiian benediction of love) in your next letter to that venerable lady of ninety years. She is two years older than I am lacking two months, and I trust that we shall meet ere long in that house not made with hands, eternal in the heavens.

Matrimonial! In your letter to Guss the other day you congratulated him in the prospect of his soon becoming a married man. Well, on the evening of the 17th of March he was married to a grand daughter of one of the pioneer missionaries to these Islands in 1820. At the request of the parties, the ceremony was solemnized by his aged father. A brief notice of the marriage appeared in our morning paper. . . . Guss said he would send a copy of the same to you.

Son's Marriage

The Jubilee of Punahou College is to come off in June. Invitations have been sent to all the alumni, far and near, to revisit their alma mater on that occasion. Emma and her husband have invited their children to come home and spend their next summer vacation, and by letters just received they are overjoyed at the idea.

Punahou Jubilee

General S. C. Armstrong of Hampton, Va., is to be the orator of the day. Now can't you and your good husband arrange your summer vacation so as to come and be our guests on that eventful occasion? Such a journey, voyage and visit would be worth far more to you than the few hundred dollars you would spend. It would so renew your youth and fill you with new views and thoughts that you would return far better qualified to teach the rising generation. Please take the subject into serious consideration and let me know the result.

According to the newspapers the weather this winter and spring has been unusually cold and stormy and caused a great

amount of suffering among the poor and destitute, both in
Europe and in America and upon the sea as well as upon land.
We have not been afflicted here with storms, tempests, cyclones,
blizzards, floods, freshets and destruction of property and lives
of men and beasts such as we read of in the papers, but the
thermometer has ranged between fifty and sixty instead of
seventy and eighty, our usual climate. It seems to me that we
are feeling the influence of the cold storms some hundreds or
thousands of miles off. But the change has been very invigorating, and we think the lines have fallen to us in pleasant places
and we do not hesitate to call this the "Paradise of the Pacific."

Everything is quiet at present in our political horizon. The
Queen has appointed a new cabinet, and made some other
changes, the result of which will appear in due time. She has
appointed her husband the Governor of Oahu and exalted him
(head and shoulders) above all other officers of her kingdom.
The regular routine of business, building of stores and dwelling
houses, the arrival and departure of steamers and sailing vessels and Island schooners, the ship yard and the two iron
foundries, the tram cars on the streets, and the steam rail cars
going daily on time to Pearl City, all give plenty of employment
to day laborers. The less said about the late King's moral
character the better. The Queen has never united with any
church, but goes occasionally to the first native Protestant
church. She is quite intelligent and we hope she will seek the
best good of her poor people. The public and private schools
are all doing well and are well supplied with good teachers.

I will enclose you a paper which will give you some idea of
what the Central Union Church are doing in Sabbath schools,
etc.

Let this suffice for the present. We are all well. Aloha nui
from your uncle.

Abigail was not here to greet the Queen upon her throne,
but her missionary sisters, some of whose daughters had been
schoolmates of the Princess Lydia at the Royal School,
gathered about her offering assistance and imploring her to
stand firm for temperance and righteousness throughout the
kingdom.

Lowell had faith in Liliuokalani. He dreamed not of a cloud the size of a woman's hand, as vague as a woman's vanity, as wicked as a weak will, that would darken the dawn of her reign. Nor had he a vision of the nearness of annexation to America, that proposal of bygone kings.

In 1840, in the sadness of many friends "gone home," Lowell confessed to an impatience "to go too." But added a fervent prayer:

The Lord give me patience and perseverance and a willingness to labour and toil and bear the burden and heat of the day and at length to go like a shock of corn fully ripe.

Now his prayer was to be answered. Four days before his summons came, Lowell prepared some fifteen bottles of the medicines that so comforted his dear Hawaiians, but sent them instead of taking them as usual to town. Feeling a little poorly from a seeming cold, he said he would stay at home until better. He continued his early rising and going to the *lanai*, but, although in touch as always with the family and business interests, turned in his talk to children, invisible children—for whom he seemed deeply concerned.

Answered Prayer

I can not be responsible for their souls' salvation. You are the ones to train them and teach them. . . . Oh pray with them, teach them to shun every false way. Keep them for Christ. . . . Come unto me . . . for my yoke is easy and my burden is light . . . *so light*.

The next morning as the sun "came over the shadowy hills and the sleeping fields" came also for Lowell "the dawn of eternal day."

Lowell's blue eyes that never lost their twinkle were closed. His last thoughts had been of little children, his tenderest words, for them. Sometimes he had reached as to invisible hands. What visions may he not have seen? Perhaps he was again the eldest child in the crowded home in Heath, doing a man's chores to help bear the parental load. Perhaps he was the young missionary beset with disappointments. His deaf ears were unstopped after long years of patience with this infirmity. What might he not hear? Did he hear at last the

voices of his stillborn sons? Did the preciousness of his namesake, Lowell, enfold him as, childlike before his Heavenly
Father, he laid him down to sleep? Perhaps the other little
ones loved long since and lost awhile, infant daughters, infant
grandsons, gave him wings as angels to mount "from the
lowly earth to the vaulted skies." Surely, loneliness for his
Abba was rewarded by her presence, and would not the
young teacher he had so long ago found in the schoolroom
teach him new and heavenly things?

BENEDICTUS

DAY after day have I spent up in the dusty book-stacks of the American Board of Commissioners for Foreign Missions' rooms in Boston, among huge volumes of time-stained letters from the Sandwich Islands, penned nearly a century ago. Turning from my task on the last day I looked down into the churchyard secluded from the throngs on Tremont Street. There are sown low grave-stones—some solitary, some in pairs—that with the years have leaned together; occasional baby stones cuddling against those of their mothers. The small paned windows, and constant rain blended the lines of the black, wet tree trunks with the graceful foliage of the locust, the poised white candles of horse-chestnut blossoms, the yellow green of unfolding elm leaves. Puddles in the hollowed paving stones made bird baths for the pigeons. The white spire of Park Street Church thrust its golden weather vane to light the dim sky. The little flags planted on Memorial Day were as drenched with rain as their forebears had been with blood. Westminster chimes sounded the musical prayer of noon.

The quiet stones beneath my gaze, in contrast to the signs of hurry, as umbrellas passed, as horns sounded and brakes screamed on the wet streets, said what? The written words in those musty volumes said what?

The particular pleas, heartaches, facts, fancies, glad and sorry, are over. The individual cycles are done. The great cycle goes on—goes on—

Do they sleep, living only in memories that like bodies must pass? Lowell and Abigail. Is their pilgrimage ended? Did not Abigail, having loosed her hold on Lowell's hand, beckon him along a still climbing pathway? Would he long only for rest? Or would he seek new opportunities for that zeal that had been as a cloud by day and a fire by night through nigh to ninety years? Was their life of struggle, poverty, frailties of the flesh, sorrows, unfulfilled longings, outreaching love, a realistic idyll? Whatever the answers be, who shall mark them as right? Every life we know is realis-tic. What makes the idyll, but the Dream? And had not they the Dream?

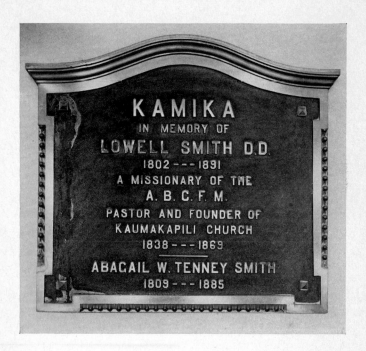

BRONZE TABLET

BEARING THE SMITH NAME IN HAWAIIAN, IN
KAWAIAHAO CHURCH, SOMETIMES CALLED
THE WESTMINSTER ABBEY OF HAWAII

*Lowell and Abigail with all their children are buried in the
Old Nuuanu Cemetery in sight of the tamarind tree
mentioned in little Emma's Journal*

APPENDIX

Family One. BROWN

Family Two. SMITH

VI   Children: Abby Jane, m. Brainerd Harrington
                        Jennie
                        William
                        George
V   iv *Russell*, b. 7 June, 1810
              v *Sarah*, b. 3 June, 1813
             vi *Augustus*
VI   Children: Frank, m. Ellen Eliza Adams, Con-
                        tent Ward Skerry, Mary Elizabeth
                        Garst
                        Abby Jane, m. Hubbard Barlow
                        Sarah, m. John Adams
                        Nellie
                        Alice, m. Albert Foster
                        Brainerd, m. Mabelle Boyd
V   vii *Franklin*
           viii *Frederic*

Family Three.   TENNEY

The ancestral home of the Tenney family is at Rowley, on the
Yorkshire Wolds, England. The church at this place dates back
five centuries. Rowley, Massachusetts, is thirty-two miles north
of Boston.

Generation

I*   I *Thomas*, arrived in Salem, Massachusetts,
                   1638; settled at Rowley, April, 1639; m.
                   Ann ——

7–II–1   II *Daniel*, b. Rowley, 16 July, 1653; m. 21
                   July, 1680, Elizabeth Stickney

48–III–7   III *Daniel*, twin of Sarah, b. 2 Mar., 1689–
                   1690; d. 21 Mar., 1756; m. Priscilla
                   Wood

127–IV–48   IV *Stephen*, b. Bradford, 20 May, 1713; d.
                   Barre, 1785; m. Mary Taylor

296–V–127   V *Gideon*, b. 16 Aug., 1759, at Northboro;
                   d. 3 June, 1842, at West Cummington;
                   m. by Rev. Thomas Holt at Hardwick, 8

* References in this column are from M. J. Tenney, *The Tenney Family*,
Concord, N. H., 1904.

Mar., 1792, to Betsey Childs, b. 27 May, 1772, at New Salem; d. 15 Mar., 1870, at Northampton

VI 1 *John Avery*, b. 12 July, 1793, at Barre, Massachusetts; d. 1874, at Willimansett; m. Nancy Lyons, sister of Lorenzo, missionary to the Sandwich Islands

VII   i *Rosey*
   ii *Frederick*
   iii *Ellen*
   iv *Lizzie*
   v *Eugenia*, m. Orange Towne. Child: Florence

VI 2 *Sarah Ann* (Sally), b. 21 Apr., 1795, at Northboro, Massachusetts; d. at West Cummington, 30 Nov., 1857; m. Joseph B. Baldwin of Brandon, Vermont

  3 *Rosey*, b. 5 Feb., 1797, at Northboro; d. 20 Aug., 1849, at Gill; m. 1 Luther Root; m. 2 William Williams

  4 *Stillman*, b. 5 Feb., 1799, at Northboro; d. 8 Dec., 1817, at Gill

  5 Infant, b. 11 Feb., 1801; died same day

  6 *Lionel*, b. 10 Apr., 1802, at Northboro; d. 1868 at Northampton; m. Mary Smith. Child: Infant

  7 *James Tyler*, b. 15 Sept., 1804, at Gerry, Massachusetts; d. 18 May, 1807

  8 *Louisa*, b. 29 July, 1806, at Barre; d. 1840, at Deerfield; m. Rev. Pomeroy Belden

VII   i *James*
   ii *Louisa*

713–VI–296   VI   9 *Abigail Willis*, "named in remembrance and to bear the name of her Hon'l Grandmother"; b. Sunday, 4 Dec., 1809, at Barre; d. 31 Jan., 1885, at Honolulu; m. 2 Oct., 1832, at Brandon, Vermont, Rev. Lowell Smith, b. 1802 at Heath, Massachusetts, s. of Moses and Lucretia (Brown). *Family Two*

VII   i, ii Two sons, one born and died each date, 31 Mar., 1839, and 8 Feb., 1840

iii *Lowell*, b. 2 July, 1841; d. 30 Apr., 1842

iv *Emma Louisa*, b. 9 Apr., 1843; d. 11 Apr., 1843

1706–VII–713   v *Emma Louisa*, b. 4 June, 1844, at Honolulu; d. 15 August, 1920, at Honolulu; m. 26 April, 1869, Benjamin Franklin Dillingham, b. 4 Sept., 1844, at West Brewster, Cape Cod; d. 7 April, 1918, at Honolulu, s. of Benjamin and Lydia Sears (Howe). *Family Four*

vi *Ellen Amelia*, b. 17 Mar., 1847; d. 10 Dec., 1848

vii *Lowell Augustus*, b. 25 Nov., 1851; d. 10 Oct., 1891; m. 17 Mar., 1891, Clara Benfield, granddaughter of Rev. Asa Thurston

VI   10 *James Augustus*, b. 28 Apr., 1812, at Wendell, Massachusetts; m. 19 Dec., 1838, Beulah S. Fay, b. 2 July, 1816, da. of William and Elizabeth (Lankton)

VII   i *Arethusa Louisa*, b. 29 May, 1840; m. 19 Dec., 1860, Albert T. Babbitt

ii *Augustus Fisher*, b. 8 Jan.,
1850; m. 18 Jan., 1877, Ada M.
Bennet, b. 25 Jan., 1858, da. of
B. G. and Loretta (Parsons)
VI 11 *Arethusa*, b. 14 Aug., 1814; d. 21
May, 1840

Family Four. DILLINGHAM

Generation
VII *Emma Louise*, da. of Lowell and Abigail Willis (Tenney)
Smith, m. 26 April, 1869, Benjamin Franklin Dillingham
VIII   1 *Mary Emma*, b. 30 June, 1870; m. 1 Aug., 1893,
Walter Francis Frear, b. 29 Oct., 1863, of early
Dutch, English and French colonials
IX   i *Virginia Dillingham*, b. 6 Apr., 1900; m. 26
May, 1923, Urban Earl Wild, b. 24 Aug., 1891
X   Children: Mary-Mae, b. 22 Aug., 1927
Urban Earl, Jr., b. 30 June, 1930
Walter Frear, b. 23 Mar., 1932
IX   ii *Margaret Dillingham*, b. 3 July, 1908
VIII   2 *Charles Augustus*, b. 19 Dec., 1872; d. 21 May,
1874
    3 *Walter Francis*, b. 5 Apr., 1875; m. 2 May, 1910,
Louise Olga Gaylord, b. 3 Nov., 1885, of English,
Scotch and Irish forebears, long established in
America
IX   i *Lowell Smith*, b. 17 June, 1911
      ii *Benjamin Franklin*, b. 14 Oct., 1916
      iii *Henry Gaylord*, b. 20 Apr., 1918
      iv *Elizabeth Louise*, b. 1 Jan., 1921
VIII   4 *Alfred Hubbard*, b. 21 Apr., 1880; d. 23 Oct., 1880
    5 *Harold Garfield*, b. 9 Oct., 1881; m. 24 Feb., 1908,
Margaret Bayard Smith, b. 20 Nov., 1885, of
American colonial paternal forebears, maternal,
English and Scotch
IX   i *Walter Hyde*, b. 23 Nov., 1908
      ii *Harold Garfield, Jr.*, b. 8 Oct., 1911
      iii *John Henley*, b. 21 Sept., 1915

iv *Bayard Harrison*, b. 6 June, 1918

v *Peter Harding*, b. 4 Mar., 1921

VIII   6 *Marion Eleanor*, b. 23 Sept., 1883; m. 10 Aug., 1904, John Pinney Erdman, b. 6 Dec., 1874, of early German and English settlers in America

IX   i *Harold Randolph*, b. 18 June, 1905; d. 26 Aug., 1931; m. 11 Sept., 1929, Mary Chickering, b. 2 April, 1905

X   Child: Mary Louise, b. 4 June, 1930

IX   ii *Emma Louise*, b. 7 Nov., 1906; m. 25 May, 1929, Charles Henderson, b. 5 Sept., 1903

X   Child: Harold Erdman, b. 30 Apr., 1933

IX   iii *Dorothy*, b. 31 Aug., 1911; m. 4 Aug., 1933, Ronald Kamehameha von Holt, b. 11 Aug., 1898

iv *Jean Marion*, b. 20 Feb., 1916

v *Marjory*, b. 27 Oct., 1919

"296–V–127

"Captain Gideon Tenney born in Northboro, Mass., 16 Aug., 1759 son of Stephen and Mary (Taylor); m 8 Mch 1792 Betsey Childs daughter of Ebenezer and Abigail (Willis) of Hardwich N.H. She was born 27 May 1772 & died 15 Mch., 1870. Residence Barre and Northboro, where he gave a silver cup to the church of that place. Gideon Tenney, gentleman, . . . entered the army 17 May 1775, served eight months, company of Samuel Wood. Gideon Tenney, private, spelled Tinney & Tiney, residence Northboro, served under Capt. Manasseh Sawyer in Colonel Dyke's regiment, Dated Dorchester Heights, 30 Nov., 1776; also served in Capt. Jotham Houghton's company, under Col. Josiah Whiting; enlisted 31 July, 1779, discharged 14 Sept., 1779. Dated Petersham. Also served in Capt. Moses Harrington's company, under Colonel Dyke, from 1 Dec., 1776 to 1 Mch., 1777. He also served in Capt. Benj. Noyes' Company, under Col. Nathan Sparhawk, from 21 Aug., 1777, to 25 Aug., 1777. They marched to reinforce the army at Bennington under General Stark. At that time he gave residence as Barre. He was at Stillwater (Army Roll). He moved

to Vermont, lived at Ludlow, Brandon, and at Rutland. In 1842
removed to Gill, Mass., where he died 3 June, 1843."*

From *The Tenney Family*, M. J. Tenney,
Concord, N. H., 1904.

BRANDON 16, July 1830

DEAR SON

Your letter received. happy to hear of your safe arrival at
Greenfield. and of the improvement of your health, and of the
health of the other children. I should have return'd an answer
much sooner, but was waiting the result of the church [meet-
ing] which took place a day or two ago, relative to candidate
for the ministry. They have given a call to a Mr. Ingraham,
and I think he will settle on this place. As to A, I went immediately to Doctor S-d, got the necessary information, he has
applyed to hand, thinks he knows a benefit, but his health is
very poor unable to labour much. Doctor Moss thinks he can
help him and is making the trial. Touching our ancestors, I can
inform something about something not far from 178 years ago
two brothers and a sister came from the west of England and
to make, their residence for some time near Newburyport in
Mass. from thence one of them and the sister went to Connecticut and settled not far from new London, the sister married but the name I have forgotten, the name remains their
now, of the Tenney, one of the decendence removed to Bennington Vt. The other brother settled in Rowley, Mass and I
believe the farm has ever been kept in the name. I once visited
them. found them very prosperous. Your grand father's brother
by the Name of Nathaniel Tenney occupied the farm, Your
great grandfather's name, Dan'l, his father's name I believe
was Thomas, can go no farther back. Your Grandpa Stephen
was born in Bradford near Rowly, on the 20th of May 1713.
He moved in early life, or rather came to Belingham in Mass.
where he married a Miss Horbit, she died in early life—had one
son who was at the age of 24. Crush to death in a saw mill.

* The Bible Family Record gives West Cummington, Mass., as the place
of Gideon Tenney's death.

Your grandpa after the death of his wife came to Mendon and thereabouts soon after married to Mary Tyler who was a native of Connecticut in the town of Roland his fathers name was David Tyler I know but little of their successors, only their has been several eminent Minister and Attorney of their name and blood. Your grandpa had two sisters, one married a Bracklebank whom I was [once] visited. The other married a Plummer, had a numerous family of very proud haughty sons and daughters, the late Governor of H. hampshire [New Hampshire], I believe to be one of the decendence, tho I have nothing to say as to his good qualifications, tho I am happy to say that their has [been] many eminent men both in church and State in the name of Tyler, Tenney and Plummer, yet I have not [set] my aim to write you particulars on that account you will excuse me as another subject presents itself—touching my revolutionary services, which will ever be familiar to me as long as I retain my rational powers, must be brief. I entered the army on the 17th day of May 1775 at the age of 15 years. That was called the 8 months service, my Capt. was Sam'l Wood of Northboro Co. Worcester—Sometime after returning home in the winter, 75, I enlisted for a year, march to Dorchester near Boston, was put under the command of Capt. Sawyer, who commanded until late in fall of 76, not being pleased[?] of the army returned Capt Moses Harrington of Graftor in the County of Worcester took the Command till the expiration of our enlistment which brought near the opening of the spring of 77. I then returned home. Soon after there was a call to raise more men to go the west, orders for enlis[t]ing men were out from all quarters, I enlisted again, was [settled] on to march to the west. We arrived at Benington in the Month of Aug't 77— a severe battle took place on the 11 of Aug't—the Americans were victorious—the enemy retreated and joined the main army under Burguoine who with his army consisting of nearly 10,000 men, officers and soldiers, fell into our hands near Stillwater on the 7 of Oct'r, 77 if I recollect right. They were marched from their to the Co. of Worcester in the Town of Rutland where there was barracks provided for their accommodation I was on the guard to guard them through the winter under the command of Capt. Tim'y Ruggles, After the opening of the Spring in '78 we were called on to march to Rhode Island. We landed on Newport Island the fore part of summer, where soon a large army was collected under the command of Gen. Sullivan. Our object was not gained—we were obliged to retreat and leave the Island. I was then a Serg't. was immediately detailed to command a guard called the fat cattle guard—had a cor'l and 12 men—duty to drive the cattle and sheep, get pasturage and forage—after rec'g [receiving] my orders, the army went to the south, I never saw them after. A Capt. Dan Kellogg came late in the fall and relieved me. My time of enlistment had long been out, but it would not do to quit my duty. Their was nearly 1000 cattle and sheep on this command. I spent to the guard nearly 100$ of good money, had the promise from Capt. Kellogg that I should receive the same again, but never have rec'd a cent, nor for my service that year nor for '77 except the bills you have in your hands. My hand fails me to write more. Will answer the remaining part of your letter another time. My crops look very promising. Yours etc.

GIDEON TENNEY

Love to all—you must put in small words where they are omitted.

INDEX

AAROA, 163
Abby Jane (Taft, Mrs. Harrington), *see* Nieces
A.B.C.F.M. (American Board of Commissioners for Foreign Missions), 36, 57, 62, 72, 88, 101, 111, 112, 117, 120, 121, 127, 128, 136, 159, 160, 176, 181, 191, 210, 213, 231, 232, 234, 236, 244, 245, 246, 248, 249, 273, 274, 293, 294, 295, 301
Acacia (probably *Cassia glauca*), 240
Adams (Governor), 163
Adams, Samuel, 5
Admiral, Thomas, 165, 166, 167, 168, 169, 220
Adobe, 94, 95, 124, 134, 149, 159
Agricultural Society, 204
Ah Fat, 261
Ah Ling, 264
Albatross, 44
Albert (Judd), 256
Alexander (Rev. James M.), 117
Alexander, Liholiho, *see* Kamehameha IV
Alexander, Prof. W. D., 233
Algaroba (*Prosopis julifera*), 116, 266, 267
Aloha (Aroha), 55, 56
America, 37, 51, 75, 87, 98, 191, 192, 202, 298, 299
American(s), 63, 67, 81, 136, 155, 161, 162, 163, 165, 198, 223, 231, 243, 261, 283, 284, 288, 310
American Board, *see* A.B.C.F.M.
American churches, 202
Amherst, 21, 23, 26, 120, 297
Anderson, Dr. R., 231, 244, 294
Andover, 20, 26, 31
Andrews, Judge and Mrs. Lorrin, 119, 120, 201
  Children: Robert, 243; Sam, Willie, 235
Andrews, Dr. and Mrs. S. L., 117
Apiang, 229
Arethusa (Tenney), 7, 8, 11, 307
Armstrong, Captain, 169
Armstrong, Caroline, 150
Armstrong, Rev. and Mrs. Richard,

112, 150, 151, 152, 154–159, 163, 217, 220
Armstrong, Gen. S. C., 67, 297
Armstrong, William Nevins, 235
Arnold (Benedict), 229
Artesian wells, 268
Ascension (Island), 221
Ashford, C. W., 284
Aspinwall, 236
Asthma, 154, 216, 232
Auburn (Theological Seminary), 18, 25, 35, 147
Auburndale, 291
Augustus (Smith), son, *see* Gus
Augustus (Smith), Lowell's brother, 304
Augustus (Tenney), Abigail's brother, 6, 7, 8, 9, 271, 277, 306
Auhea, 74, 75, 78, 94, 137. *See also* Kekauluohi
Aulick, Captain, 154
Autograph album, 19, 20, 21, 22
Avery, John, 6
Awa, 164

BACHELOT, FATHER, 116, 117
Bailey, Rev. and Mrs. Edward, 117
Baldwin, Dr. Dwight, 135
Baldwin, Hattie (Mrs. S. M. Damon), 233
Barre, 3, 6, 26, 128, 308
Barter, 10
Bates, Katharine Lee, 277
Bates, Sissy, 201
Beckley, Captain, 140
Beckwith, President E. G., 221
Beecher, Miss C. E., 21
Beecher, Henry Ward, 235
Belle (Carter) (Mrs. Crehore), 254
Bellingham, Massachusetts, 309
Bell telephone, 267
Bennington, 308, 309, 310
Beretania Street, 123, 178, 266
Berkshire Hills, 24
Bermuda grass, 120
Bernice Pauahi Bishop, 258, 276, 277
Bethel Church (seaman's chapel), 53, 150, 151, 160, 197, 198, 243

Smith, 303, 304, 306, 307
Smith, Augustus, *see* Gus
Smith, Chiliab, 27
Smith, Emma, *see* Emma
Smith, Joseph A., 36
Smith, Dr. and Mrs. Judson, 293
Smith, Rev. Lowell and Mrs. Abba W. T., *passim*
Smith, Lucia G. (the second Mrs. L. Lyons), 117
Smith, Marcia (of Punahou fame), 117
Smith Street, 123, 178
Smoking, 107, 125, 134, 147, 150, 164, 171, 236
Society Islands, 170, 229
Solomon, 141
Sorcerer (*kahuna*), 156
South America, 45, 109
South Seas, 117, 223
Southern California, 116
Spanish missions, 109
Sparhawk, Col. Nathan, 308
Spaulding, Mr. and Mrs., 68
Spencer, Mr., 286
Spooner, 3
Spooner, Hannah, 2, 3
Spooner, Thomas, 2
Spooners, 26
Stars, 242, 247, 248
Stark, General, 308
Stephens, 243
Stillwater, 308, 310
Stone, Dr., 238
Stonington, 24
Stores, Dr., 293
Stoughton, 12, 17
Strangers' Friend Society, 220, 278
Strawberries, 148, 179, 205
Strelisky, Count, 134
Stribling, Captain, 107, 169
Strongs' Island, 170, 229
Sugar bags, 182
Sugar cane, 72, 192, 193
Sugar, maple, 236
Sugar works, 143
Sullivan, General, 311
Sulphur, 146
Sumac, xv
Sumatra, 177
Sunderland, 120
Supreme Court, 293

Suspension, 133, 134, 164
Sweet, Mr., 174
"Sweet Home" (Judd house top of Judd Hill), 254

TABU, 58, 59, 162
Taconic Range, 30
Tahiti, 160
Tamarind, xiii, 157, 198, 203, 256
Tapa, 58, 62, 71, 72, 103, 104
Taro, xiv, 178, 202, 214, 215, 247
Teacher, 8–16, 18, 32, 112, 117, 120, 171; Government school teachers, 171; teaching, 194, 227, 246, 249
Tell, Capt. William, 252
Tenney(s), 26, 304–311; Arethusa, 7, 8, 11, 307; Abigail, xiii, and *passim*; Augustus, 6, 7, 8, 271, 277; Betsey (Childs), 4, 6, 7, 8, 188, 206, 242, 245, 246, 304, 308; Daniel, 4, 6, 304, 309; Frederic, 183, 305; Gideon, 1, 4, 5, 6, 304, 308, 309, 310, 311; James Tyler, 305; John or John A., 183, 248, 305; Lionel, xiii, xiv, 173, 174, 202, 215, 246, 305; Louisa, 7, 20, 153, 305; Mary (Smith), Lionel's wife, 215, 241, 305; Mary (Taylor), wife of Stephen, 308; Nancy Lyons, sister of Rev. L. Lyons of Hawaii, 305; Nathaniel, 4, 309; Sarah, 7, 305; Stillman, 7, 305; Stephen, 4, 6, 304, 309; Thomas, 304
Tenney Family Bible, 4
Territory of Hawaii, 172
Thanksgiving Day, 135, 234, 288, 291
Thomas, Admiral, 165, 166, 167, 168, 169, 220, 283
Thurston, Mrs. Asa, 150, 188
Thurston, L. A., 284
Ti (or *Ki* or *Lai*) (*Cordyline terminalis*), 59, 94, 144
Tidal wave, 121
Tierra del Fuego, 41, 45
Tiney (Tinney), 308
Tinker, Rev. Reuben and Mrs., 69, 98, 106, 107
Toohane, Mr. John, 36, 43
Treaty, 259
Turnell, Dr., 9
Tyler, David, 310
Tyler, Mary, 310

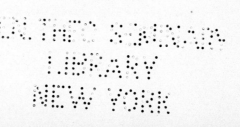

Privately Printed
Under the Direction of the
Yale University Press